DOCTOR WHO
THE HANDBOOK
The Seventh Doctor

By the same authors:

Doctor Who The Handbook – The Third Doctor
Doctor Who The Handbook – The Fifth Doctor

By David J. Howe, Mark Stammers & Stephen James Walker:

Doctor Who The Handbook – The First Doctor
Doctor Who The Handbook – The Second Doctor
Doctor Who The Handbook – The Fourth Doctor
Doctor Who The Handbook – The Sixth Doctor
Doctor Who The Sixties
Doctor Who The Seventies
Doctor Who The Eighties

By Jon Pertwee & David J. Howe:

Doctor Who – I am the Doctor

By David J. Howe & Mark Stammers:

Doctor Who – Companions

By David J. Howe:

Doctor Who – Timeframe

DOCTOR WHO
THE HANDBOOK
The Seventh Doctor

David J. Howe
and
Stephen James Walker

First published in Great Britain in 1998 by
Doctor Who Books
an imprint of Virgin Publishing Ltd
Thames Wharf Studios
Rainville Road
London W6 9HT

Reprinted 1999

ISBN 0 426 20527 8

Cover illustration by Alister Pearson

Typeset by Galleon Typesetting Ltd, Ipswich
Printed and bound in Great Britain by Mackays of Chatham PLC

CONTENTS

Acknowledgements

Our thanks go this time first and foremost to our good friend and fellow researcher Andrew Pixley, who has selflessly offered advice and shared his incredible knowledge with us throughout the preparation of this series of handbooks.

Special thanks to those few knowledgeable and generous souls who have provided sections for the 'Selling the Doctor' chapter: Ian Wheeler, who took on the bulk of this work, and Michael J. Doran, Robert D. Franks, David Robinson, Richard Prekodravac, Paul Scoones, Damian Shanahan and Dallas Jones. Thanks too to Rosemary Howe, who spent many, many hours reading all seven handbooks in order to create the incredible (and hopefully useful) index that appears herein.

A big thank-you to Sophie Aldred for the introduction and for her help in general.

Thanks also to Mark Ayres, Jonathan Blum, David Brunt, Mary Carroll, Michael J. Doran, Gary Gillatt and *Doctor Who Magazine*, David Golding, Susan James, Misha Lauenstein, Lance Parkin, Gary Russell, Philip Segal, Mark Stammers, Martin Wiggins and all *Doctor Who* fanzine editors past and present.

Finally, we would like to raise our collective glasses to our editor-in-chief at Virgin Publishing, Peter Darvill-Evans. It was he who encouraged us to submit ideas to him back in 1990, and this series of seven handbooks would never have happened, and may never have been completed, if it had not been for Peter's faith in us and in the show that we all love.

To Peter, and also to Virgin editors past and present, Rebecca Levene and Simon Winstone, we say thanks for your advice, for your enthusiasm and for your trust. We hope we've repaid it.

Dedication

For Nicole Adams (a.k.a. Suki), who threatened bad things if this book was not dedicated to her, and nice thoughts if it was. Some decisions are easy (**DJH**)

For Claire (**SJW**)

Introduction

Last year I travelled down to Wiltshire to open a small *Doctor Who* exhibition in a museum in Trowbridge. There were all the usual suspects: beautifully crafted Cybermen models, display cabinets stuffed with well-treasured boxed sets of monsters, vehicles, Doctors even. And, guarding the entrance to the exhibition, the most menacing and terrifying creation of the lot – poised at the head of the stairs, lethal weapons pointed towards an unsuspecting Mum and her seven-ish-year-old son who'd popped up from the shopping centre below to see what all the fuss was about.

As I watched, the boy stopped short, pointed and exclaimed: 'Mum, what are those?'

'Daleks, darling,' she replied. 'They had them on telly when I was your age.'

So there we have it. A whole generation growing up without that knowledge we used to take for granted. As I stood there, musing rather sadly, I started wondering how long it's going to take for the *Doctor Who* references to pass out of popular culture altogether. At least at the moment we can be assured of the odd mention of the TARDIS or Daleks on afternoon game shows and panel games.

But of course there are the fans. You lot out there who keep *Doctor Who* alive by organising and attending conventions, by writing and reading books such as this one, by supporting magazines, keeping *Doctor Who* on the video shelves, introducing new people to the show . . . the list is endless. And you're doing it not from a sense of duty or loyalty, though that does come into it somewhere along the line, but because you love this programme and these characters and don't want to see them disappear. There's a growing library full of excellent books like this to remind and inform us. There's a lot of stuff in here that I had no idea about even after all the trawling through my memory banks for my own book on the subject, *Ace!*. All the details you could ever wish for, and a bonus chapter on the eighth Doctor, and hope for the future.

So maybe it's not all doom and gloom. Sylvester and I have recently spent a couple of days working together on a spin-off audio project created by one of that band of fans who have grown up to become professional writers, directors, production companies and so on. I wondered how difficult it would be, almost ten years on, to walk back into the relationship, to remember how it was. I needn't have worried. Something that wasn't quite me and wasn't quite acting took over the moment Sylv and I stood together at the microphone; a voice and an attitude that's not quite mine came back to me, like slipping an arm into a familiar old jacket that has been hanging in the back of a wardrobe for some years, waiting and hoping that one day it'll come back into fashion. It's a bit of a saggy old jacket now, lightly faded from lack of use. But the thing is, it's still there . . . and the badges are nice and shiny.

Sophie Aldred

Foreword

Bolts of glowing energy seared through the blackness of space, unerringly seeking out the blue boxlike shape of the TARDIS, which tumbled and rolled from the multiple impacts.

The TARDIS's engines howled in protest. The attack had come suddenly and unexpectedly, and the incongruous police-box shell of the craft was creaking and groaning as the battering it was undergoing stressed the dimensional bonds that held the ship together. 'The TARDIS is indestructible,' the Doctor had boasted in the past, and now his claim was being tested to the limit.

Inside the main control room, the buffeting was intense. An exercise bike collapsed and, nearby, two highly contrasting figures lay unconscious on the floor. One was a young red-headed girl called Mel. Normally bubbly and talkative, she currently lay silent and still, unaware of what was going on around her. On the other side of the central control console, which shuddered and rocked under the continued onslaught, lay the Doctor, currently in his sixth incarnation. Mel had been unable to do anything about his appalling taste in clothes, but her persistent nagging had at least prompted him to submit to a strict regime of healthy food, carrot juice and exercise, and he was now looking rather trimmer than in the past. Anything for a quiet life, he had told himself.

This was anything but a quiet life.

The engines screamed like a cavalry of tortured horses as the TARDIS, out of control and under attack, took the only remaining course of action open to it. Its automatic systems located the nearest planet, and it plummeted through the atmosphere in a final attempt to avoid the blistering pulses of power that raked across its exterior.

A final dimensional shift brought the ship safely down on to the barren surface of the planet Lakertya, where it came to rest on the sand.

In the console room, all was now calm. Mel was still out cold, but the Doctor, his Time Lord body more able to withstand such rough treatment, slowly drifted back to consciousness.

There was something wrong. Without moving an inch, the Doctor mentally checked himself over. There was definitely something wrong. His body had suffered a mental and physical battering from the forces that had attacked the TARDIS. The symbiotic link that he enjoyed with the sensitive consciousness buried deep within his ship had communicated much of the stress of the bombardment to him, and his alien physiognomy had interpreted the attack in perhaps the only way it could.

He felt a by now familiar rush of blood to his brain, the opening of normally dormant glands to release unique Gallifreyan chemicals into his system. It was happening again. His Time Lord genes had responded automatically to the assault and he was on the verge of regenerating for the sixth time.

He dimly registered that the TARDIS had arrived somewhere, and a low purring sound told him that the external doors had been opened. Then there were other sounds. The clacking of high-heeled boots on the TARDIS floor. A harsh breathing accompanied by a furtive shuffling, as though a massive beast had entered the ship.

Then. Suddenly. A voice. 'Leave the girl. It's the man I want!'

A woman . . . but who?

The Doctor thought he recognised the voice . . . someone he knew . . . someone he had encountered only recently.

'Take him to my laboratory,' the voice ordered sternly.

The chemicals flooding through the Doctor's system made it hard for him to think. All at once, something grasped his side and pulled him over on to his back. He caught a faceful of breath that smelt like rotting vegetables before the final neural switches tripped and his regeneration started in earnest.

Memories – sights, sounds, smells, tastes and feelings – flooded through him. He felt his mind and body twist as the process overtook him.

The last thing that he was aware of before falling unconscious once more was being picked up by something strong and hairy, and thrown carelessly over a muscular shoulder.

Adapted from *Time and the Rani* Episode 1
by Pip and Jane Baker

Thus was the era of the sixth Doctor ignominiously brought to an end. Colin Baker had been fired by the BBC and producer John Nathan-Turner instructed to cast a new actor to star in the 24-year-old series. The problem was that Baker, understandably sore at the treatment he had received, had refused to return simply to record a story in which he would be written out, and so, for the first time in *Doctor Who*'s history, a regeneration had to be achieved without the participation of the outgoing Doctor.

To complicate matters further, the only other regular cast member, Bonnie Langford, was a newcomer who was still settling into her role as computer programmer and health-and-fitness fanatic Melanie Bush; and the series' long-serving script editor Eric Saward had resigned the previous year following disagreements with Nathan-Turner, leaving that post temporarily vacant.

The actor chosen to take over as the Doctor was Sylvester McCoy. Previously known mainly for children's television work and daredevil comedy stunts – including, famously, stuffing ferrets down his trousers in one particular show – he grasped the opportunity that *Doctor Who* presented him to establish himself in a different kind of role with a higher public profile. For the next three years the Doctor became a lively fellow with dark wavy hair and a faint Scots accent, sporting a paisley-patterned scarf and a question-mark pullover and brolly. McCoy's was a uniquely different interpretation of the nation's favourite Time Lord. Behind his sometimes clownish façade, this was a more introspected and thoughtful Doctor; a more mysterious Doctor; a Doctor who could take command of a situation with simply a suggestion here and a quiet adjustment there.

In the wider world during McCoy's time as the Doctor, the Archbishop of Canterbury's special envoy, Terry Waite, was kidnapped in Beirut, not to be released until some five years later; a car ferry capsized off Zeebrugge killing two hundred passengers; Margaret Thatcher was elected for a third term as Prime Minister of the UK; hurricane-force winds killed seventeen people and left a £300 million trail of destruction across southern England; and the bottom fell out of the London Stock Market, wiping ten per cent, or £50 billion pounds, off the value of shares on a day forever to be known as 'Black Monday'.

In our research for this book we have, as usual, spoken to many different people involved in the making of *Doctor Who* during the period in question. In addition to covering the three seasons transmitted between 1987 and 1989, after which the BBC effectively cancelled *Doctor Who* – although they never actually announced this fact, they just stopped making the series – we have also brought the story up to date by looking at the 'wilderness years' that followed, and at the 1996 television movie in which Paul McGann took over the mantle of the Doctor.

As well as articles examining the seventh and eighth Doctors, describing all their on-screen adventures and looking at how the mythology of the series developed during these final years, this volume contains an index to the entire series of handbooks and an errata rounding up a few annoying glitches and errors that have regrettably slipped through the net over the years that we have been working on this project.

Join us as we revisit the eras of the seventh and eighth Doctors, and bring to an end – at least for the time being – our coverage of the ever-developing, ever-popular chronicles of that mysterious traveller in space and time known only as the Doctor.

PART ONE – THE DOCTOR

1: Sylvester McCoy – In His Own Words

ON HIS EARLY LIFE AND CAREER:

'[I was born in] Dunoon, Argyll, Scotland, on a rainy day, 20 August in the year of our lord 1943 . . .

'I was a lively little lad. I'm sure there were times when people thought I should have been put in prison, but I didn't get caught! . . .

'I used to go to Saturday cinema and watch those dreadful but wonderful serials like *Flash Gordon* . . . I collected jam jars which were worth a ha'penny each, so I could get in to see *Flash Gordon* for four jam jars. The first horror film I saw was *The Beast with Five Fingers*, which I watched through the buttonhole in the top of my school mackintosh, because I was so scared. I remember *Quatermass* too, which terrified me.'

Interviewed by Johnny Black in 1987 for *Starburst* Issue 110.

'I was raised by my grandmother and sometimes my aunt . . . My father was killed in the war a couple of months before I was born. He was blown up in a submarine. And my mother subsequently had a nervous breakdown. It lasted . . . well, it lasted until the end of her life, really. She died when I was twenty-one. She spent most of her life in hospitals.'

Interviewed by uncredited writer in 1988 for *Whovian Times* Volume 17.

'Being a Catholic, I went to the local Roman Catholic primary school where we used to have vocational talks from people . . . We had a priest one day, and they asked if anybody would like to be one. Three of us put our hands up – me, Danny Sweeney and Mary O'Malley. Naturally Mary wasn't called out, but Danny and I were!

'This had never happened before, and we were sent off post haste to see the priest . . . When we got there, Danny lost his bottle. Being a cocky little thing, I knocked on the door and said, "I want to be a priest". Next thing I knew, I was on a train to Aberdeen to study for the priesthood. I got so holy, I had housemaid's knee from praying. At first I wanted to be the Pope, then I decided to be much humbler and become a mere monk. I wrote off to the Dominicans, and they replied, a very encouraging letter. When I left [Aberdeen] they all kneeled down and prayed and praised me as a saint, because no one had ever left to become something even more hard and harsh, a monk.

'Luckily, when I got home, another letter arrived from the Dominicans saying I was too young to start. I was just fifteen. It was the best thing that ever happened, because I had to cram in some education that year, so I was sent off to the local unisex grammar school, where I discovered those wonderful creatures . . . girls. I gave up all thoughts of Popes and monks right away.'

Interviewed by Johnny Black in 1987 for *Starburst* Issue 110.

'I worked in the City of London [for a time. It] was much more Dickensian than it is now. It [was] a very uptight place, especially in the matter of attire . . . Once I was a trainee executive in charge of the liaison between the computer and auto insurance. In fact, I was more a trainee alcoholic. It was driving me mad. You see, I didn't know I wanted to be an actor. All I knew was that what I was doing wasn't fulfilling, whatever it was. I was very unhappy in that world. You weren't allowed to take your jacket off on a warm day unless you got permission. I knew that this was madness, lunacy, dictatorial and unfair. It wasn't that we were in an office with people coming in to see us. We were just in an office all together, and there was no air conditioning.'

Interviewed by Lou Anders in 1995 for *Dreamwatch* 17.

'I remember once my grandmother – who is Irish – sitting in the bay window of a lovely house we had near the River Clyde, looking out onto a rainy landscape . . . Suddenly, in a mysterious kind of way, she turned to me and said I should become an actor. It came from nowhere and I thought it was a completely barmy, silly idea. But it was there and it took root, I suppose.

'What then happened was that I was working in London for a company that went bust. I ended up working in the box office of the Roundhouse Theatre, and one day Ken Campbell came in. He was setting up the Ken Campbell Roadshow with Bob Hoskins and various others, and someone had let him down. Brian Murphy was collecting the tickets I was selling . . . Ken went to Brian and said, "I need someone for this wild show starting in the north of England," and Brian said, "Well, ask the guy in the box office – he's completely out of his head!"

'So he came up to me – and in those days I was a hippie with a moustache, long hair, beads, the lot – and he asked me to join the Roadshow. I told him I wasn't an actor and he said, "Do you want to be?" I said, "Yes," and he said he'd come back on Monday. He did – and I became an actor!'

Interviewed by Richard Marson in 1987 for *Doctor Who Magazine* No. 130.

'It was supposed to be for one night, but I stayed with the Roadshow for two years. We toured all over Europe, Britain and Ireland and Israel too, and it became a bit of a cult on the fringe. I left there and went to Joan Littlewood's theatre workshop at Stratford East and worked with her for a while, then from there I went to Nottingham Playhouse with Richard Eyre . . . and I worked with him for two or three years. At the same time television started for me, and a kind of parallel career went on. It was about sixteen years ago I started as an actor and about twelve years ago I started *Vision On* for the BBC . . . Then every year I did another television series: *Jigsaw*, *Eureka*, *Tiswas*, *Starstrider* . . .

'So I had two careers going on: one in the theatre, [where I was appearing in productions of] Shakespeare, Beckett [and] Brecht and . . . having plays written for me by Adrian Mitchell, Ken Campbell and Ken Hill; [the other] paying for my mortgage in a sense by doing television and children's stuff. I also did *The Last Place on Earth*, which was a very adult piece for television – seven one-hour films about Scott's race to the Antarctic, which we actually filmed in the Arctic. [I did] *Tiny Revolutions* for Granada, which was an adult film about a professor stuck in prison in Czechoslovakia for telling jokes against the state.'

Interviewed by Gary Levy and Robert Cope in 1987 for *DWB* 50.

'[At first] I had no idea what sort of actor I was. But because of the nature of working with Ken Campbell and Bob Hoskins, who are both physical performers, I started doing very physical theatre. Then people would come up to me and say I reminded them of Buster Keaton, Stan Laurel or Charlie Chaplin. So I thought I'd better have a look at the work of the comedy pioneers – and by discovering them, I also discovered my own acting "self".'

Interviewed by Graeme Wood and Andrew Lennard in 1992 for *TV Zone* Special # 4.

'The name I used at first was Kent Smith – part of a very long name I've got. There was another actor in America called Kent Smith and I always had ambitions beyond my . . . rights. I thought perhaps I might do something in America, not realising I'd end up doing *Doctor Who*. Also, I thought Kent Smith was more of a matinée idol name and I didn't think I was that kind of actor. I was doing a show called *An Evening with Sylvester McCoy, the Human Bomb*, and in it we wanted the audience to believe that there was this little man who could do all these amazing stunts. So we printed a programme stating,

"Sylvester McCoy played by Sylvester McCoy," and it stuck, really. I thought it was quite a good name, so I kept it.'

Interviewed by Paul Travers in 1988 for *Doctor Who Magazine* No. 142.

ON WATCHING EARLIER ERAS OF *DOCTOR WHO*:

'I started watching *Doctor Who* with Patrick Troughton when I was about twenty odd, then I watched it with Jon Pertwee and Tom Baker, but when I became an actor – because of the nature of the job – I got out of the habit of watching series and serials . . . You can never follow them, because you are working. I really didn't see Peter Davison very much, or Colin [Baker].'

Interviewed by Gary Levy and Robert Cope in 1987 for *DWB* 50.

ON BEING CAST AS THE DOCTOR:

'It was a role I had wanted for some time. I remember that three years earlier when Colin Baker got the part, I heard about it a bit too late, but I still thought to myself, "I wish I'd known about that – I'd quite like to have tried for it". So though I wasn't actually pursuing it all the time, it was a role that I fancied doing. Then when I heard on the news that Colin was leaving I phoned my agent and told him that there was a job going at the BBC . . .

'Actually, what happened was that my agent phoned John Nathan-Turner, and immediately he had put the phone down [a producer named] Clive Doig also came on the line and told John he should take a look at me. Apparently John said, "Wait a minute, are you and his agent in cahoots?" '

Interviewed by Peter Haining in 1988 for *Doctor Who – 25 Glorious Years*.

'I was at the National Theatre doing *The Pied Piper*, which was actually a very good audition part for the Doctor. Then I had a two and a half hour interview with John Nathan-Turner.'

Interviewed by Johnny Black in 1987 for *Starburst* Issue 110.

'It was two and a half hours of charm, because you go into these interviews and try to be charming.

'I don't know what I talked about but I kept thinking, "I hope this interview finishes soon, or I'll run out of charm" . . . I managed to con my way through that one. Then I went back and did another two hour interview, and then I met the Head of Series and Serials, Jonathan Powell, who only gave me five minutes, thank god! They decided that they quite liked my quirkiness and humour but they weren't sure I had the seriousness and the power to overcome the many enemies that I would meet in my time travels.

'So we did two screen tests – two scenes – and one of those was overpowering the enemy and I passed that, so they gave me the job.

'Janet Fielding did the test with me, and she'd rehearsed this stuff on another day with me and a few others that were also up for the part, so I had to hang around quite a lot. At first I wasn't too bothered one way or the other, as you go up for a lot of parts, but then I began to think, "Oh my god! They're serious!" '

Interviewed by Richard Marson in 1987 for *Doctor Who Magazine* No. 130.

ON THE DOCTOR'S CHARACTER:

'He's someone who loves the Earth, and therefore humanity. But he is also a very wise man who sees the follies of man – and also those in himself. Those are his strengths. But he also has his weaknesses which are equally interesting. Take his passion for minutiae, and innocently wandering into dangerous situations that perhaps he should see: maybe does, maybe doesn't. He's also a rebel and doesn't really like authority, which is something I like in him. Because, you know, authority has to prove its worth – just because it *is* authority, it shouldn't be accepted. It should be questioned – and the Doctor does and it gets him into trouble. He's also a bit of an anarchist as well! There is even a bit of Doctor Johnson in him – you know, one of those people you admire who stand up and say what they think.

'In fact, he is a mixture of all sorts of things, but at his most basic he loves the Earth. He is a man who should not use violence, I believe, but his wits and his intelligence to get him out of any tight corner.'

Interviewed by Peter Haining in 1988 for *Doctor Who – 25 Glorious Years*.

ON HIS DOCTOR'S COSTUME:

'The hat emerged because I wore one to the interviews. I did wear a hat just like that [in my private life] but I can't now, really. Sad. They wanted the hat, though. I wanted my costume to be the sort of thing that could be seen on the street and that there was only something strange about when people get close. Not too alien. I've actually worn it in the street in Wales when we were [on location] and people who didn't recognise me or realise what was going on didn't notice anything odd. One guy came up to me and said, "I like your jumper; very nice that. Where did you get it from?" I said my mother had knitted it!'

Interviewed by Richard Marson in 1987 for *Doctor Who Magazine* No. 130.

'I knew I wanted a baggy jacket with lots of paraphernalia in the pockets. I think the Doctor should be something of an Edwardian character, like in those wonderful Jules Verne novels . . . It was basically a combination of various ideas put forward, and I'm really pleased with it.'

Interviewed by Gary Levy and Robert Cope in 1987 for *DWB* 50.

'The jumper is based on a 1930s golfing sweater. We did consider the idea of the Doctor wearing glasses – as I normally do – but it was decided that my eyes could be seen better without them. The umbrella with the red question-mark handle was all my own idea.'

Interviewed by Peter Haining in 1988 for *Doctor Who – 25 Glorious Years*.

'I like the pullover, but . . . the costume is too loud for my taste. I'd like to tone it down. As for the question-marks, they're a nice motif. I don't know whether it matters. I'd miss the [question-mark handle] umbrella if it went . . . but I think the scarf could be darker, and the hatband too. Perhaps the jacket could be brown.'

Interviewed by Paul Travers in 1988 for *Doctor Who Magazine* No. 142.

'I personally would have liked to have got rid of the question marks on the jumper. I thought that was a bit too much, but I think the umbrella is all right because at first people don't actually notice it. The pullover I would have preferred to be just plain. I tried to get rid of it last year along with the jacket change, but the producer said no, really because it was his idea, and the umbrella was mine so that was fair enough.'

Interviewed by Mark Attwood in 1990 *DWB* No. 77.

ON *TIME AND THE RANI*:

'I had to dress up in Colin's costume with a silly wig and I looked like Harpo Marx. I had to lie down on my face and then turn over. For just an instant I did look surprisingly like Colin, and then the picture went all funny and [when] it returned to normal, I was me – much to my horror when I looked in the mirror! . . .

'Right from the beginning there was a good feeling both in front of the cameras and behind them. No one made me feel I was the new boy and had to prove my worth. The director of that first story was Andrew Morgan, who had done my screen test for the series. And because I sensed right from that initial meeting that he was the sort of guy who would give me a chance, it was wonderful to work with him on the first story. It felt almost like coming home, and I said to myself, "Hey, I belong here." It was very funny – I didn't worry. I felt relaxed. I just had to learn my lines and not bump into the monsters!'

Interviewed by Peter Haining in 1988 for *Doctor Who – 25 Glorious Years*.

ON *PARADISE TOWERS*:

'There seemed to be so much to learn in the way of words! The Doctor had so much to say! Most of the speaking was on one set, and because we taped it in sets, rather than in order, I was on that set talking non stop. By the end of it, I was completely bored by the sound of my own voice, and exhausted at having to remember all those words. It wasn't all that enjoyable to do, but when I saw it, it really worked. I was surprised by how well it came across, considering the mountain I had to climb.'

Interviewed by Joe Nazzaro in 1993 for *TV Zone* Special # 11.

ON *DELTA AND THE BANNERMEN*:

'It was a fun story to do and all the people in it were a great laugh. Nobody was trying to act the star – which some of them had every right to do. I was still a bit of a new boy as the Doctor, but they were very welcoming and good fun to be with . . .

'We were [recording a] sequence on a rooftop with explosive charges going off all around me. One of them went off a little too early and this banged my head a bit, but we were able to keep on. Mind you, with the tight schedules we have, we *had* to – and I suppose that I learned right there and then that the one thing one would like more of on *Doctor Who* is time!'

Interviewed by Peter Haining in 1988 for *Doctor Who – 25 Glorious Years*.

ON *DRAGONFIRE*:

'The bizarre thing was, John Nathan-Turner wanted Bonnie [Langford] to stay on for another two stories in the next season. That way, the first story would have us arriving in the new season, and the next story would be about why Bonnie's character had to leave. Because of her commitments in the theatre, she couldn't say, "I'll give you eight weeks," so she said, "I'll give you four, and do the first story".

'I think John felt, "I don't want to do that with the first story in the twenty-fifth season; having someone leave," so he said, "Maybe you should leave now," and we would start afresh. Originally it was going to be a very quick scene, but I said, "We've got to get more into it." The Doctor had been with this character for two personas, and he was obviously very fond of her, so we should have some sort of goodbye scene.

'I'd done a really lovely goodbye scene with that character for my screen test, which had been written by the script editor Andrew Cartmel, and I suggested we use that scene to give it more impact. It seemed terribly curt to just say goodbye.'

Interviewed by Joe Nazzaro in 1993 for *TV Zone* Special # 11.

ON *REMEMBRANCE OF THE DALEKS*:

'I didn't feel as if I were a real Doctor until I'd worked with the Daleks. But it's incredibly difficult to move them around – it's also very boring hanging around waiting for them. The new ones have these great round balls, you know, like under those wheelbarrows, and that made them wobbly Daleks! It's like a big joke. I said I'd like to work with the Daleks because I'd like to find out what was underneath their skirts – and now I've found out, they've got three balls!'

Interviewed by Mark Attwood in 1990 *DWB* No. 77.

ON *THE HAPPINESS PATROL*:

'*The Happiness Patrol* was slightly disappointing, because it was done in the studio. I think it was a bit over-ambitious.

'If they've got to do a story in studio, it would be better to do something actually indoors. Trying to create a planet, it obviously doesn't work. You have to suspend a lot of [disbelief], especially as the other stories [in the same season] were so successful at creating wherever we were on location.'

Interviewed by Paul Travers in 1989 for *Doctor Who Magazine* No. 154.

'It was a great story, I thought. Really good. It had the underlying theme against the more extreme Thatcherite policies of our time. It had a neo-fascist feel about it as well. The harmonica music and the sense of longing . . . It would have been great in black and white. Maybe we should encourage everyone to turn their colour off when they watch it and see what it looks like.'

Interviewed by Nick Briggs in 1994 for *Doctor Who Magazine* No. 216.

ON *SILVER NEMESIS*:

'If you ever see the [American] documentary made [on *Silver Nemesis*] . . . you'll see me sitting on a table, cross legged, with my hair standing up, having a nervous breakdown. The asbestos scare [at the Television Centre studios] had affected us badly. We only had one and a half days' rehearsal left after *The Greatest Show in the Galaxy* to do the story, and we had to make the documentary on the same day. We were just going potty . . . I didn't know where I was.'

Interviewed by Mark Wyman in 1989 for *TARDIS*, spring 1989 edition.

ON *THE GREATEST SHOW IN THE GALAXY*:

'We had a very difficult time with *The Greatest Show in the Galaxy* because of the asbestos scare at the BBC – we had to [record the studio scenes in a] tent at Elstree. The cameras broke down, we had to stop every time a car went by or a bird whistled. Amazing.'

Interviewed by Paul Travers in 1988 for *Doctor Who Magazine* No. 142.

ON *BATTLEFIELD*:

'To work with Nick [Courtney] was lovely! I've always been a great fan of the Brigadier, ever since I watched it when Patrick Troughton and Jon Pertwee were in it. He's a lovely man and we got on very well. I'd met him at conventions before, but it's not the same as working with someone.

'Jean Marsh was lovely too! . . . They're all lovely! I'm a luvvy now! You know how sometimes you just get on with people? The chemistry was great. She could have stayed in *Doctor Who* forever as far as I was concerned. And James Ellis was a great, big-hearted Irishman with all the charm and warmth of that.'

Interviewed by Nick Briggs in 1994 for *Doctor Who Magazine* No. 216.

ON *GHOST LIGHT*:

'I'm enjoying [making] *Ghost Light*. I don't like doing studio work, but I'm happy [that] this one's set inside a building. It will give it much more [credibility]. It's got a brilliant cast, and it's a good story . . . once we work it out!'

Interviewed by Paul Travers in 1989 for *Doctor Who Magazine* No. 154.

ON *THE CURSE OF FENRIC*:

'There was a great moment in *The Curse of Fenric* where Sophie [Aldred] and I ran out of a hut and could literally feel the heat of [an] explosion [set off by] the visual effects guys . . . I enjoyed that!'

Interviewed by Graeme Wood and Andrew Lennard in 1992 for *TV Zone* Special # 4.

'It was very well written. It made sense and there weren't too many holes in it. I liked it because it was about another time. Personally, I liked to travel back in time . . . My attraction to *Doctor Who* in the beginning was the fact that we could go back in time. I've always been interested in history, so it was rather nice to go back to the time of World War Two.'

Interviewed by Nick Briggs in 1994 for *Doctor Who Magazine* No. 216.

ON *SURVIVAL*:

'We were filming in the deserts of Dorset. There's a big sandpit in Dorset. Vast thing . . . It was over 100 degrees in the heatwave, and it was just like doing a spaghetti Western . . . It was incredibly hot and all these girls had to be dressed up in catsuits and all this fun fur stuff; I mean it was just too hot for them! Too unbearably hot. But then again they were very patient except for one, who suddenly freaked out and ripped all her clothes off and was last seen running for the train. It was a lovely sight though . . .'

Interviewed by Bob Furnell, Bonnie Gale, Misha Lauenstein and Pat Burt on 28 January 1996.

'It was lovely to work with Anthony Ainley. It was interesting finding, in acting terms, that he had a way of playing the character. I kept thinking, "Now he's a Time Lord," and so I tried to act similar to him. As Time Lords, when you go round the universe . . . you respond differently to different people. But when you meet your own, there would be that kind of similarity of movement as well as various other things.'

Interviewed by Paul Travers in 1989 for *Doctor Who Magazine* No. 154.

ON HIS DOCTOR'S COMPANIONS:

'Bonnie [Langford] was a specific type of actress and she was definitely employed to act against [Colin Baker's] coat. It was so colourful! . . . You needed a very colourful person there, so there was Bonnie. The pairing was excellent for them, but then I came along. I was a different kettle of fish, and so it wasn't the right kind of pairing. Bonnie and I got on really well, 'cause we're good mates, and we'd worked together before on stage, but it didn't work. It was just the state of play; she didn't have to act against such a colourful coat.'

Interviewed by Darren Floyd, Jeremy Taylor and Huw Griffiths in 1991 for *The Global Times*.

'We are developing the relationship between Ace and [the Doctor] . . . I don't know in depth about the other Doctor/ companion relationships, but this is definitely different from [the] relationship with Ace last year, or the one with Mel. It's deeper; and we have arguments – strong arguments.'

Interviewed by Mark Wyman in 1989 for *TARDIS*, spring 1989 edition.

'The companion shouldn't be someone who screams all the time, and shouldn't be the token woman. She should be a fully fledged character in her own right. I'm sure that others have been; I'm just going by my own prejudice of what I thought. Sophie [Aldred] is great, and we're great mates.'

Interviewed by David J. Howe, Mark Stammers and Stephen James Walker in 1989 for *The Frame* No. 11.

ON HIS DEPARTURE FROM THE SERIES:

'To be very, very honest, when the third year actually came up, I was thinking of jacking it in then, thinking that this is maybe too long. I also had at the back of my mind that Peter Davison had told me that Patrick Troughton had told him: "Only do three years." But then John [Nathan-Turner] said, sometime during the negotiations for the third year, "You must agree to do a fourth term." So I thought, "Okay, I'll do it," and decided to go for it.'

Interviewed by Nick Briggs in 1994 for *Doctor Who Magazine* No. 216.

'I was upset at the end of *Doctor Who*, but I think in a way the fates have taken charge, so perhaps it's right. Otherwise I might have been tempted to stay on for quite a long time; part of me thinks that would have been a bad thing, another part of me thinks I would have enjoyed it. [For my career] as an actor outside . . . *Doctor Who*, it's been much better that I did only three short seasons . . . If I'd stayed for a long time I might

. . . still be typecast. I don't know yet. I'm not that far away from it.'

Interviewed by Darren Floyd, Jeremy Taylor and Huw Griffiths in 1991 for *The Global Times*.

'It was pretty painful for the first couple of years. I was a bit pissed off, really, at the way it had been handled, which seemed to be unfair, but I got used to it as time went on. You just have to carry on.'

Interviewed by Joe Nazzaro in 1993 for *TV Zone* Special # 11.

ON THE PLEASURES OF HIS TIME AS THE DOCTOR:

'I enjoyed working on it very much . . . Just for purely acting charms, it's a great role to play. You're asked to call upon all sorts of acting in it, from kind of merry to mad, and all the various things in between . . . melancholy and manic and murderous . . . and all those various things! It's a terrific role and I had a very happy time. I got on incredibly well with all the technicians and the cameramen and also the production staff. My companions were very good friends. One was an old friend, Bonnie, who I knew before, and Sophie became a good friend . . . I felt that our job as the regulars on the show was to make sure that all the other actors who came to it had a very good time, and as far as I know everyone did.'

Interviewed by Mike Doran, Andrew Gurudata and Kristian LeBlanc in 1993 for *The Chameleon Circuit* Issue 15.

'As we only did five months of the year, I had seven months to go off and do other things. So that made the job even more wonderful, because it afforded me the luxury of experimenting. I went off around England with an Iranian theatre group, doing a play about Iran. Because of the wage from *Doctor Who*, I could afford to find out what it was like working in another culture. And, of course, I went back to the National Theatre and did various other things, plays and *What's Your Story?* for the BBC.'

Interviewed by Nick Briggs in 1994 for *Doctor Who Magazine* No. 216.

ON THE PRESSURES OF HIS TIME AS THE DOCTOR:

'It's exhausting in the studio. The first studio I did was with Kate O'Mara, and . . . we were on set from ten thirty in the morning to ten at night, just the two of us doing these scenes. By the end of the day I couldn't stand up, I was completely shattered!'

Interviewed by Richard Marson in 1987 for *Doctor Who Magazine* No. 130.

'I don't like the loss of privacy. I get lots of letters. I find it a terrible responsibility trying to answer them, finding the time. I'm delighted to get them, obviously. My family would have preferred that I hadn't done [the series]. I've been on television for twelve years regularly . . . People are used to seeing me in the street and saying hello and all that. But *Doctor Who* had a different effect. People do invade your privacy a great deal.'

Interviewed by Mike Doran, Andrew Gurudata and Kristian LeBlanc in 1993 for *The Chameleon Circuit* Issue 15.

ON FAN REACTION TO HIS DOCTOR:

'I was told that there were such things as science-fiction conventions, but that's like saying there are bumps on the moon. I didn't know what they were really. Conventions in Britain at that time were very few and far between. My only knowledge of conventions came from the Laurel and Hardy film *Sons of the Desert*, where they run off; their wives don't want them to go, but they end up at a convention. So I had a sort of comedic view of conventions. I had no idea what they were like. I got the job on

Monday, and on Thursday I was flown to Atlanta, and there was a convention. People dressed up as various Doctors, companions and monsters from *Doctor Who*. Such great fun.'

Interviewed by Mike Doran, Andrew Gurudata and Kristian LeBlanc in 1993 for *The Chameleon Circuit* Issue 15.

'It amazed me at the beginning. I had no idea. At first I was a bit scared, frightened of it. I didn't quite know how to handle it. Then slowly I've grown to like it. I would miss it now. I mean at one time I used to go to conventions more out of duty – but also because they took me to parts of the world I'd never been to . . . But now, you get to know people and various faces and I look forward to going back to places I've been before and meeting people I've met before – seeing old friends.

'In the early days there were some bad moments because some fans . . . especially in Britain . . . became very critical . . . before they'd seen a shot I'd done. In a way *Doctor Who* is a strange role, because normally you don't have that comparison. The only other similar kind of roles are Shakespearean roles – you [have people talking about] good Hamlets and . . . bad Hamlets, [saying one's] not as good [as another, and so on]. In television you really never have that, but with *Doctor Who* you do. So that was a bit of a problem to deal with at first.'

Interviewed by Bob Furnell, Bonnie Gale, Misha Lauenstein and Pat Burt on 28 January 1996.

'There was a tour I did which was on a ship that went from Florida to Mexico and back. [It was] a wonderful convention. But one of the fans, she got a bit emotional, in fact she was so happy that she didn't want to carry on living, and we had to talk her down from jumping off the side of the boat because she was just so happy! That was a bit sad really.

'There was [once] an American guy who stood up and said [something like], "Excuse me, Doctor, but when you were in your third persona, what were you thinking when you opened the TARDIS door onto the planet Skaro?" He believed it, obviously.

Then someone else stood up and said, "Excuse me, Doctor, now you're so universally famous are you worried about being shot?" That was quite an interesting question. I just said, "Next question, please," and hid behind a chair!'

Interviewed by Mark Attwood in 1990 *DWB* No. 77.

ON THE 1996 TELEVISION MOVIE:

'It's wonderful. The only piece of the original costume is the hat, and when I put that on I felt, "Oh I'm wearing this hat again. How good!". . .

'They've treated me wonderfully. They've been very good to me – treated me with a great deal of respect, which is nice . . .

'There's more time and money to it. It's still very British. The director's British. It's a very calm and happy crew as well, and everyone's very enthusiastic . . . What is actually lovely is the Canadian crew who keep saying, "It's wonderful. We're going to get our names up on BBC Television." That's very lovely. They're really excited about it. So there's a great feeling of excitement and joy and people are really working hard to make it as good as they can, and I'm mightily impressed by the crew. They've been wonderful.'

Interviewed by Bob Furnell, Bonnie Gale, Misha Lauenstein and Pat Burt on 28 January 1996.

ON THE RELATIVE MERITS OF STAGE, FILM AND TV WORK:

'Theatre [is my favourite]. I'm a show-off. I like live theatre. I like standing on the stage and performing to a lot of people. I enjoy it immensely. I like to feel the instant feedback.

'I like doing film. On the stage you paint with a broad brush, and with a film you paint with a minute brush, sort of like little Chinese miniatures . . . Television I sometimes found a bit odd because the multicamera shoots are very odd. You never quite know which one you're on, and it's like two mediums married together – theatre and film – which doesn't quite gel.'

Interviewed by Bob Furnell, Bonnie Gale, Misha Lauenstein and Pat Burt on 28 January 1996.

ON HIS HOME LIFE:

'I have a family that I love very much and [mixing private and professional activities] it's like schizophrenia. It's a very schizophrenic profession and I'm a very schizophrenic person. Someone once read my palm and they said it was the most schizophrenic palm they'd ever seen. I think that's acting all the different parts. I go home and though I obviously talk about acting, I try to give as much energy there as when I'm working.

'My wife isn't in the business and doesn't really want to be a part of it. She enjoys the fact that I am . . . I'm not looking forward to finding a *Sun* reporter in my dustbin. If I do, I'll stick the lid back on and chain it down. I presume people are going to pry, but if they do they'll get a poke in the eye, or they'll be told in a very Scottish way where to go. They'll no doubt carry on doing it, though, and I'll just have to learn to live with it.

'As for my other interests, I go out to the theatre a lot, I like ballet and I like films and opera.'

Interviewed by Richard Marson in 1987 for *Doctor Who Magazine* No. 130.

'My wife's name is Agnes. We've been married for fifteen years. We have an eleven year old son whose name is Sam and another boy named Joe, who will be ten in November.'

Interviewed by uncredited writer in 1988 for *Whovian Times* Volume 17.

'I like classical music a lot. But I do enjoy all other sorts of music. The other day I was sailing up the Thames on a barge and we stopped at this supposedly boring place called Staines. We went into the square [and] there was an opera on at the Town

Hall, so I went to the opera . . . Then [after the opera I] came out and went across the road . . . into [a] pub where they had heavy metal, and I enjoyed that as well . . .

'I watch documentaries [and] the news [on television]. I rarely watch series or comedy shows any more. Films if there is a film on. But I have a secret and terrible addiction I must confess . . . I don't want anyone to know about it. I watch *Prisoner: Cell Block H* . . . I sit there and roar with laughter. It is *so* bad – I love it.'

Interviewed by Bob Furnell, Bonnie Gale, Misha Lauenstein and Pat Burt on 28 January 1996.

ON HIMSELF:

'Sylvester McCoy was born at the height of a Scottish summer, i.e. it was raining, it was cold, it was windy. He came out crying. I can't say he's been crying ever since, but he's been trying to make sure that not too many people around-about him cry too much. He's always felt slightly outside society, as if he was looking in and should be commenting on it. He was quite pleased about that. He was delighted to have eventually ended up as an actor, and agrees very much with the idea that actors should be, like gypsies, buried outside the walls of a city. They should not be allowed to be put in consecrated ground. He's delighted by that fact. He finds society comical, cruel, interesting and he's sometimes incredibly critical of it. He doesn't want to become a knight, because then he'd know that he'd really been bought by society.'

Interviewed by Nick Briggs in 1994 for *Doctor Who Magazine* No. 216.

2: The Doctor

Unlike when he had overseen the transition from the fourth Doctor to the fifth in 1981, or that from the fifth Doctor to the sixth in 1984, producer John Nathan-Turner had no opportunity to lay careful plans to take *Doctor Who* through the difficult process of the departure of the sixth Doctor and the arrival of the seventh. The unexpected nature of Colin Baker's exit from the role in October 1986 – Michael Grade, the then Controller of BBC1, having instructed Nathan-Turner to dismiss the actor after the completion of work on the series' twenty-third season – meant that arrangements for the casting, characterisation and introduction of the seventh Doctor had to be made between seasons. This was a task that Nathan-Turner had not expected to have to manage himself. He had acceded to his superiors' request to inform Baker of his ousting from the series only on the understanding that he would then be allowed to move on to a different project – something that he had been requesting for some time. On his return from a period of extended leave over the winter, however, he was informed that if he wished to remain on staff at the BBC he would have to continue as producer for the following season.

The most pressing problem requiring attention at this time was the lack of any suitable scripts lined up for production. Nathan-Turner therefore set about urgently finding a new script editor for the series (the previous one, Eric Saward, having resigned amid controversy) and, in the meantime, contacted Pip and Jane Baker – who had written for the sixth Doctor's era – and asked if they would consider contributing the new Doctor's introductory story.

They agreed, and on 22 December 1986 were commissioned to provide the scripts for a four-parter entitled *Strange Matter* (adapted from an earlier unused storyline).

The fact that a new Doctor was required for the series had been picked up by many actors and actors' agents, who were eager to put forward suggestions. On 18 December 1986 Nathan-Turner was contacted by Sylvester McCoy, whose agent subsequently sent in a photograph and information about his client. 'I had endless lists of possible Doctors,' recalled Nathan-Turner in a 1988 interview for Peter Haining's *Doctor Who – 25 Glorious Years*. 'I also got lots of calls from actors' agents suggesting their clients. It really is a plum job, you see, even with all the demands on both private and public life. One of these calls was from Sylvester McCoy's agent who suggested that I went to see him at the National Theatre in London where he was appearing in *The Pied Piper*. It was 6 January 1987 [when I went], I remember. I was very impressed with Sylvester's performance and decided to meet him. He later came in to my office and we sat chatting for about two hours. There is this wonderful, natural, eccentric quality about Sylvester. There is a sort of disjointed way that he speaks – the gestures are never quite in the right place at the right moment. I found myself riveted and quite happy to go on listening to him.' Nathan-Turner also viewed videotapes of some of McCoy's television appearances and was particularly impressed by a Channel 4 interview in which the actor had spoken about himself and his role in *The Pied Piper*, and exhibited the same kind of fascinatingly offbeat quality that the producer had noted in his office. He was keen from the outset to give the part to McCoy, but his immediate superior, Head of Series and Serials Jonathan Powell, asked him to cast his net a little wider and to carry out some screen tests.

Nathan-Turner and director Andrew Morgan, who had been assigned to handle *Strange Matter* (later retitled *Time and the Rani*), eventually came up with a short list of actors, three of whom – including McCoy – were subsequently screen-tested, as Powell had requested, on 18 February 1987. This involved their being recorded on the TARDIS set performing two short scenes written by Andrew Cartmel, the new script editor found by Nathan-Turner for the series, and directed by Morgan. Former companion actress Janet Fielding was contracted to act opposite them, playing an evil adversary in one of the scenes and a departing companion in the other. 'I did the tests with Sylvester and some other actors,' explained Nathan-Turner, 'and – with no disrespect to the others – Sylvester was the Doctor I was looking for. I had always envisaged a Troughtonesque quality and here it was. Mind you, I don't think Sylvester and Pat Troughton are madly similar, but there are little characteristics which are the same. I also wanted somebody who was much smaller than Colin Baker.' In addition, the producer favoured casting a relative unknown. The final decision to go for McCoy was made by Nathan-Turner in consultation with both Powell and Grade. The actor's accession to the role was officially announced by the BBC on Monday 2 March, although news of it had leaked to the press over the previous weekend as Nathan-Turner had made his own announcement in the USA on the Friday (see Chapter 9).

Nathan-Turner had briefed Pip and Jane Baker when they started work on their story to make the new Doctor a more humorous character than the old one. He also wanted to have him behaving 'semi-normally' by the time he had his first confrontation with his adversary the Rani (in contrast to some previous occasions when the Doctor had been seen to act in a decidedly erratic manner for an extended period following a regeneration). 'We were well into writing the story when we were shown a video of Sylvester McCoy,' revealed the husband-and-wife writing team in a 1988 interview. 'We had to find a) a way of regenerating the Doctor and b) a character for him. John asked for a pre-credits teaser. All of us felt that we couldn't go straight into the story. If we had to regenerate in this way we needed to start with it, then have a full stop and then start the story. It would have been impossible to open with Sylvester's title sequence otherwise; it would have looked silly.'

The apparent implication of the teaser as seen on screen was that the Doctor's regeneration was precipitated by nothing more serious than a fall from an exercise bike when the TARDIS was attacked in flight by his renegade Time Lord adversary the Rani – although it is possible that far more momentous events had occurred before this, of which the viewer was simply left unaware.

McCoy himself was very much in sympathy with Nathan-Turner's wish to bring a degree of humour into the portrayal of the seventh Doctor – at his initial press conference he told reporters that he wanted to play the part with 'more zest' as a combination of the eccentric scientist figures Magnus Pyke and David Bellamy; as someone who was 'madly interested' in everything he did and would get enthusiastic about tiny things amidst mayhem. He was inspired in part by Patrick Troughton's approach to the role, which he recalled as being predominantly humorous. He was in any case naturally inclined towards taking a comedic approach in his work, having been greatly influenced by figures such as Buster Keaton, Stan Laurel and Max Wall and having started his acting career in madcap comedy roles in Ken Campbell's Roadshow. 'I said in my [initial] discussion with [John Nathan-Turner] that I wanted to be a very Troughtonesque type of Doctor and have the contrast between the comedy and the seriousness,' he told Gary Levy and Robert Cope in a 1987 interview for *DWB* 50. 'He accepted that, but there was one time where he came in and said it was too comedic in the first rehearsal. I think the first story was a learning process for all of us, because it wasn't written for me, it was written for an unknown Doctor and by people who had only written for Colin. Some of the lines are just pure Colin's lines – you can *hear* Colin saying them.'

The 'learning process' of McCoy gradually finding his feet as the Doctor and the writers coming to reflect and cater for his characterisation in their scripts was something that continued throughout the remainder of the twenty-fourth season. 'The first season was just a hotchpotch, really . . .' noted McCoy when interviewed by Mark Wyman for the spring 1989 edition of *TARDIS*. 'The writers didn't know who to write for, and I arrived not really knowing . . . Although I'd said at the interview, "This is how I want to play the Doctor," I was just talking off the top of my head. I hadn't seen *Doctor Who* for quite a few years, and the memory I had of it was what I was vaguely selling. When I came to do it, half way through the season I suddenly thought "Now I know what it's about", but by then it was too late and we could only carry on.'

McCoy was in fact able to have a limited degree of input into the scripting of the Doctor's character as the season progressed, as he told an uncredited writer in a 1988 interview for *Whovian Times* Volume 17: 'When the opportunity presented itself, I was able to make a few changes. Very few, but important things. I was even allowed to add a few scenes. If I believed in it and I was enthusiastic enough about it and could get them enthusiastic about my idea they would put it in.' Another way in which the actor was able to bring his influence to bear was by placing an interpretation on the script that the writer might not have anticipated. Sometimes, for instance, he would deliver a line much more angrily than might have been expected from its immediate context – an attempt, as he later explained, to evoke memories of William Hartnell's Doctor, who, he had been told, was often irascible. On other occasions he would endeavour to suggest hidden depths to the Doctor's character, such as through his adoption of a melancholy tone and faraway look when commenting, 'Love has never been known for its rationality' in *Delta and the Bannermen*. It was only when work on Season 24 had been completed, however, that he had the opportunity to get together with the series' production team for a detailed discussion of how the seventh Doctor ought ideally to be portrayed. 'We sat down and chatted between seasons,' he told Wyman, 'and I said, "I want him to be more mysterious – to show the inner side of him. He's not just clear cut." Of course, he may have been all those things before that I wanted him to be, but it wasn't clear in my mind.'

The standard brief on the Doctor's character that the production team made available to prospective writers at this time was relatively minimal, and read:

> THE DOCTOR
>
> The DOCTOR is a Time Lord from the planet Gallifrey which is in the constellation of Kasterborous. He possesses

> two hearts, has a body temperature of sixty degrees Fahrenheit and is over seven centuries in age. He has the capability of regenerating himself into different appearances – his present form being his seventh guise.
>
> He no longer resides on his own planet due to his boredom with his own super-advanced planet and fellow Time Lords – he roams through time and space in his own personalised ship – the TARDIS.
>
> The DOCTOR himself is not infallible. Part of his appeal is his problem-solving capacity when things go wrong, making do with bits and pieces of electronic gadgetry that just happen to be around.

Cartmel, rather than leaving his writers to rely on these basic notes, preferred to talk through with them the way in which the character ought to be depicted, in line with the discussions that he and Nathan-Turner had had with McCoy. The fruits of these discussions became readily apparent in the transmitted stories. In Season 24 the Doctor had been seen to act – particularly at first – in a quirky, somewhat clownish manner, taking near-slapstick tumbles, playing the spoons (an example of McCoy drawing on his own talents for the role – something that Nathan-Turner was keen to take advantage of) and coming out with scrambled adages and mixed metaphors (an adaptation of his predecessor's trait of offering pertinent – and generally accurate – quotations). In Seasons 25 and 26, however, he was shown to be a far more serious, brooding character. He also appeared more able than in any of his earlier incarnations to influence and control events occurring around him: far from being simply an aimless traveller, doing his best to help the underdog and to fight injustice wherever he encountered it, he was now seen to adopt near-Machiavellian strategies in order to achieve his objectives, leaving his new companion Ace to handle the more physical aspects of his battles.

The idea emerged of the Doctor as a master strategist,

manoeuvring his adversaries and manipulating his allies like a galactic chess player – literally so in the case of Fenric in *The Curse of Fenric*, although the chess motif was also made explicit in *Silver Nemesis*. In *Remembrance of the Daleks* there were suggestions that, contrary to previous indications, the Doctor might somehow have been a contemporary of Rassilon and Omega – the legendary founders of Time Lord society. Then, in *Silver Nemesis*, the seventeenth-century sorceress Lady Peinforte claimed to be in possession of momentous secrets about his past 'from the dark time', although in the event she never had an opportunity to reveal what these were. There were even hints that some aspects of the Doctor's established history might have been deliberate fabrications on his part.

'[We wanted] to increase the mystery,' confirmed the actor in a 1995 interview conducted by Lou Anders for *Dreamwatch* 17. 'The only way we could do that was to make the audience uncertain of him, to find out whether he was this loveable character or he was dangerous. [I wanted to toy with the viewer,] to actually open up another area, peeling an onion, another layer. You'd been given the Doctor that you'd known for the last twenty-odd years, and all the mystery had been stripped from him. In order to create mystery we had to peel another layer and invent another dimension, as it were. Perhaps he was one of the three creators of Gallifrey, and where would that lead you? Well, into a whole new sphere [that] the writers could go and explore.

'[The change didn't happen overnight.] It was like turning a great ship in the ocean. It takes a long time to turn it round, because the scripts have already been written for the next season and all that stuff. It wasn't until half way through . . . the second season that the scripts started to arrive that fitted the Doctor that I wanted to do; and by the third season, we were getting there. [Had the series continued, the Doctor's character would have become] much darker, keeping the comedy all the time, but in layers. This was part of the defence system of the Doctor.'

McCoy also felt that the Doctor should be a nonviolent person who solved his problems through the use of his wits and ingenuity. 'It's a combination of unarmed vulnerability and eccentric imagination that makes the Doctor so appealing as he confronts evil,' he asserted in an interview for the 5 October 1988 edition of the *Morning Star*.

In gaining agreement to all these changes McCoy found an enthusiastic and like-minded ally in Andrew Cartmel. 'He's played a hell of a big part,' he admitted to Mark Wyman. 'It's often instant agreement between us. I'll say "What about . . ." and he says, "Yes, what a good idea . . ." We seem to have agreed a lot . . . I'm getting a trifle worried now about the lack of humour. I have to find the humour as well, because I think it's very important that he has that kind of "front". Now and again, he opens a door, and behind it there is great dark foreboding, or mystery, and anger, really. The Doctor has spent nine hundred years travelling around, and seen such destruction; love and wonders too, of course, but all that terrible destruction. So I want to bring that out.'

'We certainly did want to build up the mystery,' commented Cartmel in a 1994 convention interview. 'Having said that, we had no agenda. I think that we did say on several occasions that we wanted the Doctor to be more mysterious and also more powerful, because he didn't seem to be this huge, dangerous, interesting alien, and I think we managed to recapture some of that with Sylvester.'

The nonviolent aspect of the Doctor's character was reflected in scenes such as the one at the end of *Remembrance of the Daleks* in which he effectively talked the Dalek Supreme into committing suicide by convincing it that it was the last of its kind still alive; this was substituted for a sequence in Ben Aaronovitch's original script in which the Doctor blasted the Dalek Supreme with a gun in a pastiche of a Western shoot-out.

Interviewed in 1994 by Nicholas Briggs for *Doctor Who Magazine* No. 216, McCoy described how he had hoped to take the development of the character further, had he gone on to make a fourth season as the Doctor:

'I wanted to bring a much darker side to the character – not all the time, but I was enjoying mining this part of the character, you know? The misery that the man, this jolly person, carried around.

So that's what the fourth term was going to be about.

'He'd been around for, they told me, nine hundred and fifty years – it kept changing. I thought about my grandmother, who'd lived for one hundred years and three months. She got to one hundred and then decided that was it. In the three months left, she took up alcohol and merrily knocked herself out, went to sleep one night and didn't wake up. She'd never drunk throughout the whole of the rest of her life. But she used to tell me that she was tired; not so much physically tired – she was incredibly fit with a very sharp brain – but all her friends had died; her immediate family had all gone before her. There was that sadness of old age, the sadness of longevity.

'I found that interesting, because the Doctor had lived for all this time. I thought of [the Biblical figure of] Methuselah (who was supposedly nine hundred and sixty-nine years old) and the Ancient Mariner [in Coleridge's poem]. These people who lived for so long . . . there was a great sadness in their lives. I thought, that ought to be part of the Doctor's baggage. He goes through all these experiences, and although time is relative and all those kind of things, I felt we had to feel those nine hundred and fifty years. He'd lost so many companions, some happily, but generally it was tragically. He'd seen so much violence and misery! So I wanted to bring that baggage with me – to be part of what he was carrying.'

The discontinuation of *Doctor Who* as an ongoing BBC series denied McCoy the opportunity of exploring these ideas. The seventh Doctor did, however, make a brief reappearance in the 1996 *Doctor Who* television movie, giving the actor a chance to fulfil a promise he had made to the series' fans that he would return for a regeneration story if ever he was asked to do so, and thereby help to give his successor a smoother introduction than he himself had had. Interviewed by Bob Furnell, Bonnie Gale, Misha Lauenstein and Pat Burt on 28 January 1996, while in the Canadian city of Vancouver to film his scenes for the movie, he summarised the development of his portrayal of the seventh Doctor over the course of his three seasons in the role:

'Starting up in an incredibly naïve way, not knowing really

anything about it, diving in the deep end, relying on my own kind of natural bent towards comedy and then realising what the job was, then trying to work towards getting it, not quite achieving it – because really I needed another season to get where I wanted to. And in a sense I kind of arrogantly wanted to bring it back to a more mysterious, dangerous Doctor – not necessarily evil, but questionable. To get back that mystery. I also wanted . . . I was very interested in the fact of his longevity. I wanted somehow to start carrying that longevity to the screen . . . I wanted all that. [I wanted to make him darker, but to keep] the comic façade. You know, that kind of Patrick Troughtonesque quality. My first Doctor was Patrick Troughton and I always remembered him as light and amusing and still at the same time having the ability to switch back and forth. That was the idea. I don't know if I really ever achieved that, but that's what I wanted. I thought [that] *Ghost Light* [had] the best written part for the Doctor. It didn't work on the screen – *Ghost Light* was a bit confusing, you have to read the book to understand what's happening – but I liked what the writer had done for the Doctor . . . That was really good. I thought, "Oh good! This is how I want to play him. These are the words I want to say." '

–

PART TWO – FICTION

3: The Stories

'. . . the Doctor is unceremoniously lifted over the hairy shoulder of a Tetrap and carried out of the TARDIS . . .'

Note: In the following listings, the technical details are as follows: 'Time' refers to the starting time, rounded to the nearest minute, of the original transmission of an episode in England; 'Durn' indicates the exact duration of the episode on the master tape (where known) or otherwise the duration of the original transmission; 'Viewers' gives the official viewing figure in millions; 'Chart Pos' is the position of the episode in the top 200 programmes for that week. Where a dash appears in the 'Viewers' or 'Chart Pos' column, this signifies that no information was collected by the BBC for the transmission in question.

SEASON TWENTY-FOUR

Time and the Rani (7D)

EP	DATE	TIME	DURN	VIEWERS	CHART POS
1	07.09.87	19.35	24'44"	5.1	71
2	14.09.87	19.34	24'36"	4.2	85
3	21.09.87	19.36	24'23"	4.3	81
4	28.09.87	19.36	24'38"	4.9	86

PRODUCTION DETAILS
OB Recording: 04.04.87–08.04.87
Studio Recording: 20.04.87, 21.04.87 in TC8, 03.05.87–05.05.87 in TC1

On the planet Lakertya, the Rani (Kate O'Mara) finishes supervising two Lakertyans, Beyus (Donald Pickering) and his daughter Sarn (Karen Clegg), as they store the kidnapped genius Einstein (unknown) in a sealed cabinet alongside a number of others. The Doctor meanwhile regains consciousness in the Rani's laboratory. He seems manic and disorientated but recognises the Rani. Examining her equipment, he sees an asteroid which he identifies as being composed of strange matter.

Sarn runs away and encounters Mel, who has been rescued from the TARDIS by another Lakertyan, Ikona (Mark Greenstreet). Sarn panics and trips a wire, which creates a transparent bubble, trapping her inside. The bubble bounces around before exploding, reducing Sarn to a smoking skeleton.

The Rani orders Urak (Richard Gauntlett), a batlike creature known as a Tetrap, to reset the trap while she injects the Doctor with something to give him amnesia. When the Doctor comes round, the Rani pretends to be Mel in order to persuade him to repair a faulty machine in her laboratory.

Ikona believes Mel to be in league with the Rani. She saves him from another of the bubble traps and thus convinces him that she is friendly.

The Doctor is puzzled and confused and refuses to continue work. He and the Rani return to his TARDIS to fetch a radiation-wave meter. There, the Doctor changes his clothes, trying on those of his fourth, third, fifth and second incarnations, among others, before settling on a new outfit for himself.

Mel sees Urak and stumbles into a bubble trap. She is caught inside the bubble, which bounces over a cliff and lands on a lake. Ikona rescues her and they retrieve some weapons before being attacked by another Tetrap. Escaping, they head for the Rani's fortress, where Ikona meets Sarn's mother, Faroon (Wanda Ventham). Faroon discovers her daughter's skeleton and goes to speak with Beyus.

The Rani goes to fetch some vital material for the Doctor to use in the machine, but is captured by Urak, who mistakes her for Mel. Mel meanwhile makes her way into the Rani's control room, where the Doctor believes her to be the Rani. The two travellers eventually convince each other that they are who they say they are by feeling each other's pulses. Beyus helps them to escape by telling the Doctor the combination to unlock the control-room door – it is 953, which is both the Doctor's and the Rani's age.

Outside the control room, Mel finds the cabinets containing the kidnapped geniuses and sees that one is reserved for the Doctor. The Rani returns and, while Mel, Beyus and Faroon escape, the Doctor hides in a dark Tetrap eyrie. The Rani locks the gate behind him and he finds himself surrounded by the awaking Tetraps (Mark Carroll, Lea Derek, Ian Durrant, Paul Goddard, Daryl Book, Ricardo Mulhall, Paul Page-Hanson).

Beyus rescues the Doctor and tells him to go to the Lakertyans' Centre of Leisure, where the reason for his obedience to the Rani will be revealed. The Doctor takes a micro-thermistor from the Rani's machine and leaves.

Mel is captured by the Tetraps and paralysed by a sting from the tongue of one of them. The Rani tells Faroon to give the Doctor a message that she will exchange Mel for the micro-thermistor.

At the Centre of Leisure, the Doctor and Ikona find that the Lakertyan people are indolent and apathetic. There is a new globelike device suspended from the Centre, but no one will tell the distressed Ikona what it is for. The Rani, using remote control, suddenly stops the globe from spinning, causing killer insects to emerge from it. The Doctor, Beyus and the other Lakertyans run screaming from the Centre.

Faroon delivers her message to the Doctor, who agrees to the proposed exchange. The Rani tricks him, however, as the 'Mel' she releases is revealed to be only a holographic projection. The renegade Time Lord reinserts the micro-thermistor in her machine, making it operational, but finds that the combined brain power of the kidnapped geniuses is still not sufficient for her purposes. Urak suggests that she link her own brain in. She refuses and orders that the Doctor's cabinet be prepared.

The Doctor notes that the Rani has a fixed-trajectory rocket launcher and realises that she must be working to meet a specific deadline. Ikona distracts the Tetrap guarding the entrance to the Rani's fortress and the Doctor enters. He is caught by Urak, paralysed and placed in his cabinet. The Rani then enters a sealed room, followed by a recovered Mel. Inside is a massive brain (voice: Peter Tuddenham, Jacki Webb). With the Doctor's input, the brain is able to start carrying out the calculations that the Rani desires.

Urak and the other Tetraps leave the fortress to punish selected Lakertyans by placing around their leg a bracelet-like control device that will reduce them to a skeleton if removed.

The Rani finds that the Doctor is confusing the brain and orders him disconnected. The Doctor jumps from his cabinet, and he and Mel then trap the Rani inside it. In the control room, the Doctor finds that the Rani's rocket is intended to strike the asteroid of strange matter. He and Mel watch a recording of a supernova on a screen. Mel realises that the Rani is using the brain to come up with a lightweight substitute for strange matter in order to detonate the asteroid.

The Rani escapes from the cabinet and explains her plan to the Doctor and Mel. She needs helium-2. This will fuse with the upper Lakertyan atmosphere to form a shell of chronons – discrete particles of time – and then the brain will multiply, filling the gap between shell and planet, thereby creating a time manipulator, a cerebral mass capable of dominating and controlling time anywhere in the cosmos. Urak overhears the Rani boasting that all life on Lakertya will be destroyed. The Doctor gives the brain the correct formula and it devises loyhargil as the substance required. As the production of loyhargil starts in the Rani's laboratory, the Doctor and Mel escape from the fortress.

The Doctor helps safely remove the control devices from the Lakertyans, then returns to the fortress and places them around the brain. Beyus stays to complete this task as the Doctor, Mel and Faroon escape.

The Doctor confronts the Rani, who detonates the devices. The brain nevertheless completes its countdown and the rocket launches, but because of the Doctor's interference it misses the asteroid.

The Rani escapes to her TARDIS, but it has been commandeered by the Tetraps, who take her prisoner.

The Doctor takes all the captured geniuses on board the TARDIS so that he can return them home. He also gives the Lakertyans the antidote to the killer insects, but Ikona pours it away as he believes they should solve their own problems from now on.

WHO FAX

- Novelised as *Doctor Who – Time and the Rani* by Pip and Jane Baker in 1987.
- Story released on BBC Home Video in 1995.
- Working title: *Strange Matter*.
- Locations: Cloford Quarry, Cloford, nr Frome, Somerset; Whatley Quarry, Whatley, nr Frome, Somerset; Westdown Quarry, nr Nunney, nr Frome, Somerset.
- *Time and the Rani* featured only the third pre-titles sequence in the series' history. This showed the TARDIS being attacked in space and crashing on Lakertya. The Rani and Urak enter and the Doctor regenerates. The previous uses of a pre-titles sequence had been on Season 19's *Castrovalva* and the twentieth anniversary special *The Five Doctors*.
- For the first time, *Doctor Who*'s opening titles were created by

computer. The work was carried out by BBC graphic designer Oliver Elmes in collaboration with Gareth Edwards at CAL, a freelance computer graphics company. John Nathan-Turner was so pleased with the finished result that he commissioned CAL to create more images of the TARDIS in space, which were used for the Rani's attack on the TARDIS in the pre-titles sequence.

- John Nathan-Turner felt that the original version of the title sequence did not feature the Doctor's face prominently enough and so asked that it be more clearly superimposed. The original version was, however, used by mistake to open the fourth episode of *Time and the Rani*.
- To accompany the new title sequence, composer Keff McCulloch was called upon to provide a new arrangement of Ron Grainer's theme, replacing the previous Dominic Glynn version.

QUOTES

- 'I think I might wince at the Rani story if I saw it again.' Director Andrew Morgan interviewed by Marcus Hearn for *Doctor Who Magazine* Issue 204.

COMMENT

DJH: Time and the Rani *has got to take the title of worst opening story for a Doctor ever, beating even the sixth Doctor's debut,* The Twin Dilemma, *which was bad enough. There are virtually no redeeming features in this runabout, and for once even the musical score is simply dreadful, totally at odds with the action and simply highlighting the deficiencies of an appalling set of scripts. The actors seem lost, Kate O'Mara is wasted, and the Tetraps, while impressive, are given virtually nothing to do. The plot hinges around the incredible fact that, despite having masses of technology – including a refinery – at her disposal, the Rani has not thought to build her rocket launcher with an adjustable trajectory. A total waste of time. (1/10)*

SJW: Time and the Rani *is an impressive-looking story. It boasts* *some fine location recording, good sets and absolutely superb electronic effects – particularly for the Rani's bubble traps, which are wonderfully realised. What lets the whole thing down is the lacklustre quality of the scripts by Pip and Jane Baker, which are poorly plotted, full of ludicrous ideas and terrible dialogue and, perhaps even worse, fail to engage the viewer's interest. Sylvester McCoy makes a reasonable debut as the Doctor but is clearly still finding his feet in the role and would perhaps have benefited from some stronger direction. (3/10)*

Paradise Towers (7E)

EP	DATE	TIME	DURN	VIEWERS	CHART POS
1	05.10.87	19.34	24'33"	4.5	88
2	12.10.87	19.38	24'39"	5.2	84
3	19.10.87	19.36	24'30"	5.0	79
4	26.10.87	19.35	24'21"	5.0	93

PRODUCTION DETAILS

OB Recording: 21.05.87, 22.05.87
Studio Recording: 04.06.87, 05.06.87, 17.06.87–19.06.87 all in TC1

A young woman (Astra Sheridan), the last surviving member of a gang known as the Yellow Kangs, is killed in the corridors of a huge tower block called Paradise Towers. The Doctor and Mel arrive in the TARDIS, Mel hoping to take a dip in the Towers' swimming pool, but find that the building is run down and defaced with graffiti. They are captured by the Red Kangs (Christina Clark, Louise Clifford, Helen Fung, Elizabeth Gardner, Nisha Nayar, Julietta Norde, Jennie Slade, Martha Stylianou, Roberta Wells, Lottie Winter) and the Doctor makes friends with their leaders, Bin Liner (Annabelle Yuresha) and Fire Escape (Julie Brennon). The Kangs decide to take the two travellers to their 'hide-in', but they are attacked by Caretakers

(Sean Bowden, Andrew J. Bush, James Carrington, William Perrie, Nick Santini, Don Weinstein, Rupert Clive, Barrimore) and the Doctor is arrested.

Mel escapes and meets two old ladies, Tilda (Brenda Bruce) and Tabby (Elizabeth Spriggs), known as rezzies. The old ladies are friendly, offering her tea and cakes, but her stay at their apartment is interrupted by a young man named Pex (Howard Cooke), who breaks down the door in order to 'save' her. She leaves, and Pex insists on accompanying her to protect and guide her.

The Doctor is taken to meet the Chief Caretaker (Richard Briers), who believes him to be the Great Architect responsible for creating Paradise Towers and orders a 327 Appendix 3 Subsection 9 death for him. The Doctor escapes by tricking his guards into following nonexistent rules.

Mel and Pex – the only young man left in the Towers when all the others left to fight a war – are captured by the Blue Kangs (Suzanna Cardash, Tanya Davidson-Jones, Iona Dean, Harriet Eedle, Leigh Funnell, Heather Mair Thomas, Liz Wood). The Doctor meanwhile finds his way back to the Red Kang 'brainquarters', where he is recaptured by the Caretakers and in turn rescued by Bin Liner and Fire Escape.

The Chief Caretaker visits a mist-shrouded area in the basement of the building and speaks with something that proclaims it is hungry. The Chief Caretaker calls it his 'pet' and refers to himself as its 'daddy'.

Mel manages to talk her way out of the clutches of the Blue Kangs. She then encounters Tabby and Tilda again, but their friendly façade vanishes as they wrap her in a shawl and threaten her with a toasting fork, apparently intent on eating her. She escapes when first Tabby and then Tilda are dragged into their apartment's waste-disposal outlet by a robot arm that emerges from within it. A large robot cleaner transports the bodies of the two old ladies to the thing in the basement.

Mel and Pex make their way to a lift and, after many failed attempts, finally arrive at Floor 304 where the pool is situated. Mel intends to go swimming, failing to notice that there is a bright-yellow cleaning robot in the water.

The Doctor postulates that the Kangs' parents trapped the Great Architect, Kroagnon, in the building to stop him from completing it. The Kangs reveal that there is a 'door with smoke' in the basement. The Doctor, Fire Escape, Bin Liner and Air Duct (unknown) prepare to go and investigate. Before they can do so, however, the Blue Kangs attack, their Leader (Catherine Cusack), claiming that they have won the game. The Doctor intercedes and gets the two groups of Kangs to work together.

The Chief Caretaker is escorted to the basement by a robot cleaner and again talks with the mysterious creature. The Doctor, Fire Escape, Bin Liner, Air Duct and the Blue Kang Leader arrive. They watch as the Chief Caretaker is forced to stand under a tube but are then attacked and chased away by robot cleaners. When they have gone, the tube retracts to reveal that the Chief Caretaker has now been taken over by Kroagnon.

Mel is attacked by the cleaning robot in the pool. Pex is too scared to help her, but she grabs his gun and destroys the robot. The Doctor gathers all the Kangs together and takes them to the pool, where he is reunited with Mel.

As Kroagnon systematically 'cleanses' the floors of Paradise Towers by having the cleaning robots kill all the inhabitants, the remaining rezzies, including Maddy (Judy Cornwell), and caretakers, including the Deputy Chief Caretaker (Clive Merrison), also arrive at the pool. The Doctor gets everyone to work together to try to defeat Kroagnon.

The Deputy Chief Caretaker explains that on Floor 245, Sodium Street, Corridor 75, there is a store of explosives that they can use to destroy the cleaners. The Doctor plans to set a trap for Kroagnon and Pex volunteers to lure him there. When they arrive, the Doctor tries to topple Kroagnon into the mined store but is unable to do so. Pex plucks up courage and pushes Kroagnon in, but falls in after him. The store explodes.

The Kangs hold a ceremony to celebrate Pex's life and apparent death. The Doctor is made an honorary Kang – red and blue – and he and Mel leave in the TARDIS. On the wall nearby is a graffito reading 'Pex Lives'.

WHO FAX

- Novelised as *Doctor Who – Paradise Towers* by Stephen Wyatt in 1989.
- Story released on BBC Home Video in 1995.
- Working title: none, although the commissioning documents refer to the story as *Paradise Tower*.
- Locations: Elmswell House, Chalfont St Giles, Buckinghamshire.
- Catherine Cusack, playing the Blue Kang Leader, is the youngest daughter of Irish actor Cyril Cusack, who was at one point considered for the role of the first Doctor in 1963.
- Annabel Yuresha, playing Bin Liner, is the daughter of Belinda Wright and the Yugoslav Jelko Yuresha, who both danced regularly with the London Festival Ballet.
- For the scenes in the swimming pool where Mel is attacked by a robot, Bonnie Langford was doubled by stunt woman Ellie Bertram.
- The part of the Deputy Chief Caretaker was originally offered to Edward Hardwicke but he was unable to take it as he was working on a film.
- The incidental-music composer originally assigned to *Paradise Towers* was David Snell. He completed a score for all four episodes but was informed by John Nathan-Turner in a letter dated 11 September 1987 that it was unsatisfactory. Nathan-Turner commented that while the original sample music that Snell had provided had been fine, the completed work tended in his view to detract from the action of the story rather than enhance it. Snell responded in a letter dated 18 September, expressing disappointment and commenting that, when he had completed the music for the first two episodes, director Nicholas Mallett had assured him that Nathan-Turner was very happy with it. Snell was willing to rewrite, free of charge, any sequences that Nathan-Turner disliked, but this offer was not taken up and instead Keff McCulloch was contracted at a very late stage to supply an alternative score.

QUOTES

- 'I suppose the real starting point was when Andrew [Cartmel] asked me what SF I'd read. I responded by telling him "Not very much," but that I did like J. G. Ballard and in particular a story of his called *High Rise*. It's about a futuristic automated tower block . . . which experiences a breakdown. Following on from that initial seed of thought, it took a very long time to get the meat on the bones. However, it was a very liberating experience as I wasn't being asked to fit into any particular mould but was allowed to bring to my story what I wanted.' Writer Stephen Wyatt interviewed by John B. McLay for *Private Who* Issue 16.
- '*Paradise Towers* started from our desire to present a distorted view of what most tower blocks are like. From there, I added characters and features which were pushed to extremes, deliberately exaggerated versions of reality. The lifts are a good case in point. I'd recently visited a tower block in the East End [of London], pushed the button for the floor I wanted and was then trapped inside that little metal box for what seemed like an eternity, as it just travelled up and down totally at random. When I finally escaped (fortunately only two floors away from the one I wanted) someone told me that kids get in, press all the buttons and then get out again. And as there are no indicator lights, the next person may be stuck going up and down for hours without knowing why! So that part was certainly based on truth.' Writer Stephen Wyatt interviewed by John B. McLay for *Private Who* Issue 16.

COMMENT

***DJH:** The poor start to the season continues with this confused and corridor-bound adventure. Richard Briers delivers a dreadful performance as the Chief Caretaker, and Bonnie Langford's Mel is painful to watch as she seems to think that she is acting on stage rather than on television. With its cannibalistic old ladies, cowardly heroes and red- and blue-rinsed gangs of teenaged girls,* Paradise Towers *is an incomprehensible mess. Its one redeeming feature is Annabelle Yuresha's excellent performance as Bin Liner. (4/10)*

SJW: Paradise Towers *certainly has its problems, most notably the astonishingly awful performance by Richard Briers as the Chief Caretaker, the miscasting of Howard Cooke as Pex (a role that really demanded a muscle-bound Sylvester Stallone type, as writer Stephen Wyatt had originally intended), the terrible incidental music and the complete lack of naturalism in the production, which makes it look rather too literally like a televisual comic strip. In essence, however, it is a very encouraging story, in that it marks a complete change of style for* Doctor Who *and can be seen as the first step towards the series climbing out of the hole into which it had dug itself over the previous few seasons. There is a wonderful quality of freshness and originality about Wyatt's writing, and for the first time in years there is no reliance placed on, or even reference made to, the Doctor's past adventures. The scripts actually feature some quite horrific ideas – including Hitleresque fascists, street gangs, killer robots, animated cadavers and sweet little old ladies with cannibalistic tendencies – and the inappropriately lightweight production style may actually have been adopted deliberately in order to disguise this, given the controversy that had surrounded the series' content a couple of seasons earlier. All in all, a promising first indication of the direction in which the series would move with Andrew Cartmel as script editor. (5/10)*

Delta and the Bannermen (7F)

EP	DATE	TIME	DURN	VIEWERS	CHART POS
1	02.11.87	19.35	24'47"	5.3	90
2	09.11.87	19.36	24'23"	5.1	93
3	16.11.87	19.35	24'22"	5.4	87

PRODUCTION DETAILS

OB Recording: 24.06.87–27.06.87, 29.06.87–04.07.87, 06.07.87, 07.07.87

Studio Recording: 12.08.87 in TC3

On an unnamed planet, Delta (Belinda Mayne), a Chimeron queen, takes cover in one of the ships of the attacking Bannermen in order to escape from them. Gavrok (Don Henderson), leader of the Bannermen (Philip Babot, Terry Bennett, Darrell Brook, Russell Diamond, Ricky Garrett, Derek Hartley, Ian Lawrence, Jared Morgan, Bill Malin, Robert Patton, Rob York), ambushes her there, but is shot by another Chimeron (Tim Scott), and falls outside. The wounded Chimeron gives Delta a box and tells her to keep it with her. He then dies, leaving her as the last survivor of her race.

The TARDIS arrives at Tollport G715, where the Doctor and Mel meet the Toll Keeper (Ken Dodd), who informs them that they are the ten billionth customers and have therefore won a trip to Disneyland, Earth, in 1959. They are to travel with Nostalgia Trips, a specialist company run by the Navarinos, in a spaceship that looks like an old bus. Mel agrees to board the bus with the other holidaymakers, but the Doctor opts to follow in the TARDIS. Just before they leave, Delta arrives in the stolen Bannerman ship, and also boards the bus.

In space, the bus crashes into a satellite recently launched from Cape Canaveral and plunges to Earth. The Doctor, by using the TARDIS's vortex drive to create an antigravity spiral, manages to ensure it a safe landing. Instead of Disneyland, however, it arrives at Shangri-La, a Welsh holiday camp in 1959. The holidaymakers are greeted by Burton (Richard Davies), camp manager, who agrees that they can use their facilities until the bus is mended. He introduces Billy (David Kinder), a mechanic who will help to fix the bus, and Ray (Sara Griffiths), a girl who fancies Billy and who lends him some tools. The bus's power crystal is damaged and a spare, supplied by the Doctor, is accidentally broken by the driver, Murray (Johnny Dennis). Murray is disappointed to learn that it will take 24 hours for the Doctor to grow a further replacement.

Gavrok arrives at the Tollport in pursuit of Delta and threatens and then kills the Toll Keeper before heading to Earth in search of the bus.

At a 'get to know you' dance, Billy, who is also a singer,

dedicates a song to Delta, whom he has taken a shine to. Ray leaves in tears. The Doctor follows and comforts Ray in a laundry room, but they are interrupted by one of the other alien holidaymakers, Keillor (Brian Hibbard), who uses a transmitter device to contact Gavrok and tell him of the Chimeron Queen's location. Gavrok is pleased, but kills Keillor by blowing up his transmitter. The explosion also knocks out the Doctor and Ray.

Delta's box has meanwhile been revealed to contain a large egg. Before Mel's horrified eyes, this hatches to reveal a green baby. Billy arrives with flowers for Delta and she explains everything to him and Mel. Then she suggests to Billy that they go for a walk to allow Mel to sleep. Billy takes her and the rapidly growing baby (Jessica McGough) off in the sidecar of his Vincent motorbike.

The Doctor recovers and tries to convince Burton that they are in danger from a Bannerman attack. Burton is sceptical, so the Doctor shows him around the TARDIS in order to convince him that he is speaking the truth. Mel rouses Murray, who helps wake everyone and get them on board the bus. The power crystal needs another half-hour to finish growing. The Doctor and Ray meanwhile head off to find Billy and Delta.

Gavrok and his men arrive near the holiday camp, having homed in on a transmitter owned by Weismuller (Stubby Kaye) and Hawk (Morgan Deare), two American agents in England to monitor the satellite. He reaches the camp before the bus can leave and destroys it and everyone on board. The Doctor and Ray return with Billy, Delta and the Chimeron child (Amy Osborn) but manage to escape again. Gavrok takes Mel and Burton hostage to use as bait to obtain Delta.

Delta and her child (Laura Collins) are summoned by bees owned by Goronwy (Hugh Lloyd), an old Welsh beekeeper. They stay with him in his cottage while the Doctor goes to rescue Mel and Burton. The Time Lord blusters his way past Gavrok and leaves with his two friends unscathed. At the cottage, Billy takes a pack of the Chimeron child's special food.

Gavrok finds the TARDIS and places on top of it a sonic cone that will destroy anything that comes close.

The Doctor sets a trap for Gavrok and the Bannermen at Goronwy's cottage before leaving the place empty. Gavrok is alerted to Delta's presence at the cottage, and he and his men make a raid. They find themselves covered with honey and attacked by bees.

The Doctor enlists Billy's help to set up a powerful amplifier device that he hopes to use to defend Shangri-La against the Bannermen, who are susceptible to shrill noises. Delta discovers that Billy has been eating the Chimeron food so that he will change into a Chimeron and be able to leave with her.

Gavrok and his men return to the camp in their ship. The Doctor's device is not finished and is destroyed by the Bannermen, but as an alternative measure the screams of the Chimeron youth (Carley Joseph) are transmitted via the camp's public address system. The Bannermen collapse in pain and Gavrok, similarly affected by the sound, accidentally falls into the sonic cone's field and is vaporised.

Delta, Billy and the Chimeron child leave in the Bannermen's spaceship with the tied-up Bannermen also on board. The Doctor is now able to enter the TARDIS as Gavrok's death drained the power from the sonic cone. With Burton distracted by the arrival of the Skegness Glee Club, he and Mel slip away. Hawk and Weismuller are astonished by the TARDIS's dematerialisation, but Goronwy glances up at the sky and gives a knowing smile and a wink.

WHO FAX

- Novelised as *Doctor Who – Delta and the Bannermen* by Malcolm Kohll in 1989.
- Working title: *The Flight of the Chimeron*.
- Locations: Springwell Lock Quarry, Rickmansworth, Buckinghamshire; Sutton Farm, Fort Road, nr Penarth, S. Glamorgan, Wales; Psygollyn Mawr, Hensol Forest, nr Welsh St Donats, S. Glamorgan, Wales; Coed Y Wallas, Castle-Upon-Alun, S. Glamorgan, Wales; Majestic Holiday Camp, Barry Island, S. Glamorgan, Wales; Hangar 50, Llandow Industrial Estate, British Tissues Hangar, nr Nash, S. Glamorgan, Wales.

- The part of Ray was one of two considered to be potential companion characters. The final decision as to whether the one to be kept on would be Ray or Ace (from *Dragonfire*) depended partly on when Bonnie Langford decided to leave the series. Ultimately Langford stayed until the end of the season, and it was decided that Ace would be the character to become the new companion.
- Ray was originally to have been played by Lynn Gardner, but the actress was injured during a driving lesson and had to be replaced at short notice by Sara Griffiths. By way of compensation, Gardner was given a speaking role in the following story, *Dragonfire*.
- The Lorells, the singing group seen in this story, were actually the incidental music composer, Keff McCulloch, and sisters Tracey and Jodie Wilson, the former later to be married to McCulloch.
- Bob Gabriel, a director on the BBC's *EastEnders*, was originally slated to direct *Delta and the Bannermen* when his work on the soap opera was completed. It is unknown why he did not in the end take the assignment.

QUOTES

- '[John Nathan-Turner] wanted to use a different location from the ones they usually used in the south of England. He was thinking possibly of using something in Wales, and he asked if I was familiar with Wales. I said that I was; my brother lives in Wales [and] I spend quite a lot of time there. So I was then thinking of a project which could be set in Wales. Another of the criteria was that it should be in the recently recognisable past, rather than a period piece. So to some extent I had a couple of parameters within which to work – . . . the location and the time period. Thereafter it was a case of tossing ideas backwards and forwards with Andrew [Cartmel] and eventually latching onto this idea, at which point he said "Go away and work it into a storyline".' Writer Malcolm Kohll interviewed by David Brunt and Nigel Griffiths for *Space Buns for Tea*.

- 'The Bannermen's motives [were not apparent due to timing cuts but] were more clearly explained in the script. They had in fact made their own world uninhabitable; they had polluted it, they had despoiled it, they had abused it in every way so that it simply became no longer capable of sustaining a life force. They knew that the Chimeron planet was abundant in natural resources and they knew that the Chimerons in general were an amiable and non-warlike people. So, quite simply, they decided to move en masse onto [the Chimerons'] planet, annihilate the race and take over by force. There was no other way for them to survive, so their motive in a word was simply "survival". But [they had been forced to this] not by any cataclysmic accident of nature, it was simply [a result] of their own greed, selfishness and ineptitude; they had ruined whatever attributes their own planet possessed.' Writer Malcolm Kohll interviewed by David Brunt and Nigel Griffiths for *Space Buns for Tea*.
- 'I loved doing *Delta and the Bannermen* on location. It was a liberation and I think, though it was very tricky, we were managing to shoot about seven minutes a day. We had three days' rehearsal for it, which I found very useful.' Director Chris Clough interviewed by Richard Marson for *Doctor Who Magazine* Issue 135.
- 'The biggest problem was locating a holiday camp, but we found one being renovated down in Wales. It was ideal – it had that fifties madcap, bright, sunny, primary colour feel to it.' Director Chris Clough interviewed by Peter Griffiths for *Doctor Who Magazine* Issue 231.

COMMENT

DJH: *Although not quite as bad as the previous two stories,* Delta and the Bannermen *is still an incoherent mess. There are numerous holes in the plot, and Weismuller and Hawk, not to mention Goronwy and his bees, are totally superfluous. The show is saved by Don Henderson's marvellously evil portrayal of Gavrok, one of the nastiest characters to have appeared in the series for some time. Delta is vacuous, Billy is pathetic (and just how does eating* *some alien food turn him into an alien?) and Mel is, once more, acted by Bonnie Langford as if she were giving a stage performance. It all looks nice, but there is no substance. (4/10)*

SJW: Delta and the Bannermen *must be judged for what it is: a whimsical fifties pastiche, featuring – or at least making reference to – many of the things most associated with that era, including Disneyland, bus tours, pioneering satellite launches, holiday camps, rock-and-roll music and pulp sci-fi of the* I Married a Monster from Outer Space *variety. It never sets out to deliver gritty drama: it aims to provide light-hearted, humorous entertainment, and in this it is largely successful. It is refreshing to see the Doctor and Mel in a down-to-earth setting for once in the Wales of 1959. Bonnie Langford certainly seems rather more at home here than in the series' usual futuristic environments and Sylvester McCoy is also given some good material uniquely suited to his Doctor – the scene in which he comforts the upset Ray in the holiday camp laundry room, for instance, is one that it is difficult to imagine any of his predecessors playing, or at least playing this well. A whole season of stories in this vein would not work, but as a one-off diversion* Delta and the Bannermen *is never less than amusing. (6/10)*

Dragonfire (7G)

EP	DATE	TIME	DURN	VIEWERS	CHART POS
1	23.11.87	19.37	24'01"	5.5	80
2	30.11.87	19.35	24'40"	5.0	96
3	07.12.87	19.36	24'26"	4.7	94

PRODUCTION DETAILS

Studio Recording: 28.07.87–30.07.87 in TC1, 12.08.87, 13.08.87 in TC3

The Doctor, having decided to investigate a tracking signal picked up in the TARDIS, brings Mel to Iceworld, a space trading colony on the dark side of the planet Svartos. In the restaurant there they meet Sabalom Glitz (Tony Selby), who has come to search for treasure with the aid of a map. A waitress nicknamed Ace (Sophie Aldred) tells them about a mythical dragon that is supposed to live in the lower levels. The Doctor and Glitz decide to go and hunt both the treasure and the dragon.

In charge of Iceworld is Kane (Edward Peel), an alien exiled from his home planet of Proamon three thousand years earlier. He has bought Glitz's crew from him and has cryogenically frozen them, this process wiping their minds and turning them into an obedient fighting force. He has arranged for Glitz to obtain the map, which has a tracking device hidden in the seal, as he wants the dragon found for his own reasons.

The Doctor and Glitz set off. Mel is left behind because Glitz objects to her accompanying them. Ace insults a customer (Shirin Taylor) and is fired. She then takes Mel to her room, where she explains that she came to Iceworld from Earth in a freak time storm. The two girls hear an announcement over a loudspeaker system that there is an ice block at the docking bay. Ace decides to go and help clear it. She blows up the docking bay door with a can of her home-made nitro-9 explosive. She and Mel are then arrested by Belazs (Patricia Quinn) and taken to Kane.

Kane tries in vain to seduce Ace into joining his mercenary force. The two girls escape into the tunnels of Iceworld and encounter the dragon (Leslie Meadows), which fires laser bolts at them.

The Doctor and Glitz have meanwhile become separated. The Doctor climbs over a railing and hangs from his umbrella above an apparently sheer drop. Glitz finds him hanging there and helps him down. He then offers a deal: if the Doctor will help him recover his ship, the *Nosferatu*, he can have the treasure map. The Doctor agrees.

Kane sends Glitz's former crew after Mel and Ace.

In the tunnels, the Doctor and Glitz find the dragon, which gestures for them to follow it. Along the way they meet up with Ace and Mel, and also Pudovkin (Nigel Miles-Thomas), one of Glitz's crew, who is killed by the dragon.

Belazs plots with Kracauer (Tony Osoba) to kill Kane by raising the temperature. This fails and Kane kills both of them instead.

The dragon shows the Doctor, Glitz, Ace and Mel a polydimensional scanning imager. The image of an archivist (Daphne Oxenford) appears and tells of Kane being exiled from Proamon and banished to Svartos. The Doctor realises that the dragon, a biomechanoid, is itself the treasure. The dragon's head opens to reveal a crystal crackling with power. Listening via the tracking device in the seal of the map, Kane is pleased. After three thousand years, the dragonfire will be his. Kane orders his troops to eliminate the dragon and bring its head to him. He also revives all the mercenaries and orders them to spread terror throughout Iceworld, herding everyone on to the *Nosferatu*. He wants Iceworld cleared.

McLuhan (Stephanie Fayerman) and Bazin (Stuart Organ) hunt the dragon while Glitz heads back to the *Nosferatu* to obtain some explosives. He arrives just in time to see his ship taking off and then exploding in space, detonated by Kane.

The dragon is killed, but when McLuhan and Bazin try to remove the crystal, they are electrocuted by the power within it. Ace returns to her room to get some more nitro-9 and is captured by Kane. The Doctor and Mel find the dead dragon and are able to remove the crystal, since its power has now been diminished. They meet up with Glitz at Ace's room and then head on to Kane's HQ.

Kane wants to swap Ace for the dragonfire crystal, which he needs to power his equipment and enable him to return to Proamon to take his revenge on those who exiled him. Mel places the crystal in the circuit and the equipment powers up. Iceworld itself is a spacecraft, and it takes off from the surface of Svartos.

The Doctor reveals to Kane that Proamon no longer exists: it was destroyed two thousand years ago when its sun turned supernova. Kane opens a shield, allowing unfiltered sunlight to flood through, and melts away in the glare.

Glitz takes control of Iceworld and renames it the *Nosferatu II*.

Mel decides to travel on with Glitz, and the Doctor asks Ace if she would like to go with him in the TARDIS, taking the scenic route back to her home in Perivale.

WHO FAX

- Novelised as *Doctor Who – Dragonfire* by Ian Briggs in 1989.
- Story released on BBC Home Video in 1994.
- Working titles: *Absolute Zero*, *The Pyramid's Treasure*, *Pyramid in Space*.
- Locations: None.
- Kane was originally to have been called Hess, but this was changed so as to avoid any suggestion that it was a reference to the Nazi war criminal Rudolph Hess.
- *Dragonfire* was promoted as being the 150th transmitted *Doctor Who* story, but in fact it was only the 147th. The production team had arrived at their total by counting the previous year's season-long *The Trial of a Time Lord* as four stories.
- Glitz was added to the story at a relatively late stage in place of a similar character called Razorback in the original storyline.
- When it was decided that Ace would travel on with the Doctor and become the new companion, the production team requested that Ian Briggs sign a waiver of all rights in the character. This was done in order to avoid problems that had occurred on two occasions in the past with writers disputing the BBC's ownership of companion characters that they had claimed to have created in their stories.
- See Chapter 6 for more details on the making of this story.

COMMENT

DJH: Dragonfire *is without a doubt the best story of the twenty-fourth season, but only because it is more coherent than the others and not because it is anything particularly special in itself. The plot is still clumsy and strained. One unresolved mystery is why Kane waited three thousand years before sending his people to kill the dragon. Another is why the people of*

Proamon, if they wanted to ensure that Kane remained in exile, put the key to his salvation on the same planet, no matter how well guarded. The best performances come from Edward Peel as Kane – a superb portrayal of icy evil – and Sophie Aldred, making her debut as Ace and outshining Bonnie Langford at every turn. Other saving graces are the return of Glitz, which is nicely handled even if it stretches credibility a bit, and the well-conceived and impressive sets. A good end to possibly the worst season in the series' history. (6/10)

SJW: Dragonfire *is a more traditional story than the two that preceded it and just about wins out as the best of the season. Ian Briggs's fine scripts are well served by Chris Clough's typically polished direction, and there are some moments of genuine tension. Sophie Aldred makes a promising debut as Ace and works particularly well in partnership with Bonnie Langford as Mel, making the latter's departure almost – but not quite – regrettable. It is nice to see Tony Selby back as Glitz, and Edward Peel gives a suitably 'chilling' performance as Kane. The story does have its flaws, however, and the most notorious and unforgivable is the ludicrous cliffhanger ending to Part One, where the Doctor climbs over a railing and, for no apparent reason at all, literally hangs from a cliff. Overall, though, a pleasing end to a season that showed a great deal of promise, even if it did not always fulfil it. (7/10)*

SEASON TWENTY-FIVE

Remembrance of the Daleks (7H)

EP	DATE	TIME	DURN	VIEWERS	CHART POS
1	05.10.88	19.35	24'33"	5.5	78
2	12.10.88	19.35	24'31"	5.8	78
3	19.10.88	19.34	24'30"	5.1	91
4	26.10.88	19.34	24'36"	5.0	96

PRODUCTION DETAILS

OB Recording: 04.04.88–09.04.88, 11.04.88–13.04.88
Studio Recording: 27.04.88–29.04.88 in TC8

The Doctor and Ace arrive on Earth in 1963, in an alleyway just outside Coal Hill School. The Doctor investigates a van parked in the street while Ace goes to get some food from a nearby café, where she meets a young territorial army sergeant, Mike Smith (Dursley McLinden). Moving away from the van, the Doctor wanders into the school playground, where four scorch marks can be seen on the ground. He is watched by a little girl (Jasmine Breaks) who appears to know who he is.

The Doctor returns to the van and bursts in through the back doors. Inside he meets Professor Rachel Jensen (Pamela Salem), a scientific adviser to the army, who tells him that she has been monitoring some unusual transmissions. She then receives a message to return to 'the secondary source' and shouts to Mike Smith, who is returning from the café with Ace. They both jump into the van and drive off, heading for a junkyard in Totter's Lane.

On arriving at the junkyard, the Doctor meets Group Captain Gilmore (Simon Williams), who reveals that he has a 'hostile' penned in one of the sheds there. More soldiers arrive as re-inforcements, but the 'hostile' is a Dalek, which attacks them. The Doctor uses some of Ace's nitro-9 to destroy the creature.

Ace and the Doctor head back to the school in the van. On the way, the Doctor explains that the Daleks are after the Hand of Omega, a relic from Gallifrey that he brought to Earth in a previous incarnation. At the school, the headmaster (Michael Sheard) initially refuses the Doctor and Ace permission to look around, but then changes his mind as if receiving orders from elsewhere.

Mike brings in a man named Ratcliffe (George Sewell) to help clear up the debris after the army operation. Ratcliffe, however, has his own agenda and arranges for the damaged Dalek casing to be removed to a builders' yard. There, someone sitting in a Dalek base before a complex piece of equipment demands in

Dalek-like tones (John Leeson) that he report.

The Doctor and Ace find a transmat system in the school cellar. A Dalek starts to appear, but the Doctor fiddles with the equipment and it vanishes again. The two travellers are suddenly attacked by another Dalek. Ace manages to get out of the cellar, but the waiting headmaster knocks her to the ground and locks the Doctor in with the Dalek, which is ascending the stairs towards him. Ace recovers and head-butts the headmaster, freeing the Doctor before the Dalek can reach him. They escape from the school. The Dalek blows the door away and orders the headmaster to repair the transmat.

Outside, an army truck has delivered some antitank missiles. The Doctor and Ace take one and return to the school. The Doctor intends to destroy the transmat but Ace uses the weapon on the Dalek, and destroys it. The Doctor is perturbed; he fears a Dalek attack and wants the area evacuated. He hurries off, leaving Ace to stay with Mike in a boarding house owned by Mike's mother (Kathleen Bidmead).

That night, while the Doctor sits in the café pondering on the ripples in time created by momentous decisions, more Daleks arrive at the school via the transmat.

The next morning, the Doctor arrives at an undertaker's parlour to collect a mysterious box that he left there on a previous visit to Earth. He is left alone with the box while the undertaker's assistant (William Thomas) contacts his boss. The Doctor orders the box to open and 'processes' Ace's baseball bat. He then orders it to close again and leaves, the box floating along behind him. The Doctor takes the box to a cemetery where a blind priest (Peter Halliday) leads him to an open grave, into which the box sinks.

Ratcliffe, having been told by the Dalek creature in his yard that obtaining the Hand will give them great power, receives a message from his agent that the device has been located.

Outside the cemetery, the headmaster accosts and struggles with Mike. He demands to know the location of the renegade Dalek base, but Mike claims not to know what he is talking about. The headmaster suddenly collapses.

Mike and the Doctor return to the boarding house, where they learn that Gilmore wants them back at the army headquarters. Ace, however, is excluded – an arrangement to which she unhappily agrees. She mopes about and switches on the television, then leaves as the start of a new science-fiction show is announced at 5.15 p.m.

At the army headquarters, the Doctor requests that space tracking stations be alerted to look for spaceships, and warns that the enemy should not be engaged. A mother ship is detected in geostationary orbit and the Doctor realises that there are two opposing Dalek factions at work. He creates a device to interfere with the Daleks' control systems. Then, when Ace is reported missing, he hurries off to the school, Rachel's assistant, Alison (Karen Gledhill), having reported the reception of multiple signals from that source.

Ace arrives at the school to retrieve her ghettoblaster, which got left behind there earlier. She switches it on and picks up Dalek transmissions revealing that they are planning to attack. She hurries away, using the mysteriously enhanced baseball bat to destroy any Daleks in her way, but becomes trapped by three of the creatures near the school entrance. The Doctor arrives in the nick of time and disables the Daleks with his device while soldiers place plastic explosive on them. The Daleks are destroyed.

Returning to the school cellar, the Doctor smashes the transmat with the baseball bat. He explains to Ace that he is simply trying to keep the army out of the way as the Dalek forces battle for ownership of the Hand. The Hand, he explains, is really a remote stellar manipulator device. The Daleks want it in order to gain full mastery of time travel. The Doctor intends to let the Daleks have the Hand, but wants to avoid Gilmore and his men from being killed in the process. He must also try to ensure that the Hand goes to the right faction of Daleks.

At the cemetery, Ratcliffe finds the grave containing the Hand. He pushes a metal probe into the soft earth and it suddenly crackles with energy. The energy is detected by the Dalek mother ship in space, and the Dalek Emperor orders that an assault shuttle be prepared. Ratcliffe meanwhile arranges for the Hand to be dug up and transported to his yard. A Black Dalek is waiting there and takes possession of the Hand before ordering the extermination of Ratcliffe's men. In Ratcliffe's office, the Dalek creature is revealed to be the young girl, who is being used as a human element in the Daleks' battle computer. The Black Dalek orders that the time controller be activated.

The Doctor and Ace make their way to Ratcliffe's yard. When the opportunity arises, the Doctor deactivates the Daleks' time controller. He also checks with the Hand that it knows what to do. He and Ace then leave, avoiding patrolling Daleks along the way.

The renegade Daleks (operators: Norman Bacon, David Harrison, John Scott Martin, Hugh Spight, Tony Starr, Cy Town, Nigel Wild; voices: Brian Miller, Royce Mills, Roy Skelton) and soldiers battle outside the school as the imperial Dalek shuttle heads for Earth. The renegade Daleks withdraw on the orders of the battle computer and the shuttle lands in the school playground. Imperial Daleks emerge, intent on capturing the Hand. Mike is revealed to be a traitor working with Ratcliffe and is put under arrest by Gilmore.

The two Dalek forces clash, and the imperial Daleks deploy a Special Weapons Dalek to wipe out the opposition. The Doctor meanwhile disables the control Dalek in the shuttle and finds that the imperial Daleks will be returning to Skaro.

The imperial Daleks storm Ratcliffe's yard and take control of the Hand. Ratcliffe is killed by a bolt of electricity fired by the young girl from her hands, but Mike, who has escaped from custody, absconds with the time controller. The imperial Daleks take the Hand back to their mother ship in the shuttle.

The Doctor uses the broken transmat system in the school cellar to build a transmitter with which to communicate with the Dalek mother ship. After sending Ace after Mike, he contacts the mother ship. The Dalek Emperor is revealed to be Davros (Terry Molloy), and the Doctor goads him into using the Hand against Earth. When activated, however, the Hand destroys Skaro's sun (which also destroys Skaro) and then returns to the mother ship. Davros leaves in an escape pod as the mother ship is destroyed.

Ace finds Mike back at the boarding house. They are interrupted by the young girl, who kills Mike with a bolt of energy and then advances on Ace.

The Doctor and Gilmore find the Black Dalek outside Ratcliffe's yard. The Doctor convinces it that it has been defeated and is the last of its kind still alive, and it self-destructs.

At that moment, the young girl collapses. Ace comforts her.

Later, the Doctor and Ace follow Mike's coffin into a church. They leave just as the funeral starts. Ace asks the Doctor if they 'did good'. He replies: 'Perhaps. Time will tell. It always does.'

WHO FAX

- Novelised as *Doctor Who – Remembrance of the Daleks* by Ben Aaronovitch in 1990.
- Story released by BBC Home Video along with the first Doctor story *The Chase* as a part of a limited-edition boxed set in 1993.
- Working title: *Nemesis of the Doctor*.
- Locations: 12 Theed Street, Lambeth, London; Kew Bridge Steam Museum, Green Dragon Lane, Brentford, Middx; railway bridge, Windmill Walk, Lambeth, London; Willesden Lane Cemetery, Willesden Lane, London; bridge at Wulfstan Road/Brunel Road, Ealing, London; TA Hall, Horn Lane, Acton, London; John Nodes and Sons Ltd, 181 Ladbroke Grove, London; railway bridge, Old Oak Common Lane, North Acton, London; streets near Kendal Avenue, London; St John's School, Macbeth Street, Hammersmith, London; alley off Macbeth Street, Hammersmith, London.
- A crane was hired to lower the Daleks' shuttle craft down into the playground of St John's School.
- This story was the fourth in the series' history to feature a pre-titles sequence. This one shows the Dalek mother ship approaching Earth, accompanied by soundtrack extracts from famous early sixties speeches by a number of prominent figures – John F. Kennedy, General Charles de Gaulle, the Duke of Edinburgh, Martin Luther King and John F. Kennedy (again).
- Ratcliffe was originally to have been called Gummer. The part was originally offered to Stratford Johns.

- The following actors were considered for roles in this story: Neil Stacy, Ian Ogilvy (Gilmore), Peter Tilbury (headmaster), Mark McGann (Mike).
- The following records were used as part of the soundtrack for this story: 'Return to Sender' by Otis Blackwell and Winfield Scott, arranged by Keff McCulloch; 'Do You Want To Know A Secret' by the Beatles; 'Children's Favourites' by White, arranged by Keff McCulloch (this piece had also been used in *Delta and the Bannermen*); 'Apache' by Jerry Lordan, arranged by Keff McCulloch; 'Lollipop' by the Mudlarks; 'A Taste of Honey' by the Beatles.

QUOTES

- 'I was quite proud of [*Remembrance of the Daleks*]. Within the limits of the time and the budget I thought I'd done quite a good job.' Director Andrew Morgan interviewed by Marcus Hearn for *Doctor Who Magazine* Issue 204.
- 'I do like to pick scenes out of things. The head-up display for the Dalek was straight out of *Predator*, but it's an old idea anyway. Madcap technology from *Back to the Future*, comedy films, *Blade Runner*, lots of things. Throwaway technology is one of my favourites, where you have technology and don't explain anything about it, and someone just uses it.' Writer Ben Aaronovitch interviewed by John B. McLay for *Doctor Who Magazine* Issue 147.
- '[The thought process behind] *Remembrance of the Daleks* went like this. It was the twenty-fifth anniversary year and it was the Daleks; the most famous, and the first, monsters. I thought I *had* to go back to 1963. I had to go back to the beginning. However I had to find a reason to go back to 1963, and if the Doctor was back in 1963 the Daleks had to have a reason for being there too.' Writer Ben Aaronovitch interviewed by Marcus Hearn for *Doctor Who Magazine* Summer Special 1993.

COMMENT

DJH: *What a difference a year makes. After the 1987 season saw*

Doctor Who *descending into mindless drivel, the 1988 one gets off to a flying start with the strongest Dalek story since* Genesis of the Daleks. *Aaronovitch's tale of rival Dalek factions battling for control of an ancient Gallifreyan weapon is superb, and the characters that populate it are all well conceived and believable. Much of the mystery is returned to* Doctor Who *in this adventure, which combines the idea of the Doctor manipulating events to ensure a good outcome with a cracking, action-packed Daleks-versus-humans yarn. The only regrettable aspect is the unnecessary inclusion of Davros; and unfortunately Terry Molloy again plays him as a ranting oaf rather than an evil and calculating survivor. Nevertheless, this is the best season opener for many, many years. (8/10)*

SJW: *Now this is more like it! The first* bona fide *classic of the Sylvester McCoy era,* Remembrance of the Daleks *has a wonderfully nostalgic quality, perfectly capturing the spirit of the era in which it is set – and indeed of the Dalek stories of that era – although in other ways it is very up to date and postmodern in approach. The Daleks themselves look great – particularly the imperial ones in their distinctive cream-and-gold livery – and are very well handled. The surprise revelation of Davros as the Dalek Emperor is also a good twist, and the fact that it is held back until the end of Part Four is even more welcome as it means that he does not overshadow his creations in the way that he did in the previous four Dalek stories. A great start to the season. (9/10)*

The Happiness Patrol (7L)

EP	DATE	TIME	DURN	VIEWERS	CHART POS
1	02.11.88	19.35	24'51"	5.3	96
2	09.11.88	19.35	24'48"	4.6	104
3	16.11.88	19.35	24'25"	5.3	88

PRODUCTION DETAILS
Studio Recording: 26.07.88–28.07.88 in TC3, 10.08.88, 11.08.88 in TC8

The Doctor and Ace arrive on the Earth colony planet Terra Alpha. The Doctor has heard disturbing rumours of something evil on the planet and intends to get to the bottom of them. They meet Trevor Sigma (John Normington), an official from Galactic Centre who is on the planet conducting a census of the populace.

The Doctor intends to start his investigation by getting himself arrested, so when some members of the planet's pink-garbed Happiness Patrol (Argie Alaime, Olwyn Atkinson, Heather Downham, June Easther, Selina Gilbert, Julie Lawrence, Carole Mudie) arrive and start painting the TARDIS pink, he points out that he and Ace are without official offworlder badges. The leader, Daisy K (Georgina Hale), has them arrested. They are taken to a holding zone controlled by Priscilla P (Rachel Bell), where they meet Harold V (Tim Barker) who used to be Harold F and whose brother (Cy Town) has been sentenced to death for a display of public grief. Harold V tells the Doctor and Ace of Helen A (Sheila Hancock), the ruler of Terra Alpha, and her executioner the Kandy Man (David John Pope).

Harold V is killed by an electric shock from a fruit machine and the Doctor and Ace escape from the holding zone in a motorised go-kart after the Doctor first disarms a bomb that has been planted on it.

Ace is re-arrested, but is allowed to escape by Susan Q (Lesley Dunlop), a disaffected Happiness Patrol member. The Doctor meanwhile narrowly avoids being rearrested by Happiness Patrol spy Silas P (Jonathan Burn), who is knocked unconscious by a man named Earl Sigma (Richard D. Sharp). When Silas P comes to, he is killed by a Happiness Patrol because he is unhappy.

Earl explains that he is a holidaying medical student who has got stuck on Terra Alpha. He also plays blues music on a mouth organ. He and the Doctor head for the Kandy Kitchen, where they are captured by the Kandy Man, which plans to use them in its experiments. They escape when the Doctor verbally confuses the Kandy Man and gets it to spill some lemonade, which sticks it firmly to the floor.

The Doctor and Earl run into a network of pipes and tunnels under the Kitchen, where they meet up with a group of Pipe People (Wences: Phillip Neve; Wulfric: Ryan Freedman; other Pipe People: Bilent Hassan, Charles Martin, Steve Martin, Lee Pearse), the original inhabitants of Terra Alpha. On learning from the Kandy Man what has happened, Helen sends Fifi, her pet Stigorax, a vicious doglike creature, into the pipes to flush them out.

Ace is rearrested once more and taken to a holding zone with Susan Q. She is rescued by one of the Pipe People, but Susan Q is taken off for a 'routine disappearance'.

The Doctor emerges from the pipes and again meets Trevor Sigma, whom he persuades to take him to see Helen A. They arrive at her office and she tells Trevor that she has managed the population down by 17 per cent. The Doctor takes a fire extinguisher from the inner office and a lemonade siphon from the outer.

Fifi chases Ace and a Pipe Person down the tunnels. Ace uses a can of nitro-9 to blow up the pipe behind her but then falls down another pipe and emerges to join Susan Q on the execution platform. The Pipe Person scurries off and escapes.

The Doctor returns to the Kandy Kitchen – on the way persuading a sniper to lay down his weapon, thus saving some striking factory workers from death – where the Kandy Man is still stuck firm. The Doctor unsticks it with a blast from the fire extinguisher in return for the Kandy Man's agreement to divert a flow of boiling candy destined for the execution platform. With Ace and Susan Q thus saved, the Doctor uses the lemonade to reattach the Kandy Man to the floor.

Helen A, furious that the execution failed, enrols Ace to appear at the forum – her death is to take place in five minutes' time. The Doctor tells Earl to bring the demonstrating factory workers to the forum square. He then persuades a couple of snipers (Mark Carroll, Steve Swinscoe) to stand down. Helen A, undaunted, orders the Happiness Patrol to wipe out the demonstrators.

Fifi survived the nitro-9 blast in the tunnel and, tended by Helen A, has now recovered completely. Helen A sends it back down into the pipes to wipe out the 'vermin' therein.

Ace and the Happiness Patrol arrive at the forum square to be greeted by the Doctor, who seems ecstatically happy to see them – which means that the Patrol cannot touch him. The demonstrators also appear happy, as do Ace and Susan Q. This leaves only the Patrol themselves, who are unhappy. Priscilla P therefore arrests the Patrol. Helen A is furious and orders her to let them go.

The Doctor, Ace, Susan, Earl and the Pipe People are chased through the pipes by Fifi. They arrive at a section of pipe encrusted with sugar and the Doctor gets Earl to play an A flat on his mouth organ in the hope that this will create a resonance and cause the sugar to collapse. This fails, so Earl tries a C instead. Fifi approaches closer and howls, which brings the sugar crashing down on the creature.

A radio announcer (Anne Hulley) reports that the Nirvana Sugar Beet plant has fallen to the guards and drones. Helen A is calm, reasoning that this is just one factory out of the thousand she has set up. She confers with Daisy K about who to send to quell the riots. Daisy K suggests Priscilla P. Priscilla P, however, is tied up and held at gunpoint by Susan Q in the holding zone.

The Doctor and Ace head for the Kandy Kitchen, where they threaten the Kandy Man with a red-hot poker and the heat from the oven. The Kandy Man escapes into the pipes but is engulfed and dissolved by a flow of boiling candy started by the Pipe People. Only a metal skeleton and some sweet remains emerge on to the execution platform.

Helen A is packing to leave Terra Alpha when the radio announcer reports that 112 factories have fallen to the rebels. Helen A's private shuttle takes off, but she is not on board. Instead it is piloted by Gilbert M (Harold Innocent), who constructed the Kandy Man and acted as its assistant, and Joseph C (Ronald Frazer), Helen A's husband. They bid her farewell via a video screen.

Helen A makes her way through the city and meets the Doctor.

She is still convinced that she was right and that unhappiness and love were unnecessary. She plans to leave on a scheduled flight. She sees Fifi, now injured and dying, and breaks down in tears. The Doctor is joined by Ace and they watch her cry. Their task is done.

Priscilla P and Daisy K have been put to work repainting the city as the Doctor and Ace bid farewell to Susan Q and Earl Sigma. The TARDIS has been mostly repainted blue, and Ace finishes the job before they leave.

WHO FAX

- Novelised as *Doctor Who – The Happiness Patrol* by Graeme Curry in 1990.
- Story released on BBC Home Video in 1997.
- Working title: *The Crooked Smile*.
- Locations: None.
- Patricia Routledge and Jill Bennett were among the actresses considered for the role of Helen A; Prunella Ransome and Rosalind Ayres were among those considered for the role of Susan Q.
- The mouth organ was played not by the Earl Sigma actor Richard D. Sharp but, from out of vision, by musician Adam Burney.

QUOTES

- 'Writing for *Doctor Who* was quite unlike anything I've ever done before, or will probably ever do again. It did seem tough at the time but I learnt a lot from doing it and was invaluable experience.' Writer Graeme Curry interviewed by John B. McLay for *Doctor Who Magazine* Issue 173.
- 'There were two or three basic ideas that made up *The Happiness Patrol*. The simplest was of a regime where you have to be happy or else you're in trouble. It comes from hearing muzak in lifts, or being greeted with "Have a nice day" and a big cosmetic smile when you go into McDonald's. The extension of that was to identify the things in society that are cosmetic and make them the benchmark of a regime – hence

the Patrol's nasty "cheerleader" aspect. When we started, the idea was to make it very American; all bright and brassy, with fifties cars on a shiny set. It was only at a design meeting, quite close to production, that we decided it would be more effective to set it against a rather seedier society in which the buildings were flaking, the whole place was collapsing and they were still trying to pretend that as long as everyone had a toothy grin, nothing would go wrong.' Writer Graeme Curry interviewed by Mark Wyman for *Private Who* Issue 15.

- 'We shot it all in studio, dealing with a totally controlled environment the whole time. Action on multicamera is a nightmare. Any action sequence relies on very specific angles and very specific lengths of shots, so it's much easier to do it on single camera and edit afterwards.' Director Chris Clough interviewed by Peter Griffiths for *Doctor Who Magazine* Issue 245.

COMMENT

DJH: The Happiness Patrol *is one of those stories that it is impossible to classify. It is both a thinly veiled attack on the policies pursued by Margaret Thatcher when she was Prime Minster of the UK, and also a bizarre, almost knockabout comedy, with the outrageously dressed and coiffured Happiness Patrol vying for attention with the incredible Kandy Man – a robot made of sweets. The sets are surreal and dark, echoing the work of German expressionist film makers of the twenties and thirties, and the dialogue is keen and witty. Some people hate it, but personally I rather like it, even though the plot involves a little too much running about, getting captured and escaping only to be captured again. What makes it for me is the Kandy Man. A marvellous concept, well handled by all concerned. (7/10)*

SJW: *If ever proof was needed of the flexibility of* Doctor Who*'s format, it is to be found in great abundance in Season 25.* The Happiness Patrol *is a totally different type of story from the one that preceded it on transmission (and indeed from the two that* *followed it), but in its own way it is almost equally successful. Graeme Curry's excellent and thought-provoking scripts are very well served by Chris Clough's imaginative direction, and the whole production has a highly distinctive quality. The contrast between the garishness of Helen A's regime and the grimness of their surroundings works extremely well. The Happiness Patrol's costumes and make-up are wonderful, and the intentionally false-looking sets are outstanding. I just wish that the Kandy Man had looked a little more humanoid, as Curry had originally intended, and a little less like Bertie Bassett. (8/10)*

Silver Nemesis (7K)

EP	DATE	TIME	DURN	VIEWERS	CHART POS
1	23.11.88	19.35	24'31"	6.1	76
2	30.11.88	19.36	24'12"	5.2	94
3	07.12.88	19.35	24'36"	5.2	98

Note: Parts Two and Three of this story were premiered in New Zealand on 25 November 1988 as part of a compilation version of the whole story. See Chapter 9 for further details.

PRODUCTION DETAILS
OB Recording: 22.06.88–24.06.88, 26.06.88–02.07.88, 05.07.88

In South America, 1988, a man named de Flores (Anton Diffring) receives confirmation that 'the landing' is to take place the next day, 23 November, in Windsor. He calls together a group of paramilitary men (Steve Ausden, Jon Baker, Sean Barry-Weske, Jamie Durdy, Keith Harvie, David Howarth, Sean McGrory, Julian Radmond, Andrew Searle, Jack Talbot) and they toast their destiny: the Fourth Reich. They leave for England, taking with them a silver bow.

In Windsor, 1638, Lady Peinforte (Fiona Walker) is anxious for a mathematician (Leslie French) to complete his calculations. He eventually tells her that the object of her interest will land in the meadow outside in the year 1988. Peinforte and her squire, Richard (Gerard Murphy), kill the mathematician to obtain blood for a potion. They then use this to travel forward in time to 1988, taking with them a supply of poisoned gold-tipped arrows and a single silver arrow. They materialise in the middle of a crowded restaurant.

The Doctor and Ace are meanwhile listening to an outdoor jazz recital given by Courtney Pine and his musicians (Ernest Mothle (double bass), Adrian Reid (piano), Frank Tontoh (drums)). The Doctor's pocket watch bleeps but he is unable to remember what this alarm signifies. The two friends head back to the TARDIS. On the way they are attacked by two men (Dave Ould, John Ould) wearing strange headphone-like devices. They manage to escape and get back to the ship, where the Doctor uses a scanner device incorporated into a new ghettoblaster that he has built for Ace to display an image of Earth. The Doctor admits that he has known since 23 November 1638 that the planet will be destroyed at this time. He takes Ace to a storage area in Windsor Castle to find a silver bow, but it is not there. They then travel in the TARDIS to Lady Peinforte's house in 1638, where the Doctor finds the dead mathematician.

The Doctor tells Ace that he has been here before and that a quantity of a silver-coloured living metal called validium, the purpose of which is destruction, fell to Earth and was used by Lady Peinforte to make a statue of herself. He also knows that Lady Peinforte has travelled forward in time to 1988.

Meanwhile a 'meteor' has landed in Windsor, 1988. It is cordoned off by the police (Darrell Brook, Christian Fletcher, Mike Mungarvan), who are then all knocked out by a gas that is emitted from alien-looking pipes that emerge from the earth around the object.

The Doctor and Ace arrive in the grounds of Windsor Castle and follow the Queen (Mary Reynolds) inside. The Doctor wants to summon help, but they are apprehended by two guards (Martyn Read, Derek Van Weenan).

Lady Peinforte and Richard watch from hiding as de Flores and his men arrive to take charge of the meteor. De Flores's second in command, Karl (Martin Yenal), places the bow on the meteor and it starts to glow in time with the statue buried inside. The TARDIS arrives and de Flores threatens to kill Ace unless the Doctor tells him where the arrow is. The Doctor explains that validium needs to have a critical mass to operate and that both the bow and the arrow are required to make up this mass.

Suddenly a massive spaceship arrives. From it emerge Cybermen (Cyber Leader: David Banks; Cyber Lieutenant: Mark Hardy; Cybermen: Paul Barrass, Danny Boyd, Tony Carlton, Bill Malin, Scott Mitchell, Brian Orrell), who attack de Flores's men. Lady Peinforte and Richard dispatch several Cybermen with their gold-tipped arrows. In the confusion, the Doctor takes the bow and leaves with Ace in the TARDIS.

The Cybermen defeat de Flores's men and take the meteor into a nearby hangar in order to cut the statue out of it. They then take the statue to Lady Peinforte's crypt elsewhere in the grounds of Windsor Castle and hide it in her tomb, where they wait in the expectation that the Doctor will bring the bow to them.

The TARDIS arrives elsewhere in the grounds and the Doctor uses the bow to home in on the statue. He explains to Ace that validium was created by Omega and Rassilon as the ultimate defence for Gallifrey in the olden times.

The Cybermen try to communicate with their fleet, but the Doctor jams their transmissions by playing a jazz tape on Ace's ghettoblaster.

Lady Peinforte and Richard arrive at the crypt. The Cybermen believe that Lady Peinforte will be driven mad by the realisation of her own death, but this does not happen. Richard instead destroys several more Cybermen with gold-tipped arrows.

Ace blows up the Cybermen's ship with some nitro-9 as the Doctor distracts its human guards (the same men who attacked them after the jazz recital). The Cybermen kill the men for failing in their task.

De Flores speaks with the Cyber Leader and explains that he wants to form an alliance with them. The Cyber Leader agrees: if de Flores can destroy Lady Peinforte, the planet will be split between them. Once de Flores has gone, however, the Cyber

Leader orders that he be killed as soon as the arrow is retrieved.

The Doctor is at first unable to locate the Cybermen's fleet on the holographic 'screen' above Ace's ghettoblaster. He then realises that it is invisible, however, and overcomes this, thereby revealing thousands of Cyber warships waiting in space.

Lady Peinforte finds the statue in her tomb, but escapes with Richard through a secret exit as de Flores arrives.

The Cyber Leader returns to the tomb with the silver arrow, which is grasped by the statue. The statue is starting to come to life. The two travellers arrive and the Doctor allows the statue to touch the bow for a moment before snatching it away again. They then run for the TARDIS as the statue awakes. The Doctor explains that it will now follow the bow.

De Flores escapes from the Cybermen by throwing a handful of gold dust at the Cyber Leader's chest unit.

The Doctor takes the TARDIS first to Lady Peinforte's house in 1638, where Ace obtains some gold coins, and then back to the meteor in the hangar.

Lady Peinforte and Richard hitch a lift into Windsor from Mrs Remington (Dolores Gray), a descendant of Lady Peinforte's neighbours in 1638.

The statue arrives and comes to rest in the meteor, where the Doctor gives it the bow. The statue talks to Ace and explains that it is whatever it is made to be – and at the moment it is Nemesis.

The Cybermen arrive and attack the hangar. They chase after Ace, who picks them off one by one by firing gold coins at them with a catapult.

The Doctor meanwhile sets up the meteor so that, when launched, it will be on course for the Cyber fleet in space. He intends Nemesis to destroy the fleet, but declines to release it once it has completed this task as he may have further use for it. He puts paid to the remaining Cybermen in the hangar by causing the meteor's in-built rockets to fire automatically. De Flores arrives and takes charge, only to be killed by the Cyber Leader after it recovers from being hit by Ace's final coin. Lady Peinforte also arrives, accompanied by Richard, and argues with the Cyber Leader over who should have the bow. Lady Peinforte gloats that she alone knows the Doctor's true identity, as this was revealed to her by the statue. The Doctor appears to concede defeat; however, he gives the bow not to Lady Peinforte but to the Cyber Leader. Lady Peinforte threatens to reveal the Doctor's secrets – of the old time on Gallifrey, the time of chaos – but the Cyber Leader has no interest in this. The Doctor returns the bow to Nemesis and the Cyber Leader orders the statue to launch. At the last moment, Lady Peinforte jumps into the meteor with the statue and merges with it. The meteor launches and destroys the Cyber fleet. The Cyber Leader goes to kill the Doctor, but Richard grabs a gold-tipped arrow that was lodged in the TARDIS door and uses it to destroy the creature.

The Doctor and Ace give Richard a lift back to 1638. Having beaten the Doctor at chess, Ace asks him who he is. In response, he simply puts his finger to his lips.

WHO FAX

- Novelised as *Doctor Who – Silver Nemesis* by Kevin Clarke in 1989.
- Story released in an extended edition by BBC Home Video in 1993. The tape also included an edited version of an American documentary, *The Making of Doctor Who*, on the making of the story.
- Working title: *The Harbinger*, *Nemesis*.
- Locations: Greenwich Gas Works, Tunnel Avenue, nr Blackwall Tunnel, London; Arundel Castle Estate, Arundel, W. Sussex; street in Arundel, W. Sussex; St Mary's, Bramber, nr Steyning, W. Sussex; Casa Del Mer, Marine Parade, Goring-by-Sea, W. Sussex; Black Jack's Mill Restaurant, Harefield, Uxbridge.
- *Silver Nemesis* was the first in-season *Doctor Who* story to have some of its episodes premiered outside the UK; Parts Two and Three were first transmitted in New Zealand on 25 November. Previously, only the twentieth anniversary special *The Five Doctors* had been seen in another country – the USA – before it went out in its home territory.
- Prince Edward was approached to play a nonspeaking 'member

of the Royal Family'. The Prince's equerry apparently wrote back stating that he would be too busy as he had just started working for Andrew Lloyd Webber's Really Useful Company.

- Several cameo appearances were made in this story. The tour guide showing visitors around Windsor Castle was director and producer Vere Lorrimer, while those in his party included production assistant Ian Fraser, directors Fiona Cumming, Andrew Morgan and Peter Moffatt, actor Nicholas Courtney, writer Graeme Curry and production unit manager Kathleen Bidmead. Kevin Clarke, the writer of *Silver Nemesis*, is also seen as a tourist at the Castle, as one of the passers-by in Windsor as Lady Peinforte and Richard make their way through the streets and as a car driver who declines to stop and give Lady Peinforte a lift in Part Three.
- The part of Lady Peinforte was offered to, in order, Billie Whitelaw, Anna Massey, Penelope Wilton and Sarah Badel before eventually being accepted by Fiona Walker, who had made her television debut in *Doctor Who* as Kala in the Season One story *The Keys of Marinus*.
- The part of the mathematician was originally offered to Geoffrey Bayldon and then to Richard Vernon.
- Dolores Gray's character was originally written as a man called Milton P. Remington.
- The role of de Flores was originally offered to Charles Gray (the note specifying 'no German accent required').
- The music performed by Courtney Pine and his ensemble was recorded at Lime Grove Studios on 12 June 1988. The pieces played in Part One were called 'Pe Pi Po' and 'Adrian's Affair'. The piece played on Ace's ghettoblaster to jam the Cybermen's signals later in the story was by the same ensemble and called 'Frank's Quest'.

QUOTES

- 'I don't think I'll ever again have the chance to write for the Courtney Pine quartet, creatures from outer space, the Fourth Reich and the Queen in one show.' Writer Kevin Clarke interviewed by Joe Nazzaro for *Doctor Who Magazine* Issue 146.

- 'Action requires an awful lot of effort for very little screen time. You've got to give it a big feel; it's quite tricky really. You wonder what you're doing next all the time.' Director Chris Clough interviewed by Peter Griffiths for *Doctor Who Magazine* Issue 245.

COMMENT

DJH: Silver Nemesis *is one of the most incoherent and garbled* Doctor Who *stories ever. There are numerous loose ends and unanswered questions (the main one probably being how the Doctor and Ace manage to escape from the guards at the Castle) and far too many characters, all of whom suffer from being underdeveloped and poorly written. The plot – which is virtually the same as that of* Remembrance of the Daleks *(Doctor tricks old enemies into obtaining a Gallifreyan relic, which then destroys them) – is buried under a great amount of extraneous incident; and the fact that the Doctor has to explain everything to Ace (and through her to the viewer) highlights the fundamental weakness of the scripts. The Cybermen are particularly badly treated, being killed by arrows and even coins fired at them with a catapult – although, inconsistently, a handful of gold dust appears to have no effect at all on the Cyber Leader.* Silver Nemesis *is a self-indulgent mess and well deserving of its popular fan nickname,* Silly Nemesis. *(1/10)*

SJW: *What a let-down! After a great start to the season,* Silver Nemesis *comes as a deep disappointment. The scripts jumble together a whole load of disparate characters and elements with no real rhyme or reason, and the end result is a dreadful mess. The idea of restoring some mystery to the Doctor's character was a good one in principle but (unlike in the similarly themed but far more effective and coherent* Remembrance of the Daleks*), it is so unsubtly handled here that it seems completely gratuitous and serves only to irritate and frustrate the viewer. Even the usually dependable Chris Clough falters in his direction for once, as if*

he didn't really have his heart in the project. A strong contender for the title of worst Cyberman story ever. (2/10)

The Greatest Show in the Galaxy (7J)

EP	DATE	TIME	DURN	VIEWERS	CHART POS
1	14.12.88	19.35	24'23"	5.0	86
2	21.12.88	19.36	24'20"	5.3	99
3	28.12.88	19.40	24'30"	4.8	108
4	04.01.89	19.38	24'24"	6.6	79

PRODUCTION DETAILS

OB Recording: 14.05.88–18.05.88, 06.06.88–10.06.88, 15.06.88, 16.06.88, 18.06.88

The Doctor is juggling and Ace is looking for her rucksack when an advertising beacon materialises in the TARDIS control room, promoting the Psychic Circus on the planet Segonax. The Doctor decides to enter the Circus's talent contest.

On Segonax, Bellboy (Christopher Guard) and Flowerchild (Dee Sadler) are running across an open area of ground. They are being tracked by kites controlled by the Chief Clown (Ian Reddington) from a hearse. Bellboy draws the kites' attention away as Flowerchild finds an abandoned bus and, entering it, locates a hidden box. Before she can open the box, however, she is attacked and killed by a robot bus conductor (Dean Hollingsworth). Bellboy, meanwhile, is captured by the Chief Clown and returned to the Circus.

The Doctor and Ace arrive on Segonax and obtain directions to the Circus from a local stallslady (Peggy Mount). The Doctor tries to hitch a lift on a bike owned by Nord the Vandal (Daniel Peacock), but Nord refuses and heads off to the Circus on his own. The two travellers have no choice but to follow on foot. On the way they meet up with the intergalactic explorer Captain

Cook (T. P. McKenna) and his companion, a young woman called Mags (Jessica Martin). Cook is taking tea while Mags investigates a giant robot mostly buried in the sand. Suddenly the robot comes to life and grabs Mags. Ace deactivates it by hitting it over the head with a shovel.

Moving on, the Doctor, Ace, Cook and Mags come to the bus. They too are attacked by the robot bus conductor, but the Doctor manages to get it to destroy itself. Ace finds one of Flowerchild's earrings in the sand outside and pins it to her jacket. Cook and Mags take off for the Circus in their jeep, leaving the Doctor and Ace to continue walking.

On reaching the Circus, Cook and Mags are invited through to the ring, where Bellboy is being punished. Mags screams, but her scream is muted by the Ringmaster (Ricco Ross) with an electronic device. Having just arrived outside, Ace hesitates as she thought that she heard screaming. The Doctor asks her if they are going in or not, and the Chief Clown appears at the entrance and waves them in. Inside, they meet Morgana (Deborah Manship), a gypsy mystic who explains that all the founder members of the Circus expressed themselves through special skills – hers was fortune telling. The Ringmaster invites the two travellers to take their seats. Morgana tries to warn them of something but the Chief Clown appears and ushers them through.

The Doctor and Ace sit next to a strange family: a mother (Janet Hargreaves), a father (David Ashford) and a little girl (Kathryn Ludlow). The show starts, and amid juggling and tumbling clowns (Patrick Ford, Paul Sadler, Phil Sadler, Alan Heap, Paul Miller, Dave Pumfrett, Jeff Davis, Karl Magee, John Alexander, Hugh Spight, Nicky Dewhurst, Earth G, Raymond Dunstan) the Ringmaster announces that the Doctor will be the next act. The Doctor leaves to prepare, and Ace runs off when the Chief Clown notices Flowerchild's earring on her jacket. The Doctor is put in a cage with Cook, Mags and Nord. Cook insists that Nord be the next to enter the ring, and the Vandal is taken away by clowns.

Hiding at the entrance to the Circus, Ace overhears Morgana

and the Ringmaster talking. Morgana is very unhappy. The Chief Clown arrives and Ace's presence is revealed. She runs, chased by the clowns. She finds Bellboy but hides when the Chief Clown arrives and asks him to repair the bus conductor robot.

Nord enters the ring and lifts a weight – a feat for which he receives a marking of three 9s from the family. He is then asked to tell a joke but finds this more difficult and receives three 0s. He is reduced to ashes by a bolt of lightning.

Another participant arrives. This is a boy (Gian Sammarco) who is a big fan both of the Circus and of Cook. The Doctor and Mags manage to escape from their cell. Ace, however, is captured by the Chief Clown and put in a darkened workshop full of partially constructed robots, which start to move. She is rescued by Bellboy, who switches off the robots.

The Doctor and Mags find their way to a stone tunnel leading to a well. The well seems bottomless, but when the Doctor drops a juggling club down it there appears at the bottom an eye symbol of a design previously seen displayed on the kites. Suddenly Cook appears, flanked by clowns. He has come to collect them all as they are due to appear in the ring. As they leave they pass under an image of a moon, which induces a strange reaction in Mags. The Doctor takes this opportunity to escape again. He returns to the Circus entrance, where he sees in Morgana's crystal ball an image of the same eye symbol. He is concerned that things are getting out of control more quickly than he expected.

Bellboy explains to Ace that his circus skill was making robots. He gives her a control box for the large robot buried in the sand.

The Doctor meets Deadbeat (Chris Jury), a mentally damaged man who appears to be a cleaner at the Circus, and is taken by him to Ace and Bellboy. Bellboy remembers that Deadbeat used to be called Kingpin. Both men haltingly recall events that brought the Psychic Circus to its present situation, and the Doctor starts to piece the mystery together. Meanwhile, Cook has graciously allowed the young fan to go before him into the ring. The boy is killed.

The Doctor, Ace and Deadbeat head off to the well. The Chief

Clown arrives at the workshop and Bellboy commits suicide by causing his robot clowns to kill him.

Deadbeat shows the Doctor and Ace how he summoned the powers that now control the Circus by lifting an amulet above the well. They realise that the centre of the amulet – the eye – is now missing and must be hidden at the bus. The Doctor asks Ace to go to the bus and fetch it. He then returns to the cage and proposes to Cook and Mags that they all enter the ring together.

The Ringmaster introduces the three newcomers to the ring. Cook asks to have a moon spotlight directed at Mags. She turns into a werewolf and chases the Doctor around the ring. Cook hopes to deal with the powers behind the Circus once the Doctor is out of the way. The Doctor confronts the family, all of whose eyes glow green. He then falls, but Mags turns on the Captain and kills him.

Ace locates the box in the bus and takes it outside to Deadbeat, where she finds that she cannot open it. She is attacked by the bus conductor robot, which has been repaired and returned to the bus, and inadvertently stamps on the box as they struggle. The box opens and Deadbeat retrieves the centre of his amulet from within and inserts it in place. His full mental faculties return and he tells Ace to hit a button on the top of the conductor's head. She does so and the robot explodes. Deadbeat – now Kingpin once more – realises he must get the amulet to the Doctor.

Mags reverts to her human state and she and the Doctor run from the ring. The family demand another act and, as there is no one left, kill the Ringmaster and Morgana instead.

The Doctor tells Mags to meet up with Ace and Kingpin. As she leaves, however, she is followed by the Chief Clown in the hearse. The Doctor asks the eye in the crystal ball to open a pathway for him. He then pushes through the barriers and emerges into a different circus ring before three stone gods (David Ashford, Janet Hargreaves, Lorne McCulloch; voices: David Ashford, Janet Hargreaves, Alan Wareing). He is in the space-time of the Gods of Ragnarok, beings he has fought through all time.

The hearse's progress is obstructed by the stallslady, whose stall is blocking the road. The Chief Clown and the robot clowns continue their pursuit on foot. Mags meets up with Ace and Kingpin. Ace leads them to the buried robot and, using the control unit given to her by Bellboy, destroys the robot clowns. The Chief Clown is also killed. The three friends then use the hearse to return to the circus.

The Doctor is performing a succession of conjuring tricks to keep the Gods amused.

Ace, Mags and Kingpin find that the Psychic Circus ring is deserted. Kingpin realises that the Doctor is in the 'dark circus' and heads for the well. Behind them Cook comes back to life. He follows them and takes the amulet from Kingpin. The Doctor finishes his act just as Ace makes Cook drop the amulet down the well. The amulet appears before the Doctor and he uses it to deflect blasts of power from the Gods. The dark circus starts to tremble and fall apart. The Doctor throws the amulet at the Gods and walks from the circus tent as it is completely destroyed behind him.

The Doctor suggests that Mags help Kingpin to rebuild the Circus. Kingpin invites the Doctor and Ace to join them as well, but the Doctor declines.

WHO FAX

- Novelised as *Doctor Who – The Greatest Show in the Galaxy* by Stephen Wyatt in 1989.
- Working title: none.
- Locations: Skinner's Road, Golden Pond and the Blue Lagoon, all at ECC Quarry (West Knighton Pit), Warmwell, Dorset; tent erected in car park of BBC Elstree Studios, Borehamwood, Hertfordshire; Borehamwood, Hertfordshire.
- Production of this story was disrupted when potentially dangerous white asbestos was discovered during building works at the TV Centre studios. It was saved from cancellation by the production team arranging for the planned studio sessions to be relocated to a large tent erected in the car park at the BBC's Elstree Studios (home of the soap opera *EastEnders*).
- The Whizzkid, the unnamed character portrayed by Gian

Sammarco, was a deliberate parody of the sort of fan that the production office perceived that *Doctor Who* attracted.

- Following completion of the story, incidental music composer Mark Ayres wrote to the head of BBC Records suggesting the release of a spin-off single called 'The Psychic Circus'. This track, inspired by the plot of the story but not featured within it, was written by Christopher Guard and performed by Guard, Ayres and other cast members. The track was apparently liked by John Nathan-Turner, who gave his blessing to its release. The BBC was not interested, however, and so the project was abandoned.

QUOTES

- 'The biggest challenge of the script for me was to create the creepy atmosphere that was required. The wonderful thing about the story, which I loved from the moment I read it, was that nothing was as it appeared to be, and that apparently innocent characters turned out to be evil. That was the biggest challenge: to get that across without giving the game away. I was quite happy that I wasn't dealing with rubberised monsters.' Director Alan Wareing interviewed by Joe Nazzaro for *Doctor Who Magazine* Issue 161.
- 'We'd already shot the location aspects of the show some weeks earlier, which represented about a quarter of the story. Then we went into rehearsal for the studio aspects of the show which represented about three quarters of it, and found out that the BBC TV Centre studios were going to be closed to clear the asbestos. There was a suggestion that the story be abandoned, and we fought very hard [against this]. They felt they could cut their losses, but John was very unhappy about the idea of a shortened season. I was unhappy about losing the show because it was going very well. The designer, David Laskey, came up with the idea of building a tent, and that's what we did. The tent in fact had plastic walls, a canvas roof and a wooden floor, and we built it in the car park at BBC Elstree, where *EastEnders* is shot.' Director Alan Wareing interviewed by Joe Nazzaro for *Doctor Who Magazine* Issue 161.

COMMENT

DJH: *After the disaster that was* Silver Nemesis *it is great to see* Doctor Who *back on form.* The Greatest Show in the Galaxy *features lots of good ideas, and the whole production is lifted by the excellent performances of a superb cast. Particular mention must go to Ian Reddington, who gives a totally chilling performance as the Chief Clown, and also to Jessica Martin as Mags, who manages to evoke both horror and sympathy from the audience. Mark Ayres's score is superbly pitched, and the visuals are both effective and sumptuous. (8/10)*

SJW: *The anniversary season ends on as high a note as it began. In fact in some ways* The Greatest Show in the Galaxy *is an even more impressive achievement than* Remembrance of the Daleks *in that, in keeping with the usual approach in the McCoy era, it is completely fresh and original in its concepts and characters, whereas the latter story relied to a large extent on the series' established mythology. The circus setting is inspired, and the clowns make wonderfully eerie villains. Alan Wareing's direction is highly atmospheric, and there are some truly memorable sequences such as the brilliantly realised transformation of Mags into a 'punk werewolf'. The only real flaw in the entire story is the inclusion of the Whizzkid, a crude and unnecessary caricature of a tiny minority of* Doctor Who *fans. (9/10)*

SEASON TWENTY-SIX

Battlefield (7N)

EP	DATE	TIME	DURN	VIEWERS	CHART POS
1	06.09.89	19.35	24'06"	3.1	102
2	13.09.89	19.35	24'07"	3.9	91
3	20.09.89	19.35	24'13"	3.6	95
4	27.09.89	19.35	24'14"	4.0	89

Repeat (BBC2)

EP	DATE	TIME	DURN	VIEWERS	CHART POS
1	23.04.93	19.20	24'06"	1.6	-
2	30.04.93	19.10	24'07"	1.2	-
3	07.05.93	19.20	24'13"	1.3	-
4	14.05.93	19.20	24'14"	1.2	-

PRODUCTION DETAILS

OB Recording: 06.05.89–08.05.89, 11.05.89, 13.05.89–17.05.89
Studio Recording: 30.05.89–01.06.89 in TC3

Alistair Gordon Lethbridge-Stewart (Nicholas Courtney) at a garden centre . . .; a sword with a glowing jewel in its handle . . .; a UNIT convoy transporting a nuclear missile . . .; Brigadier Bambera (Angela Bruce) unable to make contact with the convoy . . .; a witch looking on through a crystal ball . . .; and in the TARDIS, the Doctor receiving a distress signal from sideways in time, across the boundaries between worlds.

The TARDIS arrives in England in the near future and the Doctor and Ace hitch a lift from Peter Walmsley (James Ellis), site manager of the Carbury Trust conservation area – an archaeological dig by the shore of Lake Vortigern. The UNIT convoy has stopped at the dig and the Doctor and Ace discover that its systems have been blown by an energy pulse. Sergeant Zbrigniev (Robert Jezek) tells a sceptical Bambera about the Doctor and his ability to change his appearance and personality.

Several armoured knights (Mark Jardine, Martin Kennedy, Danny Lawrence) crash to Earth from space, and one of them finds the TARDIS. The knights start to fight among themselves.

Bambera gives the two time travellers a lift to the Gore Crow Hotel, where Ace befriends a young Chinese girl, Shou Yuing (Ling Tai). There is a scabbard hung on the wall of the hotel lounge and Elizabeth (June Bland), the hotelier's blind wife, senses something strange about it – as though it is waiting for something. Ace and Shou Yuing retire to the garden to talk about explosives.

The knights continue to clash. A grenade is thrown and one of the knights is blown up in the air and through the roof of a brewery behind the hotel, startling Ace and Shou Yuing. The Doctor and the girls investigate and find the knight. He is Ancelyn (Marcus Gilbert), who greets the Doctor as Merlin. Bambera arrives, her car having been damaged in the fighting. Finally Mordred (Christopher Bown) enters, flanked by knights. The Doctor prevents Mordred and Ancelyn from fighting. Taking advantage of the fact that both believe him to be Merlin, he orders Mordred to leave. The knight complies, but tells the Doctor that his mother has waited twelve centuries to face him.

Lethbridge-Stewart has meanwhile been directed to go to London by UNIT commanders in Geneva. He orders that an exclusion zone be placed around Carbury.

In an abandoned church, Mordred summons his mother, Morgaine (Jean Marsh). She appears and speaks to the Doctor through a mental link, warning him not to stand against her.

The next morning, Lethbridge-Stewart and Flight Lieutenant Lavel (Dorota Rae) leave London for Carbury by helicopter.

The Doctor, Ace and Walmsley investigate the archaeological site. Ace blasts a hole using some nitro-9, revealing a tunnel leading downward.

Morgaine is in a churchyard with her knights. She is honouring the dead. Seeing Lethbridge-Stewart's helicopter, she makes it crash. Lethbridge-Stewart is unharmed and goes to fetch help for Lavel, who is injured. He encounters Morgaine but they part with mutual understanding. He then hurries to the hotel and commandeers Shou Yuing's car from her.

The Doctor and Ace follow the tunnel and eventually find themselves in a spacecraft under the lake. There they find the slumped, armour-clad figure of Arthur and a sword. Ace pulls the sword from its mounting and thereby inadvertently activates a defence mechanism that knocks the Doctor out. She then finds herself trapped in an airlock as it rapidly fills with water.

The Doctor recovers in time to free Ace from the airlock by opening the outer door. Ace swims up to the surface of the lake, where Walmsley and Ancelyn see her emerge carrying the sword. Lethbridge-Stewart, having arrived along with Shou Yuing, heads down the passage and rescues the Doctor.

Morgaine sends her Knight Commander (Stefan Schwartz) to retrieve Excaliber from Ace.

Mordred is drinking at the hotel when Lavel enters and holds him at gunpoint. Morgaine arrives and forces Lavel to lower her weapon and kneel at her feet. She then kills the woman by draining the knowledge from her mind. When the hotelier, Pat (Noel Collins), complains, she disintegrates the body and pays for the drinks by restoring Elizabeth's sight.

The Doctor, Ace, Shou Yuing, Bambera, Lethbridge-Stewart, Ancelyn and Walmsley all return to the hotel, trying to avoid Morgaine's knights along the way. There, UNIT troops take steps to evacuate all the civilians. Major Husack (Paul Tomany) encounters resistance from Pat and Walmsley, but the Doctor convinces the two men that they wish to leave and they do so with no further problem. Lethbridge-Stewart has ordered up numerous weapons – and adds to the inventory, at the Doctor's suggestion, silver bullets. He has also had Bessie, the Doctor's yellow car, brought to the hotel. The Doctor heads off for the missile convoy in order to prevent a battle there. He leaves Ace with some chalk, instructing her to draw a circle and stay inside it with the sword.

Elsewhere, Morgaine has been watching this exchange through her crystal ball. She summons the Destroyer (Marek Anton), a blue demon, and then transports herself to the hotel, where Ace and Shou Yuing cower in the circle. She attempts to obtain the sword by playing mental tricks on the young women and then, when this fails, threatens them with the Destroyer.

The Doctor manages to bring a temporary halt to the fighting at the convoy. Mordred is captured and reveals that the Destroyer has been summoned. The Doctor tries to get Morgaine to stop what she is doing by threatening Mordred's life but, to Mordred's horror, she is undeterred. Morgaine cannot touch the sword so long as it is in the chalk circle. The Doctor hurries back to the hotel, but there is a massive explosion as he arrives. Ace and Shou Yuing are unharmed, but Ace admits that she gave Morgaine the sword.

There is a curtain of light in the room and the Doctor and Lethbridge-Stewart pass through it. They find themselves transported to where Morgaine and the Destroyer are waiting. The Destroyer reveals that it enabled the Doctor to come here in the hope that Morgaine would be forced to free it. Lethbridge-Stewart is knocked through a window by the creature.

Ace has meanwhile realised that the Doctor may need the silver bullets. She jumps through the interstitial vortex after him and bumps into Morgaine, giving the Doctor a chance to grab the sword. Morgaine frees the Destroyer and regains the sword. She and Mordred, who has arrived from the battlefield, then fade away, while the Doctor and Ace beat a hasty retreat with Lethbridge-Stewart, who is unharmed.

Ace gives the Doctor the silver bullets and he loads them into Lethbridge-Stewart's gun. Lethbridge-Stewart, however, knocks the Doctor out and goes to deal with the Destroyer himself. The bullets work and the Destroyer is banished. The Doctor finds Lethbridge-Stewart's prone form and, distraught, reflects that he was supposed to have died in bed. It turns out, however, that Lethbridge-Stewart is not dead after all, only unconscious. Recovering, he determines to return to his wife, Doris (Angela Douglas).

Morgaine and Mordred have returned to the UNIT convoy, where they plan to fire the nuclear missile.

The Doctor and Ace revisit the spaceship. Ace replaces the sword in its mounting and the Doctor discovers that the suit of armour in which Arthur is supposedly held in suspended animation is empty but for a note – left for him by his own future self – explaining that Arthur died in the final battle and warning that Morgaine has taken control of the missile.

As Ancelyn and Mordred fight, the Doctor goes to stop Morgaine. He convinces her that to use the missile is dishonourable and she hits the abort button. The spacecraft explodes and the Doctor tells Morgaine that Arthur died many years ago. He then incapacitates Mordred and tells Lethbridge-Stewart to lock both Mordred and Morgaine up.

Later, back at Lethbridge-Stewart's house, the women head off for a drive in Bessie, leaving the men to do the gardening and cooking.

WHO FAX

- Novelised as *Doctor Who – Battlefield* by Marc Platt in 1991.
- Story released in an extended version by BBC Home Video in 1998.
- Working titles: *Nightfall*, *Storm Over Avallion*.
- Locations: Fulmer Plant Park, Cherry Tree Lane, Fulmer, Bucks; Little Paston, Fulmer Common Road, Fulmer, Bucks; Black Park Country Park, Iver, Bucks; Dowager House, St Martin Without, Lincolnshire; Hambleton Old Hall, Upper Hambleton, Leicestershire; Hambleton Ridge, Upper Hambleton, Leicestershire; Rutland Water, Upper Hambleton, Leicestershire; Twyford Woods, Lincolnshire; Castle Cement, Pit Lane, Ketton, Lincolnshire; Memorial Cross, Upper Hambleton, Leicestershire; Church of St Andrew, Upper Hambleton, Leicestershire.
- During recording of the sequence at the end of Part Two in which Ace is trapped in a rapidly filling water tank, the tank burst and water poured out on to the studio floor. This incident was potentially life threatening both to Sophie Aldred (who was in the tank) and, in view of the many electrical cables present, to others in the studio.
- It was at one point intended that Brigadier Lethbridge-Stewart would be killed by the Destroyer at the end of this story, but this idea was abandoned before recording. The suggestion that the Brigadier might be killed off was nevertheless used by John Nathan-Turner as a publicity gimmick.

QUOTES

- 'I wasn't happy with *Battlefield*. Everything that could go wrong went wrong. I didn't write a very good script. The cast was good and it was well directed but it was really over-ambitious. And the special effects went wrong . . . Andrew Cartmel asked me to expand it [from a three-parter] to a four-parter and it just didn't work. As a three-parter it had a kind of simplistic elegance to it . . . The middle episode was stretched over two episodes and bits filtered in.' Writer Ben Aaronovitch interviewed by Marcus Hearn for *Doctor Who Magazine* Issue 201.

- 'There was one instance where, in Part One, we're intercutting between Ace and one of the armoured knights flying through the air. Now, in the script it said, "He flies through the air," and I was uncertain as to whether it was the effect of the hand-grenade going off or whether he was meant to be automaton-like and have the ability to [fly] . . . And when presented with that question, Ben [Aaronovitch] wasn't too sure either. He said, "Well, a bit of each really". I still am not sure. I deliberately played it so that once the armour came off, he lost the facility [to fly]. I think perhaps, looking back on it, that it was something we should have developed. It was, at one stage, in the original write, that when he took [the armour] off, you saw cables . . . so there was a suggestion of automaton- or robot-like action. But then you say, "If he has that facility, why didn't he use it all the way through?" . . . Perhaps we should have played it as the hand-grenade effect.' Director Michael Kerrigan interviewed by Nicholas Briggs for *TV Zone* Issue 2.
- 'I find the biggest problem is the credibility – how far you play the humour, and how far you play it for real. Certainly, as a director, the biggest problem I had was that balance, especially when Ben does write with a sense of humour. The thing I enjoyed about it was [keeping] the pace going. I feel it has to have an almost relentless pace, and I like the fact there were ninety-odd scenes. I mean, I didn't at the time! Time is always the biggest element, and you end up trimming, and never quite getting your hundred per cent. You fall slightly short . . . but then, that's very common.' Director Michael Kerrigan interviewed by Nicholas Briggs for *TV Zone* Issue 2.

COMMENT

DJH: *Kicking off what was to be the final season of* Doctor Who *as an ongoing BBC series,* Battlefield *features such disparate elements as Arthurian legend, a witch, sword-fighting knights* *and a spacecraft, not to mention the return of the Brigadier and the introduction of sundry other characters. Out of this potential recipe for disaster comes a passable yarn that intrigues and entertains but is a little rough around the edges. Jean Marsh's Morgaine steals the show, but Bambera, Ancelyn and Shou Yuing are strong characters as well. There is even an excellent monster at the end. All in all, not a bad season-opener. (7/10)*

SJW: *In each of Sylvester McCoy's three short seasons as the Doctor there is sadly one story that falls notably below par. In Season 26 it is* Battlefield. *The scripts by Ben Aaronovitch are actually not too bad, although they do contain quite a bit of poor dialogue and some rather silly ideas (such as the suggestion at the end of Part Four that UNIT will be able to keep Morgaine and Mordred in check simply by locking them up), but their translation to the screen leaves a great deal to be desired. The main problem is that, with the spectacular exception of the excellently realised Destroyer, the production has a conspicuously low-budget quality to it. The opposing factions of knights look desperately unimpressive clumping about the countryside in their stock armour and indulging in a succession of poorly arranged fights with pathetically ineffective weaponry. Michael Kerrigan's direction is also rather heavy-handed, failing to make the most of the material or to bring out the best in the cast. It is good to see the Brigadier back in action, though, and the fact that John Nathan-Turner had second thoughts about killing off this ever-popular character is something to be grateful for. (3/10)*

Ghost Light (7Q)

EP	DATE	TIME	DURN	VIEWERS	CHART POS
1	04.10.89	19.34	24'17"	4.2	94
2	11.10.89	19.34	24'18"	4.0	93
3	18.10.89	19.35	24'17"	4.0	104

PRODUCTION DETAILS
OB Recording: 21.06.89
Studio Recording: 18.07.89, 19.07.89, 01.08.89–03.08.89 all in TC3

The TARDIS arrives in a laboratory-cum-playroom in a mysterious old house. The Doctor tells Ace that their location is a surprise. Ace hopes that the house isn't haunted as she hates haunted houses – she's been in one already.

The housekeeper, Mrs Grose (Brenda Kempner), meanwhile, lets in the Reverend Earnest Matthews (John Nettleton) at the front door. He has come to see Josiah Smith, the owner. Grose leaves him to wait and, with the other day maids (Katy Jarrett, Sue Somerset), hurriedly departs from the house. The clocks strike six and the night maids (Vivienne Darke, Emma Darrell, Diana Frances, Fiona King) emerge from behind concealed panels in the hall, together with Mrs Pritchard (Sylvia Sims), head of the night staff. Josiah sends his ward Gwendoline (Katharine Schlesinger) to greet Matthews.

Ace and the Doctor find a snuff box on the floor in a hallway. It is radioactive. They then meet an explorer and big-game hunter (Michael Cochrane), who is searching for Redvers Fenn-Cooper. The explorer sees the box as proof of Redvers's presence and explains that he intends to save him from Josiah. He suddenly sees himself reflected in a window pane – and recognises this as the reflection of Redvers. Mrs Pritchard bursts in and takes Redvers away. Nimrod (Carl Forgione), a Neanderthal butler, invites the Doctor to join Matthews in the study.

In the study, Matthews assumes that the Doctor is Josiah and starts berating him for his scientific beliefs. The Doctor gives Nimrod the fang of a cave bear – a sign of knowledge – and the butler leaves to bring some tea. Ace goes with Gwendoline to get changed into something more suitable. Josiah (Ian Hogg) enters and the lights dim automatically. He is wearing dark glasses and is covered with dust.

Nimrod goes down to the cellar – revealed as being a stone spaceship – and kneels before a shape concealed behind a lighted panel. As he does so, however, he is knocked out by a creature that emerges from a previously locked cell.

Josiah is speaking to the Doctor when the telephone rings. He answers it, and a voice croaks, 'I escape.' Josiah reacts in horror but then composes himself and has Mrs Pritchard show Mr Matthews into the room. Mrs Pritchard prepares a pad of ether as the two men talk, and uses it to knock Matthews out.

Ace realises that the Doctor has brought her to Gabriel Chase, a house in Perivale that she burnt down when she was thirteen years old because she sensed evil there. Furious with the Doctor for tricking her, she runs off. Josiah joins the Doctor and offers him five thousand pounds to rid him of 'the brute' that is opposed to him. Ace meanwhile finds the lift and descends to the cellar, where she is attacked by two reptilian 'husk' creatures (Keith Harvie, Jack Talbot), while a hoarse voice calls her 'Ratkin'.

Gwendoline pulls open a specimen drawer to reveal the sleeping form of a policeman (Frank Windsor). She tells the Doctor that he is from Java.

Nimrod comes to Ace's aid, but becomes agitated when she threatens to smash the lighted panel. He struggles with her and the panel is broken, sending him into shock. The Doctor arrives with Josiah and notes that there is something hibernating behind the panel. Josiah then obtains a gun and takes charge. He tells the Doctor and Ace to operate the controls to close down the ship, but they distract him. The creature in the cell orders the husks to release it. The two time travellers run, with Josiah, back to the lift. They eventually make it back to the ground floor. Josiah's skin is flaking – he has started evolving again – and he breaks the lift before ordering Mrs Pritchard to seal the house because dawn is approaching.

In the laboratory/playroom, Josiah offers a banana to Matthews, who is starting to turn into a monkey. Gwendoline then drugs Matthews with another chemical pad.

As dawn breaks, the Doctor wakes the sleeping policeman and Ace falls asleep.

Ace is eventually woken by Mrs Grose, who has brought her a large breakfast – although it is now around 5 p.m. Ace is to join the Doctor and the policeman in the drawing room. Mrs Grose hurries away.

Nimrod is still in a coma. The policeman, Inspector Mackenzie, is eating heartily and trying at the same time to conduct enquiries into the disappearance of the house's original owner, Sir George Pritchard, which he started investigating in 1881.

The creature from the cell – Control (Sharon Duce) – leaves the cellar and listens at the door as the Doctor brings Nimrod out of his coma by shouting 'Light!' As Nimrod talks to the Doctor, Control goes to prepare for the return of Light. The Doctor has mended the lift and hopes that Control will bring 'something' up from the cellar with it.

The Doctor sets the clock in the hall forward to 6 p.m. and, as it strikes, Mrs Pritchard and the night staff emerge. Josiah also appears. He has shed another husk and now no longer needs to hide from the light. The Doctor refuses his request to stop the lift. The doors open and Control emerges. Suddenly a bright light bursts from the lift, followed by the unearthly figure of Light (John Hallam) himself. Ace comments that it is an angel, but the Doctor replies that it is just another life form; while it slept, its survey – Josiah – got out of control. Light kills one of the maids. He explains that he previously spent centuries cataloguing all life on Earth, but as soon as he finished it started to change and evolve. Control runs off. The Doctor tries to persuade Light to leave, but fails.

Josiah has plans for the British Empire and tells Gwendoline that it is time to send Ace 'to Java'.

Control meets Redvers who tells her that she can achieve her ambition to be a real lady – she is evolving fast. The Doctor arrives and Control jumps out of a window. Redvers tells the Doctor that he is hunting the crowned Saxe-Coburg – the Queen of England.

Gwendoline attacks Ace, but Control climbs in through the window and comes to her rescue. Gwendolyn is left locked in the room but soon breaks down the door and heads off after Ace.

Light checks his calculations and cannot believe that he is still on Earth. He sees one of the maids and calls her to him. Later,

Nimrod arrives to find that Light has 'dismantled' the maid to see how she worked. Inspector Mackenzie enters, and Light kills him as well.

The Doctor finds Ace and Gwendoline fighting again. He shows Gwendoline a locket containing a photograph of her mother – Mrs Pritchard.

The Doctor, Ace, Redvers and Control join Josiah for dinner. The Doctor tells Ace not to have the soup. The Doctor shows Mrs Pritchard the locket and she leaves in tears to find her daughter.

Mrs Pritchard finds Gwendoline in a bedroom and they embrace. Light appears and turns them to stone so that they will never change again. Nimrod witnesses this and is horrified.

Redvers has an invitation to Buckingham Palace and now plans to take Control there instead of Josiah. Josiah is furious because he intended to use this opportunity to assassinate the Queen. Control burns the invitation and Ace breaks down, admitting that she burnt Gabriel Chase to the ground when she was thirteen.

Light arrives in the dining room. He has a solution to his problem. He was going to reduce all life to primordial soup – like Inspector Mackenzie, currently in the soup bowl – but now intends to destroy everything with a firestorm. That way his catalogue will be complete. The Doctor points out that Light is changing too and that his catalogue still has gaps: griffins, basilisks, dragons, slithy toves, bandersnatches and crowned Saxe-Coburgs to name a few. He cannot destroy all life before he has completed the catalogue.

Light, realising that everything is changing all the time, turns himself to stone. Nimrod points out that the firestorm program has already been activated. Everyone hurries to the stone spaceship, where Control takes charge of Josiah and orders him back. The heads of the husks explode and Josiah reverts to a basic creature, which Control then locks up in the cell: they have changed places. Redvers and Nimrod decide to take over Light's task of completing the catalogue and Control notes that the Doctor is not listed . . . and probably never will be. The spaceship leaves with Josiah, Control, Redvers and Nimrod on board.

The Doctor and Ace return upstairs as Light finally disperses. The Doctor notes that the house will remember these events – it is the reason that Ace burnt it down.

WHO FAX

- Novelised as *Doctor Who – Ghost Light* by Marc Platt in 1990.
- Story released on BBC Home Video in 1994.
- Working titles: *The Beastiary*, *Life Cycle*.
- Location: 11 Greenhill, Weymouth, Dorset.
- This was the final *Doctor Who* story to be recorded as part of the ongoing BBC series.
- The song played by Gwendoline on the piano in Part One is 'That's the Way to the Zoo', composed by J. F. Mitchell. It was played out of vision by Alasdair Nicolson.

QUOTES

- 'I set out to do quite a lot in *Ghost Light*. Where other writers have gone back into the Doctor's past – which I like – I wanted to show up other people's relationships to the Doctor. I have this feeling that he doesn't really realise what exactly he does to people – the effect he has on their lives. He turns up on a location for maybe two days, solves some momentous catastrophe, goes away and leaves behind ten people in a heap saying "My God, what hit us?" and they have to come to terms with the way the rest of their lives will now change as a result of his interference.' Writer Marc Platt interviewed by Gary Russell for *Doctor Who Magazine* Issue 158.
- 'For me the stories that work better are the creepy stories, the sinister ones like *Ghost Light*. It was successful because it was a creepy story, and people are more frightened by that. . . . I was pretty certain when I finished *Ghost Light* that it had all the ingredients that would make you want to sleep with your lights on.' Director Alan Wareing interviewed by Joe Nazzaro for *Doctor Who Magazine* Issue 161.

COMMENT

DJH: Ghost Light *dragged* Doctor Who *kicking and screaming into the nineties (a good trick, since this was only 1989!). Marc Platt's script is densely packed, and almost every word has significance. This is* Doctor Who *for the video generation, a story that really can be watched over and over again with new things being spotted and heard each time. It's hugely entertaining, as well as thought-provoking, and finally Sophie Aldred finds her feet as Ace. All the cast are totally convincing and the setting is one of the best: an old haunted house. Brilliant fun, superb entertainment, let down only by being possibly a little too incomprehensible for its own good. (9/10)*

SJW: *A fascinatingly dense and imaginative set of scripts by Marc Platt, excellent direction by Alan Wareing, fine performances from a remarkable cast and outstanding production values* – Ghost Light *has all the ingredients of a bona fide classic. There is a wonderful quality of Gothic weirdness about the whole thing, and Platt's superb characterisation of the Doctor and Ace is particularly noteworthy. Great stuff. (9/10)*

The Curse of Fenric (7M)

EP	DATE	TIME	DURN	VIEWERS	CHART POS
1	25.10.89	19.34	24'23"	4.3	-
2	01.11.89	19.34	24'09"	4.0	-
3	08.11.89	19.34	24'11"	4.0	-
4	15.11.89	19.35	24'16"	4.2	-

PRODUCTION DETAILS

OB Recording: 03.04.89–08.04.89, 11.04.89–15.04.89, 18.04.89–20.04.89

Russian commandos (Sergeant Prozorov: Peter Czajkowski; Petrossian: Mark Conrad; others: Andy Combs, Ken Dee, Martin Dew, David Foster, Damon Jeffrey, Nigel Parkes Davies, Mark

Ponsford, Vince Sears, Derek Van Weenan) arrive on the English coast by dinghy. Their commander, Sorin (Tomek Bork), orders them to set up camp. They find one of their comrades lying injured on the rocky beach and Sorin tries to discover what happened to the sealed orders that he was carrying.

The TARDIS arrives just outside a secret naval base. The Doctor leads Ace to the office of the wheelchair-bound base scientist Dr Judson. There he forges letters of authority for himself, completing this task just before Captain Bates (Steven Rimkus) arrives to investigate. The two travellers are then shown to their quarters for the night.

One of the Russian soldiers, Gayev (Stephen Fitzalan), finds the sealed orders but is chased and attacked by something unknown.

The next morning, the Doctor and Ace arrive at the local church looking for Judson. The vicar, Mr Wainwright (Nicholas Parsons), shows the Doctor to the crypt. Ace meanwhile befriends two young women, Jean (Joann Kenny) and Phyllis (Joanne Bell), evacuees from London who are currently staying with an elderly woman named Miss Hardaker (Janet Henfrey). They arrange to meet later at Maidens' Point, then Ace rejoins the Doctor. In the crypt, Judson (Dinsdale Landen) is trying to translate some Viking runes. The Doctor and Ace leave him to it. After a detour through the churchyard, where the Doctor realises that some of the graves have Viking names on them, the two travellers head out to Maidens' Point. There the Doctor finds the sealed orders. He returns to the church, where Wainwright shows him some records made by his grandfather at the end of the last century. They contain translations of the inscriptions in the crypt. The Doctor and Wainwright take the translations to Judson.

Back at the base, the Doctor and Ace find a group of Wrens (Marianne Bergin, Mandy Demetrious, Claudia Lyster, Nicola Maddock, Suzi Mollett, Jane Perry, Roslyn Riley, Kate Shury, Wendy Spear) translating German messages. One of the women, Kathleen Dudman (Cory Pulman), has a baby girl (Aaron Hanley) with her, and Ace falls in love with it.

The Doctor and Ace find Commander Millington's office,

which is an exact replica of a naval cipher room in Berlin. Millington (Alfred Lynch) is trying to think like the enemy in order to stay one step ahead.

The Doctor and Ace return to Maidens' Point and find a dead soldier. They are captured by Sorin and his men but, on hearing the Doctor's story, Sorin lets them go.

Judson shows Millington the translations. As he reads the words, things move under the sea and a set of new runes appears in the church crypt. Later, Millington suggests that Judson use the Ultima machine – a code breaker – to translate the runes.

The Doctor and Ace find the new inscriptions in the crypt but are interrupted by Millington. He takes them through to a secret tunnel system where a natural poison that seeps from the walls is being collected. Millington plans to use the poison to win the war.

The Doctor goes with Millington back to the base as Ace speaks with Wainwright. The minister is suffering a crisis of faith.

Millington explains to the Doctor that the Ultima machine has been booby-trapped with a flask of the poison. The plan is that the Russians should be allowed to steal it. He demonstrates the effects of the poison in an isolation tank. The machine is programmed to detonate the flask when it receives a particular coded word: 'Love'. That word will be included in a message sent to Russia when the political climate is right.

Miss Hardacre has severely reprimanded Jean and Phyllis for going to Maidens' Point. They ignore her and return there, venturing into the water for a bathe. A mist appears and covers them, and when it lifts they are no longer to be seen.

Millington, much to the puzzlement of Captain Bates, orders that all the radio transmitters on the base be disabled and that all chess sets be burnt.

Judson sets the Ultima machine to translate the runes. The phrase 'let the chains of Fenric shatter' is printed out.

Jean and Phyllis reappear, but they have been transformed into vampires. They entice a soldier into the water, where he is grabbed by a group of monstrous Haemovores (Ian Collins,

Jennifer Crome, Ian Elliott, Perry Evans, Ann Graham, Raymond Martin, Jaqui Nolan, Tony Ryan, Graham Stagg, Cy Town, Alan Marshall, Tip Tipping, Paul Heasman, Sam Kent-Smith, Joe Kent-Smith). They then return to Miss Hardacre and kill her.

The two vampires next attack Wainwright at the church. They leave when the Doctor and Ace arrive, but threaten to return for Wainwright later. The Doctor discovers that Ace has given Judson the clue that he needed to solve the mystery of the runes: they are a logic diagram for a computer program. He, Ace and Wainwright hurry to the base to stop Judson from using this. They are too late, however, and Haemovores are summoned from the sea. Millington realises his mistake: the base has been weakened to allow the Russians to steal the Ultima machine and now they have no way of summoning help because he has also ordered that all the radios be destroyed – a task that Perkins (Christien Anholt) has carried out with an axe.

On the beach, Sorin and his men retreat as the Haemovores advance.

The two time travellers search the secret tunnels for what the Doctor describes as 'something evil'. Ace finds an old flask and, thinking that it might come in useful, stuffs it in her rucksack.

The Haemovores try to break into the church, while the Doctor, Ace and Wainwright try to keep them out. The Doctor realises that faith will repel the attackers. He whispers the names of his past companions and this sets up a screaming noise that drives the creatures away. Sorin arrives and determines to rescue his men, relying on his faith in the Russian Revolution for protection. He gives Ace his scarf before leaving. The Doctor, Ace, Wainwright and two Russian soldiers escape through the tunnels, pursued by Jean, Phyllis and the Haemovores.

Ace wants to make some more nitro-9 using the old flask, but the Doctor realises that this is the 'oriental treasure' to which the runes referred.

The Doctor, Ace and Wainwright emerge from the tunnels to find Millington and his men waiting for them. Millington orders the exit doors barred, despite protests from the Doctor and Ace that there are still two soldiers inside.

Sorin tries to make a truce with Millington, but the Commander has him locked up.

Ace finds Kathleen sitting alone. The woman has received a note that her husband is missing, presumed dead.

Ace confronts the Doctor. She realises that he knows what is going on and demands that he explain. He tells her that Fenric, an evil intelligence from the dawn of time, is trapped inside the flask. They need help to defeat it, so Ace distracts a guard and thereby enables the Doctor to release Sorin.

Wainwright waits by the exit from the tunnels as the Haemovores start to burn their way out. The creatures emerge, and Wainwright is killed as his faith proves insufficient to hold them back.

The Doctor realises that Fenric needs a body to occupy. He and Ace hurry to the cipher room, where Judson is knocked out by a discharge of power from the Ultima machine. The Doctor, Ace and Sorin look on as Millington recites the Viking legend. Behind them, Judson rises to his feet, his eyes glowing green. He has been possessed by Fenric.

Fenric/Judson states that he has been trapped in the shadow dimensions for seventeen centuries, and that now his preparations are complete. He vanishes and reappears in the tunnels, where he orders Jean and Phyllis to fetch the Ancient One (Raymond Trickett). They go to Maidens' Point and summon the creature from the sea.

The Doctor tells Ace that he needs a chess set to play his game with Fenric to its conclusion. They try to get one from Millington's office, but he has mined it with explosives and they narrowly escape being killed. Ace then remembers that Kathleen also had a chess set.

As the Doctor hurries to set up the chess game, the Wrens are trapped by the Haemovores and transformed into vampires, following which they attack the soldiers. Judson's nurse, Crane (Anne Reid), is also killed. Millington shoots down Sorin's second in command, Vershinin (Marek Anton), but is then killed by Captain Bates. Ace sends Kathleen and the baby off in a car to stay with her Nan at 17 Old Terrace, Streatham. She then finds herself trapped by the pursuing Haemovores.

Fenric/Judson tells the Ancient One to take the poison into the sea and to destroy the other Haemovores. The Ancient One carries out the latter instruction, saving Ace from an attack by Jean and Phyllis, who crumble away to nothing.

The Doctor faces Fenric/Judson, challenging him to make the final move in the chess game that he has set up in the laboratory. He then convinces the Ancient One that to poison the seas would only bring about the destruction of the world – and that the future from which the Ancient One comes would no longer exist.

Ace finds Fenric/Judson hunched over the chess set. He cannot solve the problem of the final move. She runs off and finds Bates helping the wounded Vershinin. They are now working together. Realising that this is the solution to the chess puzzle, she returns to the laboratory to find Sorin. She tells him that the solution is for the opposing pawns to join forces. Sorin, however, has now been taken over by Fenric in place of Judson. The Doctor arrives to find that Fenric/Sorin has won. A lightning bolt hits the chess set and it bursts into flame. Fenric/Sorin reveals that all those involved are his pawns – including Ace, as Kathleen's baby is her mother, whom she hates, and she has just created her own future. Fenric/Sorin orders the Ancient One to kill the Doctor and Ace. The creature is held back, however, by Ace's total faith in the Doctor. Fenric/Sorin demands that the Doctor kneel before him, but the Doctor responds by telling him to kill Ace. He claims he knew all along that Ace was a pawn and accuses her of being an emotional cripple that he would never have allowed to travel with him if he hadn't known the truth. Ace collapses. Now freed from the obstacle of her faith, the Ancient One herds Fenric/Sorin into the isolation tank and releases the poison, killing both of them. The Doctor grabs Ace and escapes before the room explodes. The Doctor tries to explain to a tearful Ace that he had to break her faith in him so that the Ancient One could act.

Later, on the rocks at Maidens' Point, Ace is still troubled. The Doctor watches as she dives into the water. When she emerges, she says that she is not scared any more. They turn and walk away together.

WHO FAX

- Novelised as *Doctor Who – The Curse of Fenric* by Ian Briggs in 1990.
- Story released in an extended edition by BBC Home Video in 1991.
- Working titles: *Wolf-Time*, *The Wolves of Fenric*.
- Locations: Crowborough Training Camp, Crowborough, E. Sussex; St Lawrence Parish Church, The Moor, Hawkhurst, Kent; Bedgebury Lower School, Lillesden, Hawkhurst, Kent; Roses Cottage, Slip Way Hill, Hawkhurst, Kent; Yew Tree Farm, Slip Way Hill, Hawkhurst, Kent; Lulworth Cove, Weld Estate, Dorset.
- An edition of the BBC children's show *Take Two* on 19 April 1989 included an item on the making of *The Curse of Fenric*, then still under its working title *The Wolves of Fenric*. This was introduced by presenter Phillip Schofield and considered the question of what frightens children. After canvassing the views of members of the studio audience (all children), Schofield read out a script extract describing the death of the vampires Jean and Phyllis. There then followed a short prerecorded documentary looking at the development and realisation of this scene.
- Sylvester McCoy's sons Sam and Joe Kent-Smith make a cameo appearance in this story as Haemovores.

QUOTES

- 'It took a lot of persuading to put *The Curse of Fenric* on location. It was absolutely frowned upon to start off with; John [Nathan-Turner] would not entertain it. I was absolutely determined because there seemed to me no other way of doing it. The script just fell into a location plot, and it just seemed to create more headaches if you tried to do it in the studio.' Director Nicholas Mallett interviewed by Peter Griffiths for *Doctor Who Magazine* Issue 230.
- 'We were doing the [series] on a shoestring, and I don't know to this day why we should have been doing it that way. It was good television. The reason it started to go downhill was that we were

making so many shortcuts and really not being allowed to do enough of the visualising, enough of the effects, because it needed an extra man here or a bit more money there. It always seemed to be down to the bare bones, and certainly I don't think that's the way to do it.' Director Nicholas Mallett interviewed by Peter Griffiths for *Doctor Who Magazine* Issue 230.

COMMENT

DJH: *Easily one of the best* Doctor Who *adventures of this period, and ranking among the all-time greats,* The Curse of Fenric *has an exciting and well-conceived story, a great new monster race and excellent performances from an impressive cast. Nicholas Parsons is perfect as Wainwright, and Tomek Bork, Dinsdale Landen and Alfred Lynch are also convincing in their respective roles as Sorin, Judson and Millington. The effects are marvellous, the action constant, and the plot engaging enough to hold the viewer's interest throughout. (9/10)*

SJW: *Following on from the excellent* Ghost Light, *the viewer is treated to another terrific story in the very different* The Curse of Fenric. *Ian Briggs's scripts and Nicholas Mallett's direction are admirable, and the Haemovores are a superbly realised monster race in the traditional* Doctor Who *vein. Unlike some of the other 'guest stars' who appeared in the series in the mid-eighties, Nicholas Parsons is well cast and treats his role with suitable seriousness and conviction, and all the other performances are also very good. The recording of the story entirely on location was a wise move, and the spirit of the forties is well conveyed. Almost faultless. (9/10)*

Survival (7P)

EP	DATE	TIME	DURN	VIEWERS	CHART POS
1	22.11.89	19.36	24'14"	5.0	89
2	29.11.89	19.35	24'13"	4.8	96
3	06.12.89	19.35	24'20"	5.0	91

PRODUCTION DETAILS

OB Recording: 10.06.89–15.06.89, 18.06.89–23.06.89

A man named Dave (Damon Jeffrey) is washing his car in a quiet suburban street when something appears before him. He tries to run, but vanishes from sight. The TARDIS arrives at the end of the street. The Doctor has brought Ace back to Perivale because she wanted to see how some of her old gang were faring. They head for the youth club where Sergeant Paterson (Julian Holloway), who has been teaching the art of survival to a group of lads (Nick Ferranti, Simon Horrill, Humph James, Keith Macey, Dominic Martinez, Jimmy Morris, Michael Savva, Lee Towsey), tells them that kids from the area keep vanishing. The Doctor is more concerned by a black cat that seems to be watching them.

The Doctor and Ace go to Perivale High Street where the Doctor buys some cat food and cheese from a supermarket run by Len (Gareth Hale) and Harvey (Norman Pace). Ace bumps into one of her friends, Ange (Kate Eaton), who tells her that she hasn't seen any of the others lately. The Doctor is thoughtful and wanders off to try to catch a cat. He opens some cat food in the street and then hides and waits.

Ace makes her way to a children's play area. She finds a black cat and, after it runs off, is suddenly confronted by a humanoid cheetah person on horseback. She is chased around the play area and shouts for the Doctor. Suddenly there is a flash of light and she finds herself on an alien planet, where she discovers the dead body of the man seen earlier washing his car.

The Doctor arrives to find the play area deserted. He returns to his bait and sees a black cat, which he pursues. He is hampered by Paterson, who chases after him in the belief that he is causing a public nuisance.

Ace is chased by a cheetah person on horseback. She manages to get away with the aid of a boy, who is killed and taken by the cheetah person. She then meets her friends Shreela (Sakuntala Ramanee), Midge (William Barton) and Derek (David John), who are hiding out, and determines to go on the offensive.

The Doctor climbs a wall to get to the cat, but Paterson follows him. They fall from the wall and arrive on the alien planet, in the middle of the cheetah people's camp. The creatures (Emma Durrell, Susan Goode, Damon Jeffrey, Samantha Leverett, Leslie Meadows, Basil Paton, Lee Towsey, Adel Jackson) herd them to a tent wherein sits the Master (Anthony Ainley), his eyes glowing yellow. The Doctor resists the Master's attempts to goad him into running, but Paterson is not so strong willed and is caught and tormented by the cheetah people. The Doctor manages to grab a horse, rescue Paterson and escape.

Ace has meanwhile set up some traps for the cheetah people. One of these fails when a cheetah person sees and disables it, and another captures only the Doctor and Paterson.

The Doctor determines to get everyone to a safe area beyond the cheetah people's camp and explains that the planet is on the point of breaking up. Warning them not to run, he starts to lead them through the camp. Suddenly a milkman (Jack Talbot) appears, exciting the cheetah people and panicking the humans. Everyone but the Doctor runs, and the cheetah people attack. Paterson and Midge manage to free Derek by throwing rocks at the creatures. Ace captures a horse and Shreela helps Derek to get away.

Ace finds herself by a lake and watches as an injured cheetah person arrives on the other side. It collapses and she goes to its aid, speaking to it and bringing it water from the lake.

The Doctor encounters the Master by some ruined buildings. The Master explains that the cheetah people are linked to the planet; when they fight each other, they bring it closer to destruction. He wants the Doctor to find a way out of the situation. He himself has been infected by the planet and is gradually transforming into a cheetah person.

The Doctor finds Ace and tells her that they need an animal whose home is Earth in order to return there. The Master overhears this and prepares a leash by stripping some skin from a dead animal. Ace confesses to the Doctor that she likes the planet and feels as if she could run for ever. She is also starving hungry. They meet up with the others. Midge attacks Derek but runs off, his eyes glowing yellow, when the Doctor intervenes. He then encounters the Master, who puts him on the leash and tells him to go hunting. He vanishes, taking the Master with him.

The Doctor tells Ace and the others that they must wait until one of them succumbs to the planet's influence and then use that person to get them home. The cheetah person that Ace helped by the lake returns. Ace is pleased, and when she looks back at the Doctor her eyes are glowing yellow. The cheetah person asks Ace to come hunting and they run off together, the Doctor giving chase.

On Earth, the Master muses that if he has to become an animal, then like an animal he will destroy the Doctor.

Ace speaks to the cheetah person, Karra (Lisa Bowerman), and wonders why she called her 'sister'. She sees her yellow-eyed reflection and realises that she must get back to the Doctor. Karra tempts her with the hunt for food, but she resists this and returns with the Doctor to the others. The Doctor explains to Ace that if she helps them to escape, she may never change back. They all link hands, and Ace transports them back to Earth. Shreela and Derek run off, but Paterson refuses to acknowledge that anything out of the ordinary has happened.

Ace wants to leave in the TARDIS but the Doctor insists they sort out the Master and Midge. They visit Midge's home and find a slaughtered cat and a young girl, Squeak (Adele Silva), who shows them the direction in which the Master and Midge went. Ace's eyes glow, and she senses that Midge is at the youth club.

The boys at the youth club are hypnotised by the Master, and when Paterson arrives they kill him. The Doctor and Ace catch up with them on a nearby hill. There the Doctor and Midge confront each other in a motorbike duel, riding directly at each other at high speed. There is a massive explosion as the bikes collide. Midge dies after the crash, but the only trace that Ace can find of the Doctor is his hat. The hypnotised boys approach, but she realises that she cannot fight them – the Doctor has warned her that if she does so she will be permanently transformed. She shouts for help. Karra appears on horseback and chases the boys away, but the Master then stabs her with an animal tooth. Ace screams.

The Master, leaving the scene, passes the Doctor's body lying in a rubbish heap. The Doctor is still alive and, recovering, he returns up the hill. He finds Ace crying over Karra, who has transformed into a young woman. Karra wishes Ace good hunting, then dies.

The Doctor encounters the Master waiting for him by the TARDIS. The Master is still infected and feels the power from the planet growing in him. He grabs the Doctor and they are both transported back to the planet, which is visibly more unstable than before. They struggle with each other, but the Doctor realises that they must stop. The Master claims that they cannot escape and goes to deliver the fatal blow. At the last moment, however, the Doctor is suddenly transported back to Earth. He finds himself by the TARDIS being berated by a housewife (Michelle Martin) about the noise of his shouting.

Ace looks on as another cheetah person appears on horseback, picks up Karra's body and then vanishes again. The Doctor arrives and retrieves his hat and umbrella from Ace. Ace is pleased when he confirms that the cheetah planet will live on inside her. They turn and walk back to the TARDIS together. More adventures beckon.

WHO FAX

- Novelised as *Doctor Who – Survival* by Rona Munro in 1990.
- Story released on BBC Home Video in 1995.
- Working titles: *Cat Flap*, *Blood Hunt*.
- Locations: 5 Medway Drive, Perivale, Ealing, London; Drayton Court Hotel, The Avenue, Ealing, London; 4 The Avenue, Ealing, London; Motorcycles Unlimited, 2 Medway Parade, Perivale, Ealing, London; Londis Food Market, 20 Medway Parade, Perivale, Ealing, London; Sceptre Financial Services, 23 Medway Parade, Perivale, Ealing, London; balcony outside flats, 63 Medway Parade, Perivale, Ealing, London; children's play area, Ealing Central Sports Ground, Horsenden Lane South, Perivale, London; Colwyn Avenue, Perivale, Ealing, London; wall in Bleasdale Avenue, Perivale,

Ealing, London; alley off Colwyn Avenue, Perivale, Ealing, London; 45 Woodhouse Avenue, Perivale, Ealing, London; EYJ Martial Arts Centre, North Ealing Sports Centre, Greenford Road, Sudbury Hill, London; notice board on Horsenden Hill, Perivale, London; Horsenden Hill, Perivale, London; ECC Quarry (West Knighton Pit), Warmwell, Dorset.

- For the scene in which the two motorbikes crash, the Doctor and Midge were doubled by Tip Tipping (for the Doctor) and the legendary stunt cyclist Eddie Kidd (for Midge). Tipping, however, walked off the production before the completion of recording in a dispute over Kidd's involvement.

QUOTES

- 'It's an adventure story with a lot of action in it and we are limited in terms of time and money. I think those types of shows take longer to do, simply because of the time it takes to set them up.' Director Alan Wareing interviewed by Joe Nazzaro for *Doctor Who Magazine* Issue 161.
- 'We're using three real cats, but there are no definite number in the story. In the script they're called kitlings and are described as having red eyes, but we couldn't quite achieve that [effect]. What we decided to do was to make them all black and give them a ruff of hair up their backs, which sort of matches the ruff on the [cheetah people].' Director Alan Wareing interviewed by David J. Howe, Mark Stammers and Stephen James Walker for *The Frame* No. 11.
- '[I decided to use the same quarry as for *The Greatest Show in the Galaxy*] because I know you can get another planet's surface there. It's a vast quarry – you can drive round it for hours. For the most part, we will be using different sections of it, including some wooded areas. It fact, we are going to just one of the same places again – it's where the hippie bus was, and this year it's going to be the cheetah [people's] encampment . . . To be honest, when we get to the [quarry] I want grey, overcast skies, because shadows and sunlight are a problem. I'm going to paint a lot of heavy skies in anyway on locked-off shots, because the planet itself is supposed to be

very stormy, with volcanoes and the like. We will be painting on volcanoes and lava flows, so I'll be looking for clean skylines and piles of sand to use for those purposes.' Director Alan Wareing interviewed by David J. Howe, Mark Stammers and Stephen James Walker for *The Frame* No. 11.

- 'The cheetah people were not as sinister as I would have liked. They *never* looked real. What I wanted was for them to be very human with perhaps just fangs and a feline look about the cheeks and strange catlike eyes. My original idea – way, way back – was to have them hunting, shooting, fishing and charging around on horses, hunting humans. That would have been much more frightening. If you have something that looks human until it bares its teeth, then that is scary. Alan Wareing, Andrew Cartmel and I all sat around talking about what these cheetah people would look like, and Alan kept saying, "As long as we don't get *Puss in Boots*". Unfortunately, I think that's exactly what we did get.' Writer Rona Munro interviewed by Liam Rudden for *Doctor Who Magazine* Issue 189.

COMMENT

DJH: Survival *is a very enjoyable story, and one that has not really dated since its original transmission. Its key theme of survival and the novel concept of the linking of a planet to its indigenous population work well. Anthony Ainley as the Master turns in his best performance since Season 18's* Logopolis *and the other guest cast are also superb, especially Julian Holloway as Paterson. The story is let down only by some less than convincing costumes and make-up for the cheetah people – if only CGI had been available to provide some computer-generated cheetahs and morphing effects for the human–cheetah transformations. Overall* Survival *is a great closing story in what was undoubtedly the best season of* Doctor Who *for very many years. (8/10)*

SJW: Survival *is another in a run of excellent stories. The scenes set in Perivale are refreshingly down to earth and naturalistic,* *making for a very effective contrast with the wonderfully fantastical and exotic sequences taking place on the planet of the cheetah people. Anthony Ainley gives his best ever performance as the Master (who at last has a decent new costume, superseding the awful penguin suit of his earlier eighties appearances), and his confrontations with the Doctor – including in particular their climactic final struggle on the disintegrating planet – are highly memorable. The cheetah people are admittedly a little too cuddly in appearance to be totally effective, but on a more positive note the story boasts some superb electronic effects – an aspect of the series' production that improved in leaps and bounds during McCoy's time as the Doctor. A fine end to what was, the occasional disappointment notwithstanding, a fine era. (9/10)*

Doctor Who (Television Movie)

EP	DATE	TIME	DURN	VIEWERS	CHART POS
	27.05.96	20.29	84'39"	9.08	9

PRODUCTION DETAILS
Location Filming: 15.01.96–19.01.96, 22.01.96–26.01.96, 29.01.96–30.01.96, 01.02.96–02.02.96, 05.02.96–08.02.96
Studio Filming: 31.01.96, 08.02.96–09.02.96, 12.02.96–16.02.96, 19.02.96–21.02.96

'It was on the planet Skaro that my old enemy the Master was finally put on trial. They say he listened calmly as his list of evil crimes was read and sentence passed. Then he made his last and, I thought, somewhat curious request. He demanded that I, the Doctor, a rival Time Lord, should take his remains back to our home planet, Gallifrey.

'It was a request they should never have granted.'

In the TARDIS control room, the Doctor (Sylvester McCoy) places an urn containing the Master's remains into a casket and locks it with his sonic screwdriver. This done, he rests with a cup of tea and a book while the TARDIS heads for Gallifrey, dateline 5725.2 Rassilon Era.

The casket shudders, gently at first and then with more vigour, and finally cracks open, releasing a jelly-like substance. The substance swiftly moves to the TARDIS control console and vanishes inside. The console starts to malfunction and the Doctor tries to stabilise it. There is a critical timing malfunction and the TARDIS prepares for an emergency landing.

On Earth, in San Francisco, a group of youths – Chang Lee (Yee Jee Tso) and two others (Michael Ching, Dean Choe) – are being chased by a car. They scale a fence into a yard and believe themselves safe, but a group of armed thugs (Darryl Quan, Byron Lawson, Paul Wu, Johnny Mah) emerge from hiding. Suddenly a wind blows up and the TARDIS materialises in front of Chang Lee. The door opens and the Doctor exits, to be met by a hail of bullets. A car pulls up and the gang members depart, leaving Chang Lee with the prone figure of the Doctor. Chang Lee calls for an ambulance and the Doctor sees the jelly-like substance emerge from the TARDIS's keyhole.

In the ambulance, a medic named Bruce (Eric Roberts) gets Chang Lee to sign a form authorising treatment for the patient. The date is 30 December 1999. Chang Lee gives the Doctor's name as 'John Smith'. On arrival at the hospital the Doctor is rushed into surgery, while in the ambulance a jelly-like snake hides itself in Bruce's jacket.

Much to the astonishment of a nurse, Curtis (Delores Drake), the Doctor's X-rays show that he has two hearts. The emergency doctor, Salinger (John Novak), removes two bullets from the Doctor's left leg – a shot to his shoulder passed right through – and requests that the cardiologist, 'amazing Grace', be summoned from her night off at the opera.

Grace Holloway (Daphne Ashbrook) arrives at the hospital still in evening wear and prepares to operate on the Doctor. In surgery she starts to probe the heart of the apparently unconscious patient, but he wakes and recognises the music playing in the background: Puccini's *Madame Butterfly*. He struggles but is anaesthetised. Grace finds that she cannot recognise the internal structure of the Doctor's body and experimentally pushes the probe hard. The Doctor convulses and his life signs vanish from the monitors. He dies at 10.03 p.m. Grace is upset and demands to see the X-rays. Chang Lee, waiting outside, is summoned and takes possession of the Doctor's belongings. Grace is suspicious of the boy, and he runs from the hospital.

At Bruce's apartment, the jelly-like snake emerges from the medic's coat and approaches the bed where he and his wife (Eliza Roberts) are lying. It rears up and enters Bruce's body through his mouth.

The Doctor's body is taken to the morgue, where it is checked in by Pete (William Sasso) and Ted (Joel Wirkkunen) and placed in a cubical.

Later, Pete is watching *Frankenstein* on television, unaware that something is happening inside the cubical. Lightning plays around the Doctor's body and he regenerates, returning to life. The new Doctor (Paul McGann) smashes his way out of the cubicle, causing Pete to faint. The Doctor leaves the morgue and finds himself in a deserted wing of the hospital where he breaks down on seeing his reflection. He doesn't know who he is.

The next morning, the Doctor raids some lockers for suitable clothes and discards a long multicoloured scarf before plumping for a selection of items, including a green duster coat intended as part of a Wild Bill Hickok fancy-dress outfit.

Bruce's wife wakes to find her husband already up and acting strangely. He tells her to call him 'Master', and then kills her by breaking her neck.

The Doctor, waiting in the hospital corridor, recognises Grace as she passes him. He starts to remember what happened.

The hospital director (Michael David Simms) tells Grace to forget about the death, and about X-rays that show two hearts. Grace refuses to cooperate and resigns. The Doctor follows her as she leaves, and manages to get into her car. There, to her astonishment, he removes the broken probe from his chest. Now realising that this is the missing, apparently 'dead' patient, she drives him back to her apartment.

The Master arrives at the hospital and is told that the Doctor is dead and that his body has gone missing. He also discovers that Chang Lee has the Doctor's possessions.

At her apartment Grace checks the Doctor's hearts again and also his blood. She is puzzled by what she finds, but the Doctor assures her that everything is all right. They decide to go for a walk in a nearby park.

Chang Lee returns to the TARDIS and gets in using a key that he found among the Doctor's possessions. Inside he meets the Master, who entrances him and takes the bag containing the Doctor's things. The Master intends to use the boy to obtain the Doctor's body, which he needs to take over as his own in order to survive, and bribes him with gold dust. They move through the TARDIS to the cloister room. The door opens of its own accord and the Master comments that the TARDIS 'likes' Chang Lee. In the middle of the vast room is the Eye of Harmony, the centre of the structure. The Master tells Chang Lee how to open the Eye – something that can be done only with a human eye – and he does so.

As the stone cover over the Eye moves back, the Doctor regains his lost memories.

An image of the seventh Doctor appears above the Eye, followed by one of the current incarnation. Seeing the Doctor's eye magnified, the Master realises that he is half human. The next image is of Grace, as the Eye 'sees' through the Doctor's own eyes.

Realising what is happening, the Doctor closes his eyes. He explains to Grace that he needs an atomic clock to fix the timing mechanism on the TARDIS. Grace, believing that he has finally flipped, hurries back to her apartment. The Doctor follows and pleads to be let in, but Grace calls for an ambulance. The Doctor frantically explains that they have only until midnight to close the Eye and leave the planet, taking the Master with them, or the Earth will cease to exist. To convince Grace, he demonstrates that molecular structures are already breaking down by pushing first his hand and then his whole body through a glass pane and into her apartment.

Chang Lee and the Master leave to supply the ambulance that Grace requested.

The Doctor sees on the television news an item about an atomic clock being unveiled in San Francisco that evening. He realises that this must be a beryllium clock and determines to obtain it.

The ambulance arrives and the Doctor and Grace go off in it, unaware that Chang Lee is driving and that their fellow passenger is the Master. The vehicle suddenly jolts to a halt in a major traffic jam and the Master's sunglasses fall off, revealing his identity to the Doctor. The Master spits a burning slime at Grace, and it hits her arm. The Doctor uses a fire extinguisher to temporarily blind the Master, and he and Grace escape out of the back of the ambulance.

The Doctor and Grace run to the front of the traffic jam and steal a police motorbike. Chang Lee and the Master give chase in the ambulance.

Eventually the Doctor and Grace arrive at the Institute for Technological Advancement and Research (ITAR) where the clock is situated. Grace uses the fact that she is on the board of trustees to get the Doctor in. They meet Professor Wagg (Dave Hurtubise), inventor of the clock, and the Doctor steals his pass in order to get to the device and remove the component that he needs. On the way out, however, he and Grace are spotted by the Master and Chang Lee. They manage to escape by setting off the fire alarm and using a fire hose as a rope to lower themselves down the outside of the building. They return to the TARDIS, where the cloister bell is tolling. The Doctor wires the beryllium chip into the circuits and the Eye closes. He discovers that this was not done quickly enough, however, and decides that they must go back in time to before the Eye was ever opened. To obtain sufficient power for this, he plans to divert energy from the Eye. Grace, however, becomes possessed by the Master as he enters the Ship, and she knocks the Doctor unconscious before he can complete the connections.

The Doctor revives to find that he is now strapped to a trolley in the cloister room. Grace places a crownlike device on his head on the instructions of the Master, who has now changed into Gallifreyan robes, and he is then chained up on a balcony overlooking the closed Eye. He appeals to Chang Lee for help. The Master, in countering this, inadvertently reveals to the boy that his earlier claim that the Doctor had stolen his lives was a lie. The Master kills Chang Lee and then kisses Grace so as to return her to normal and enable him to use her to open the Eye. The Master positions himself in the reflected light from the Eye and the transference of his mind to the Doctor's body begins. The Doctor shouts to Grace to return to the console room and reroute the power as before.

Storms break over San Francisco as the transference process continues. The countdown to the new millennium begins: thirty seconds to go.

Grace struggles to connect the correct wires beneath the console. She manages it with just one second to spare.

The TARDIS starts to roll back in time and enters temporal orbit. Grace releases the Doctor from his chains, but this act also frees the Master, who throws her from the balcony to her death. The Doctor and the Master fight. The Master leaps at the Doctor, intending to push him into the Eye, but the Doctor blinds him with reflected light and he is sucked into the Eye himself.

The Doctor sadly collects the bodies of Grace and Chang Lee as the TARDIS slips further back in time. Suddenly, their life essence emerges from inside the Eye and returns to their bodies. The Eye closes by itself and, as he and Grace embrace, the Doctor observes that the TARDIS is sentimental.

The Doctor directs the TARDIS to take Grace and Chang Lee back to Earth on 31 December 1999. When they arrive, he bids farewell to Chang Lee, letting him keep the gold dust and telling him not to be there the same time next year. He asks Grace to come with him, but she retorts that he should come with her. She says that she will miss him, and they kiss. The Doctor returns to the TARDIS alone, and Grace watches as it dematerialises.

In the TARDIS, after making some fine-tuning adjustments to the console, the Doctor again relaxes with a fresh cup of tea and his book – H.G. Wells's *The Time Machine*.

WHO FAX

- Novelised as *Doctor Who* by Gary Russell in 1996.
- Story released on BBC Home Video in 1996.
- The movie was first transmitted in Canada on 12 May 1996. The version transmitted by the BBC on 27 May 1996 was edited, with over two minutes of the programme removed. It was also this version that was released by the BBC on video in the UK (although in other countries it was the complete version that was released). The material edited out was as follows:
  - The Chinese youths continue to shoot at the car as it backs away.
  - The Chinese thugs open fire with automatic weapons and kill Chang Lee's two companions. Chang Lee stands terrified in front of them. Wind starts blowing around them.
  - Chang Lee reacts in horror as the thugs raise their guns to aim at him.
  - The thugs open fire on the TARDIS, which is unaffected by the hail of bullets.
  - Chang Lee emerges from behind the TARDIS and runs over to look at the bodies of his friends, then turns towards the fallen body of the Doctor.
  - Grace continues to operate on the Doctor. (This scene was drastically shortened and the music rearranged as a result. Grace's attempts to retrieve the probe and the efforts to revive the Doctor were significantly shortened; and Grace's mention of the probe still being stuck in the body and the Doctor's final scream were cut completely.)
  - Bruce's wife's neck snaps. (Only the sound effect of this was removed; the picture was retained intact.)
  - The Master twists Chang Lee's head.
- An opening caption, 'Based on original series broadcast on the BBC', was also absent from the version transmitted and released on video by the BBC, although no edit was made in order to accomplish this.
- Working title: none. (Executive producer Philip Segal suggested to fans that if they wanted a title for the movie other than just *Doctor Who*, they could refer to it as *Enemy Within*.

However, neither *Enemy Within* nor *The Enemy Within* was ever used as a working title during production.)

- Locations: Vanier Park; Pacific Space Centre; BC Children's Hospital, 4480 Oak Street; alley between E Georgia/Union Street; Magazine Store, 218 W Georgia; Weng Heng Ent, 221 Union Street; Golden Crow Centre, 211 E Georgia Street; 222 Keefer Street; Carrall Street/Keefer Street junction; John Livingstone Park, Carrall Street; Lombard Street. All locations in Vancouver, British Columbia, Canada.
- The studio stage where filming was carried out was located at 8651 Eastlake Drive, Burnaby, British Columbia, Canada.
- This story was a co-production between BBC Worldwide and Universal Television.
- The UK transmission of the story featured a dedication after the closing credits to the actor Jon Pertwee, who had died seven days earlier on 20 May. The idea of dedicating the transmission in this way was suggested in a fax to the Controller of BBC1, Alan Yentob, by Kevin Davies, a freelance film maker who had directed the 1993 BBC documentary *30 Years in the TARDIS*. It was also suggested independently by executive producer Philip Segal.
- A twenty-minute documentary, *The Making of Doctor Who – The Movie*, part of a programme called *Sci-Fi Buzz*, was shown by the Sci-Fi Channel on 25 May and on a number of other occasions over the next six months. This was based around the movie's 'electronic press kit'.
- See Chapter 8 for more information on this story.

COMMENT

DJH: *The first* Doctor Who *story under a new producer for sixteen years, and it's simply fabulous. The performances, the effects, the sets and the production values in general are all outstanding, and Paul McGann simply steals the show with his sensitive and well-observed portrayal of the Doctor. The pace is fast and furious, leaving little time for the viewer to ponder on some obvious plotting and structural problems, and the action* *never lets up. With a sense of style and identity of its own,* Doctor Who *(as its title has to be) is tremendous fun and highly watchable. Words fail me when I consider what delights a series produced on this basis could have held in store, and the fact that no such follow-up was forthcoming can only be considered a monumental wasted opportunity. (9/10)*

SJW: *The* Doctor Who *television movie is far, far better than anyone had a right to hope for, bearing in mind that it was destined to be transmitted on one of the major commercial networks in the USA (in contrast to earlier screenings of the series on the public service PBS channels). In fact it is superb by any standards, and Paul McGann gives a truly brilliant debut performance as the wonderfully costumed eighth Doctor. The plot is admittedly full of holes and rather simplistic, but this is more than made up for by all the good things in Matthew Jacobs's excellent script, including some nice set pieces and fine, witty dialogue. Daphne Ashbrook is great as Grace, Eric Roberts suitably chilling and pleasingly vicious as the Master, and Yee Jee Tso fine as Chang Lee. Special mention must go to Geoffrey Sax for his terrific direction, which keeps the action coming fast and furious and successfully disguises the aforementioned deficiencies in the plot. Surprisingly true to the spirit of the original BBC series, albeit inevitably an Americanised interpretation, the movie can only be considered a great success. (9/10)*

STORIES: APPENDIX

The seventh Doctor has also appeared in other productions that, while not forming a part of the established Doctor Who *canon, are detailed here.*

Search Out Science: The Ultimate Challenge

BBC2 transmission – part of the 'Planet Earth' module of *Search Out Science*.

DATE	TIME	DURN	VIEWERS	CHART POS
21.11.90	10.15	19'15"	-	-

Repeat (BBC2)

DATE	TIME	DURN	VIEWERS	CHART POS
28.11.90	10.15	19'15"	-	-
18.11.92	10.15	19'15"	-	-
25.11.92	10.15	19'15"	-	-

PRODUCTION DETAILS

Studio Recording: 20.05.90 at BBC Model Stage, 25.05.90 at Ealing Film Studios
Location/OB: 14.05.90, 15.05.90, 18.05.90, 21.05.90

The Doctor is the host of a gameshow and the contestants are the viewer, Ace, K-9 (voice: John Leeson) and, from the planet Glurk, Cedric (Stephen Johnson).
The first challenge is for Cedric: what shape is the Earth? (He ponders and, with clues from Ace and K-9, incorrectly decides that it is a cylinder.)
The second challenge: what makes day and night? (Cedric suggests that a spinning light or a spinning Earth could cause the effect. There are additional clues from Ace and K-9.)
Third: what makes summer hot and winter cold? (Cedric postulates that in winter the Earth is further from the sun than in summer. K-9 thinks that in winter the sun gives out less heat, or the heat is more concentrated.)
Fourth: why does the moon appear to change shape? (There are clues from Ace – she is reflected in a mirror, but is the light real or reflected? – and from Cedric – who explains that moonlight is really reflected sunlight.)
Fifth: how would you find out how many days there are in a lunar month? (The Doctor presents a clue: a picture showing the phases of the moon.)

The Doctor introduces a new subject: the stars. Round one is called: 'who, how, where, why, what'.

Who can see the stars in the daytime? (Ace can with a radio telescope.)
When can you see stars with an ordinary telescope?
How many stars are there?
How would you count them?
Cedric asks: where is K-9? (K-9 is floating in space. He has two questions: 'When can I come down?' and 'Which way is down?')
The final question in this round comes from the Doctor: what is yellow or red or brown or black or orange or blue? (K-9 comments that this is easy: it is a piece of metal when heated. The Doctor tells him that the answer is in the stars. K-9 trundles off and finds large coloured discs on the ground. He realises that the colours represent stars at different stages of their life. He fails to get the answer and dematerialises. The Doctor rescues him from space using the TARDIS.)

The Doctor poses the final question: the key to the universe is hidden somewhere in the universe, but where is it? Thirty seconds is allowed in which to answer. (K-9 states that the task is hopeless – which is the correct answer.)

WHO FAX

- This one-off entry in the BBC schools series *Search Out Science* featured Sylvester McCoy as the Doctor and Sophie Aldred as Ace.
- The visual effects were created by Mat Irvine, who had worked on the *Doctor Who* series and who also had a fully operational K-9 prop that he loaned to the production.
- The producer of this programme was Lambros Atteshlis, the series producer was Robin Mudge and the director was Berry-Anne Billingsley.
- The programme was the fifteenth and last in the unit 'Planet Earth' and also appears to have had the title 'Search Out Space', although this does not appear on screen.
- Many of the sound effects used in the production were from *Doctor Who* itself. A section of the theme music from the *K-9 and Company* spin-off programme was also used.

- Locations: Avalon Travel Agency, Ealing, London; The Danish Kitchen, Ealing, London; foot tunnel nr Shepherd's Bush Underground Station, London; Jodrell Bank Science Centre, Cheshire; concourse outside the Lloyds Building, Leadenhall Street, London.

COMMENT

It is a strange thing to see the Doctor and Ace taking part in a quiz show – one of only a very few instances of Doctor Who *characters appearing as such in another programme. Given that* Search Out Science *was an educational series for children, it is not surprising that the pace is fast and the mood light-hearted. The idea was that the questions posed should be investigated and answered by students after the programme was over, and in no way does it hang together as a 'story' (hence our decision not to give it a mark out of ten). However, it makes a lot more sense than* Dimensions in Time*!*

Dimensions in Time

EP	DATE	TIME	DURN	VIEWERS	CHART POS
1	26.11.93	20.08	7'34"	13.8	15 *
2	27.11.93	19.23	5'27"	13.6	10 **

* Shown as a part of the 1993 Children in Need appeal. ** Shown as a part of *Noel's House Party*. In both cases the 'Viewers' figure is for the fifteen-minute segment of the programme containing the *Doctor Who* 'episode'. The 'Chart Pos' is for the whole programme.

PRODUCTION DETAILS

Studio Recording: 21.09.93 at Fountain TV studios, New Malden, Surrey

Location/OB: 22.09.93–24.09.93

A spacecraft – the Rani's TARDIS – is suspended in space

beside a vortex. In the control room, the Rani (Kate O'Mara) and her assistant (Sam West) are surrounded by the spinning heads of the first and second Doctors.

The fourth Doctor (Tom Baker) sends a message to the other Doctors. The Rani has trapped the first two Doctors and wants to trap the others in a time loop in London's East End.

The Rani and her assistant have a Time Lord (Andrew Beech) and a Cyberman trapped inside her TARDIS. They need an Earthling to complete their menagerie.

The Doctor's TARDIS arrives beside the Cutty Sark in Greenwich, London. The seventh Doctor (Sylvester McCoy) and Ace (Sophie Aldred) emerge. The year is 1973.

The sixth Doctor (Colin Baker) and Ace are in Albert Square in London's East End. Ace tries on a jacket at the market stall operated by Sanjay Kapoor (Deepak Verma) and Gita Kapoor (Shobu Kapoor). The year is 1993.

The third Doctor (Jon Pertwee) and Melanie (Bonnie Langford) are in the market. They meet Pauline Fowler (Wendy Richards) and Kathy Beale (Gillian Taylforth). The year is 2013.

The sixth Doctor and Susan (Carole Ann Ford) are also in the market. The year is 1973.

Sarah Jane Smith (Elisabeth Sladen) is with Sharon Watts (Letitia Dean) when she spots the third Doctor across the market and runs to join him. The year is 2013. The Doctor realises that they are in a twenty-year time loop.

The Rani decides that the Doctors are getting too close to the truth and orders her specimens released.

The fifth Doctor (Peter Davison), Peri (Nicola Bryant) and Nyssa (Sarah Sutton) are nearly hit by a blast from a Cyberman's weapon. They run, bumping into Pat Butcher (Pam St Clement) as they do. The Doctor realises that no one else can see the invading monsters, which are all around them now. The Rani calls to them from the doorway of the Queen Vic public house, announcing that she is sending them all on a long journey. The fifth Doctor concentrates to try to summon his other selves. He, Peri and Nyssa disappear and are replaced by the third Doctor and Liz Shaw (Caroline John). Liz runs at the Rani and struggles with her, but Mandy (Nicola Stapleton) pulls her away. Captain Yates (Richard Franklin) arrives in Bessie and the third Doctor climbs in and drives off back to the TARDIS. A helicopter arrives, on board which is the Brigadier (Nicholas Courtney). When it lands, the sixth Doctor is there to greet it. He states that he must find his friend.

The Rani still needs an Earthling and prepares to materialise at Greenwich.

Grant Mitchell (Ross Kemp) and Phil Mitchell (Steve McFadden) find Romana (Lalla Ward) in their lock-up garage and ask her to leave. Romana is grabbed by the Rani and dragged into the Queen Vic. A TARDIS dematerialisation sound is heard and Frank Butcher (Mike Reid), passing outside, is puzzled.

The third Doctor and Victoria (Deborah Watling) are on the *Cutty Sark*. They leave the ship and head for the TARDIS. It departs and then materialises again nearby in Greenwich. The seventh Doctor exits from the ship and finds Leela (Louise Jameson) by the Rani's TARDIS – previously disguised as the Queen Vic. Leela explains that the Rani cloned her before she could escape. The Doctor realises that the Rani is trying to transfer her time tunnel to Greenwich. With her store of genetic codes for every living thing, evolution will then be hers to control.

The Doctor asks Leela what form she was in when the Rani cloned her. It was Romana. The Doctor realises that the Rani therefore has two Time Lords in her system and it will overload.

The seventh Doctor, K-9 (voice: John Leeson) and Ace intend to pull the Rani's TARDIS into the time tunnel. The plan works and the trapped Doctors are freed. As the seventh Doctor comments to Ace, he is hard to get rid of.

WHO FAX

- This was a two-part skit produced for the BBC's annual Children in Need telethon in 1993. It was intended to be watched through special polarised filter glasses to achieve a 3-D effect.
- The action centred around the fictional Albert Square, setting

for the BBC's soap opera *EastEnders*. Many of the then regular cast of *EastEnders* appeared in their usual roles.

- Locations: *EastEnders* lot, BBC Elstree Centre, Borehamwood, Herts; *Cutty Sark*, Greenwich, London; Queen's House, Greenwich, London; Royal Maritime Museum, Greenwich, London.
- The costumes for the monsters that invaded Albert Square were supplied from the BBC's own stock and from the private collections of a number of *Doctor Who* fans who made appearances in the show either as passers-by or wearing the costumes. One of the most prominent of these appearances was by Andrew Beech, former Coordinator of the *Doctor Who* Appreciation Society, who wore the ceremonial robes and collar of a Time Lord. Other monsters or characters glimpsed in the story included: Cyberman, Ogron (*Day of the Daleks*, *Frontier in Space*), Vanir (*Terminus*), Tractator (*Frontios*), Tetrap (*Time and the Rani*), Zog (from the stage play *The Ultimate Adventure*), Fifi the Stigorax (*The Happiness Patrol*), Vervoid (*The Trial of a Time Lord*), mutant (*Mawdryn Undead*), the biomechanoid (*Dragonfire*), Mentor (*The Trial of a Time Lord*), Argolin (*The Leisure Hive*), D84 robot (*The Robots of Death*), Plasmaton (*Time-Flight*), Melkur (*The Keeper of Traken*), Sea Devil (*The Sea Devils*) and a Mogarian (*The Trial of a Time Lord*).
- Between the first and second episodes, a telephone vote was held to determine which of two *EastEnders* characters – Mandy or Big Ron – would help the Doctor. The first check of the state of voting showed Mandy with 17,162 votes (57%) and Big Ron with 12,704 (43%). The final tally had Mandy with 22,484 votes (56%) and Big Ron with 17,044 votes (44%).
- The first segment of the story was shown during Children in Need on the Friday night, in a link-up with presenter Noel Edmonds's fictional house at Crinkley Bottom. Jon Pertwee was introduced and 'watched' the story with Edmonds and the studio audience in the house. The second segment was shown during *Noel's House Party* on the Saturday evening, but no guests were present.

- The K-9 prop was supplied by ex-BBC effects designer Mat Irvine, who also operated it for the production.
- The series' familiar theme music was rearranged for the production by Mike Fillis (who played a Sea Devil) and Adrian Pack, who gave Nathan-Turner a demo tape during the recording at Albert Square. Nathan-Turner had already approached both the Pet Shop Boys and Erasure to provide the theme but, according to his later recollection, both groups had declined. Fillis and Pack eventually made their version of the theme commercially available on a CD entitled 'Cyber-tech' in 1994.
- To keep costs down, the set for the Rani's TARDIS control room was borrowed from Dominitemporal Services Ltd, the commercial arm of the *Doctor Who* Appreciation Society, who had recently had it constructed for a *Doctor Who* convention.
- The spacecraft exterior of the Rani's TARDIS was adapted from a model used in the BBV independent video *Summoned by Shadows* (which also starred Colin Baker and Nicola Bryant).
- The Rani's assistant was named Cyrian, but this was not revealed in the final dialogue.
- The story as broadcast included no cast or crew credits. The cast have been identified in the above synopsis, and the main crew were as follows: director: Stuart McDonald; writers: John Nathan-Turner and David Rodan (a pseudonym for David Mansell); production manager: Gary Downie; sculptors: Susan Moore, Stephen Mansfield; visual effects: Mike Tucker; video effects: Dave Chapman; make-up: Lesley Smith; K-9 operator: Mat Irvine; costume designer: Ken Trew; assistant floor manager: Jenny Drewett; producer: John Nathan-Turner.

COMMENT

Dimensions in Time *is like* Doctor Who *on acid. The pace is frenetic and the plot is totally garbled. No attempt is made to explain why the Doctor and his companion(s) keep changing nor exactly what the Rani is trying to do. The whole thing is like some nonsensical sketch from a Benny Hill show where a whole horde of diverse characters bump into each other and then have a chase. Basically, it is just a fun skit that reunites as many* Doctor Who *regulars as were willing to offer their time and efforts for charity. It is just a shame that it contains so little that feels like 'genuine'* Doctor Who *and is, really, totally unrepresentative of the series. (0/10)*

4: Rewriting the Myth

Every era of *Doctor Who* brings new elements to the series' developing mythology. Story after story, new facts are invented by the series' writers and added to what is already known of the Doctor's universe. Some new pieces of this ever-growing jigsaw puzzle interlock neatly with what has gone before, while others fit so poorly that the viewer is forced to start rebuilding the picture from scratch. Many *Doctor Who* fans expend great amounts of time and energy trying to find an order that gives all the seemingly contradictory facts and storylines some kind of logical continuity.

In the era of the seventh Doctor, the main developments related to the character of the Doctor himself. The revelations were relatively minor to start with. In *Time and the Rani*, the Doctor's age was stated to be 953 – the same as the Rani's. The last mention of his age, in the previous year's *The Trial of a Time Lord*, had put it at 900, but this sort of discrepancy was nothing new: wildly different figures had been quoted during the course of the series' history. More remarkable was the fact that no real explanation was provided on this occasion for the Doctor's change of appearance, the viewer being left to assume that it was brought on as a consequence of the Rani's attack on the TARDIS.

The new Doctor seems to experience far less post-regeneration trauma than on previous occasions. The situation is complicated by the fact that the Rani drugs him in order to increase his confusion, but nevertheless he instantly recognises his adversary and is immediately on the alert – even if he promptly trips over and performs an impressive pratfall in her laboratory. When the effects of the Rani's drug wear off, he seems stable and fully in control.

Certain aspects of the seventh Doctor's character do, however, seem somewhat at odds with what has gone before. During his visit to Paradise Towers, for example, he seems to have no qualms about killing Kroagnon by pushing him into a mined storeroom (although in the event this task falls to the young man Pex). It is hard to imagine any of the other Doctors, except possibly the sixth, taking such an active part in the destruction of a life form, no matter how hostile. In *Delta and the Bannermen* he appears not overly upset at the death of Gavrok – in fact he seems more pleased that Gavrok's trap around the TARDIS has been drained of energy as a result. In *Remembrance of the Daleks* he blows up a Dalek and deliberately goads Davros into destroying Skaro, and similarly in *Silver Nemesis* he arranges for Nemesis to wipe out the Cybermen's fleet in space. In the Dalek story he also tells Ace that lives must sometimes be sacrificed for the greater good, suggesting that his justification for his actions is that the end justifies the means – a philosophy rejected by his earlier incarnations.

These glimpses of a darker side to the Doctor's nature coincide with a deepening of the mystery surrounding the character – a considered policy on the part of the series' production team (see Chapter 2). In *Remembrance of the Daleks* the idea is introduced that when the first Doctor came to Earth with his granddaughter Susan in 1963 he brought with him the Hand of Omega, a remote stellar manipulator device used by Omega – one of the legendary founders of Time Lord society – to detonate stars. Quite how he came by this device is left unexplained, but he is seen to be in total command of it. (It is this that he ultimately uses to bring about the destruction of Skaro.)

There are, however, a number of apparent inconsistencies between the events of this story and those of the first ever *Doctor Who* episode, *100,000 BC: An Unearthly Child*. A book about the French Revolution is seen lying in the science lab at Coal Hill School, but it looks quite different from the one on the same subject that was lent to Susan by her history teacher Barbara

Wright, and the latter book was not left in the science lab. A possible explanation for this is that it is simply a different book, and that its presence is a complete coincidence. More difficult to explain away, however, is the fact that the junkyard at Totter's Lane also looks somewhat different this time around. Quite apart from anything else, the owner's name on the entrance gates is spelt differently – in *An Unearthly Child* it was 'I M Foreman', here it is 'I M Forman'. Then there is a scene in which a television announcer is heard to introduce a new science-fiction series on BBC television. Nothing unusual in this – except that the time is stated to be 5.15 in the afternoon and yet it is still light outside, whereas if this really is November – and a calendar seen on the wall of the café visited by the Doctor and Ace seems to confirm that it is – it should really be dark by this time. More interesting still is the strong implication that the series about to start is actually called *Doctor Who*.

One way to rationalise all these apparent quirks is to assume that the action of *Remembrance of the Daleks* takes place in some kind of parallel universe where it is indeed light on November evenings in England, Davros is the Dalek Emperor and the Doctor is a contemporary of Rassilon and Omega, rather than – as implied in previous stories such as Season 10's *The Three Doctors* and Season 14's *The Deadly Assassin* – from a later era of Time Lord history.

The question of the Doctor's origins is further explored in *Silver Nemesis*, when it is hinted that he might not even be a Time Lord after all, or perhaps not *just* a Time Lord (a suggestion also contained in dialogue recorded for *Remembrance of the Daleks* but edited out before transmission). How and why the metal validium fell to Earth in the first place remains unclear, but the viewer learns that after Lady Peinforte fashioned it into a statue of herself the Doctor was on hand to send it back out into space. It transpires that validium was created by Rassilon and Omega as the ultimate defence for Gallifrey in the 'dark time', and that while in Peinforte's possession it told her secrets about the Doctor. What exactly those secrets are, however, is not revealed.

'We all knew that there was a mystery as to who exactly the Doctor was,' noted Ben Aaronovitch, the writer of *Remembrance of the Daleks*, in a 1994 convention interview, 'but we all had different ideas about what it was, so that it remained a mystery. I remember that Kevin Clarke [who scripted *Silver Nemesis*] had a completely different idea as to who the Doctor was, and he wasn't telling! So there were two objectives for me: to get more mystery back, and to get the kids back behind the sofa.'

The idea of the Doctor being 'the Other', a mysterious figure associated with Rassilon and Omega, was indeed one of those discussed by script editor Andrew Cartmel and his writers (and ultimately featured in Aaronovitch's novelisation of *Remembrance of the Daleks*), although at least one of the writers, Marc Platt, took the view that 'the Other' was actually a completely different character. Further, arguably more outlandish ideas considered at one time or another included the Doctor being twice born (first as a contemporary of Rassilon, then again in his Hartnell incarnation); being more insane than his adversaries; and even being a Christ figure (the idea particularly favoured by Clarke). As scripted, *Survival* had the Doctor explicitly confirming to his old adversary the Master that he had evolved into something more than just a Time Lord (tying in with the loose theme of evolution that had run through the last three stories of the twenty-sixth season). This, however, was vetoed by John Nathan-Turner and did not feature in the transmitted story. 'Andrew and the writers had all sorts of sensational revelations as to who the Doctor was,' recalled the producer in 1996 in the book *Ace! The Inside Story of the End of an Era* by Sophie Aldred and Mike Tucker, 'none of which I was prepared to entertain. I was prepared to accept the odd hint, but originally it was spelt out. I think that you have to be very careful with what you say to an audience, especially an impressionable one, and I felt that what Andrew and the writers were going to do went totally against making the Doctor more mysterious.' On-screen references to the Doctor's mysterious origins were consequently confined to occasional hints and suggestions.

The idea of the Doctor having had untelevised adventures was nothing new for the series; many references to such adventures had been made in the past, often in the form of throwaway remarks about meetings between the Doctor and famous historical figures. In the McCoy era, however, this plot device took on a particular importance. As well as the revelation of the earlier encounter with Lady Peinforte, there are references to the Doctor's hiding of the Hand of Omega on Earth, past battles with the Gods of Ragnarok (*The Greatest Show in the Galaxy*) and Fenric (*The Curse of Fenric*) and a future encounter with the witch Morgaine in an alternate dimension wherein he poses as Merlin and sides with King Arthur (*Battlefield*).

The Doctor during this incarnation is also revealed to have some hitherto unsuspected talents. He is seen to be a consummate magician and acrobat, able to entertain the three demanding Gods of Ragnarok for some time with a seemingly endless succession of conjuring, manipulation and escapology tricks. He is also seen to be able to incapacitate foes with his fingers, apparently transmitting some form of energy to make them sleep (although this could just be a different utilisation of Venusian aikido skills that have lain dormant since his third incarnation). More significantly, he is frequently shown to have a degree of foreknowledge about the situations into which he arrives, as in *Remembrance of the Daleks*, *Silver Nemesis*, *The Greatest Show in the Galaxy*, *Battlefield*, *Ghost Light* and *The Curse of Fenric*. He tends to keep this information to himself, however, leaving Ace – and anyone else unlucky enough to be around – to get caught up in events and learn from the experience.

'This version of the Doctor, I have a lot more respect for him,' Cartmel told interviewer David Bishop in 1994 for *TSV* 40. 'I always hated it when he was zapped on the head or knocked unconscious and tied up. I always thought that was demeaning to him. If he doesn't get tied up, it should be that it was his plan all along . . . It all goes back to "Doctor who?" The mysterious, scary, powerful Doctor . . . It struck me this was the most interesting way to do the show. You could crack on and do some really exciting television.'

These moves towards restoring some mystery to the Doctor's

character went hand in hand with a conscious policy on Cartmel's part, already evident in Season 24, to eschew the continuity-heavy approach of the sixth Doctor's era, in which every story had relied to a greater or lesser extent on the series' established mythology. 'We had a conscious junking of the mythology,' confirmed Stephen Wyatt in a 1989 interview conducted by Joe Nazarro for *Doctor Who Magazine*. 'Let's forget about the Master; let's forget about the Time Lords; let's get back to the original idea, which was [that the Doctor was an explorer in] outer space ... There was a clean sweep. [My story] *Paradise Towers* had no cross references whatsoever to any previous *Doctor Who* adventures or characters, and that was quite a conscious decision.'

Given this approach, it is perhaps not surprising that few stories of the McCoy era add anything to the viewer's knowledge of other previously established elements of the series' mythology. The exceptions to the rule are *Remembrance of the Daleks*, *Silver Nemesis* and *Survival*.

In *Remembrance of the Daleks*, it is revealed that there are, at this time, two rival factions of Daleks: renegades who report to the Black Dalek – otherwise known as the Dalek Supreme – and imperial Daleks who report to the Emperor. They can control human subjects through the use of electronic implants located behind the ear – perhaps a refinement of the Roboman technology previously seen in *The Dalek Invasion of Earth*. It is also explained that the two factions of Dalek creatures are physically different from each other. The imperial Daleks have proper limbs and are fitted with cyborg attachments, whereas the renegade Daleks are little more than blobs with vestigial limbs.

The major revelation, however, is that the Dalek Emperor is none other than Davros, now reduced to little more than a Dalek himself (an idea suggested to Aaronovitch by visual effects assistant Mike Tucker). The Emperor had not previously been seen in this form in the series, although it had appeared in Season 4's *The Evil of the Daleks* as a static creature housed in and linked to the Dalek city on Skaro. No explanation is provided as to how Davros managed to 'become' the Emperor following his capture by the Daleks loyal to the Dalek Supreme at the conclusion of Season 22's *Revelation of the Daleks*, but the splitting of the race into two rival factions is consistent with the events of that story (in which Davros's Daleks had the same cream and gold livery as the imperial Daleks in *Remembrance of the Daleks*) and also with those of Season 21's *Resurrection of the Daleks*. It is also quite understandable that the imperial Daleks are more genetically advanced than the renegades, as Davros would no doubt have been continuing his experiments to make them ever more ruthless and efficient.

Another major development in this story is the destruction of Skaro's sun, and with it Skaro itself, by the Hand of Omega. No time frame is given for this, however, and a Dalek at one point announces that the Hand is entering Skaro's time zone, which might perhaps be taken to imply that it occurs in the very far future.

One well-remembered aspect of *Remembrance of the Daleks* is the scene at the end of Part One in which a Dalek is seen, for the first time, to ascend a flight of stairs. This did not constitute a particularly major development in the series' mythology, however, as even as far back as Season 2's *The Chase: Journey into Terror* it had been implied that this was within the creatures' capabilities, and Season 22's *Revelation of the Daleks* had actually shown that both the Daleks and Davros could hover above the ground.

Earlier stories had been inconsistent in their indications of the Daleks' vulnerability to attack. In Season 9's *Day of the Daleks*, for example, the creatures had seemed impervious to anything that UNIT troops could throw at them, but in Season 11's *Death to the Daleks* one of them had burst into flames on being attacked by spear-wielding Exxilons. *Remembrance of the Daleks* places them at the more vulnerable end of the spectrum, as they are destroyed by Ace's augmented baseball bat and home-made nitro-9 explosives as well as by rockets fired at them from army rocket launchers.

The implied vulnerability of the Daleks is nothing, however, to that of the Cybermen in *Silver Nemesis*. It was well established in

Revenge of the Cybermen and *Earthshock* that the forcing of gold dust into the Cybermen's chest units could suffocate them by coating their respiratory systems. Here, however, the creatures seem to have an aversion to gold in any form (as vampires have an aversion to garlic, perhaps), and a number of them are destroyed by gold-tipped arrows and by gold coins fired into their chest units by means of a catapult. Paradoxically, however, the Cyber Leader actually survives having a handful of gold dust thrown into his chest unit.

Towards the end of *Silver Nemesis* the Doctor arranges for the Nemesis statue to destroy the Cyber fleet, which – since hints have been given throughout the story that this is their last remaining force – could be taken to imply that this is the final end of the Cybermen, or at least that they are subsequently reduced to isolated groups scavenging space, as suggested in *Revenge of the Cybermen.*

The final revelations of the McCoy era occur in *Survival*, when the Doctor and the Master become trapped on the dying planet of the cheetah people. The Master has succumbed to the planet's influence and started to transform into a cheetah person himself. It is established that the only way off the planet is for someone affected in this way to lead others back to his or her home world; thus is Ace able to lead the Doctor and her friends back to Earth at one point. At the end of the story, however, as the Master prepares to deal him a killing blow, the Doctor manages somehow to transport himself to Earth. If one supposes that he too has become 'infected' by the planet, this raises the question why he did not return to Gallifrey or perhaps to the TARDIS interior – the only other place that he could legitimately call 'home' – rather than to Earth. Perhaps, though, the answer is something more fundamental – something unique to the Doctor that links him with Earth in a manner previously undisclosed . . .

('Rewriting the Myth' continues in Chapter 8)

PART THREE – FACT

5: Production Development

John Nathan-Turner had not expected to remain as *Doctor Who*'s producer for the seventh Doctor's debut season – his seventh in that capacity. He was asked to do so by his BBC superiors only at the eleventh hour, and agreed with considerable reluctance. He consequently had less time to prepare for this season than for any other that he had worked on, and matters were not helped by the fact that he had to find not only a new lead actor but also a new script editor for the series. 'With regard to the latter,' he recalled in 1996 in *Doctor Who Magazine* Issue 246, 'I had a stroke of luck. Richard Wakely . . . [an agent] I had known from the moment I arrived in London . . . asked me to meet a young man called Andrew Cartmel, which I duly did, and found him bursting with many ideas and, indeed, firm opinions about the show. Although we didn't always agree, we instantly struck up a rapport – which I do think is a good sign. I invited Andrew to join the team and I have never regretted it.'

Cartmel had previously been working for a computer company in Cambridge but had also attended some workshops at the BBC's Television Drama Script Unit and been taken on as a client by Wakely on the strength of some unproduced scripts that he had written. 'The reason John gave me the job was that we got along,' he said in a 1994 interview conducted by David Bishop for *TSV* 40, 'and I didn't impress him as being an idiot. He'd read a script of mine, and obviously saw qualities in there [demonstrating] that I knew what a good TV script should be.'

Pip and Jane Baker had already been asked by Nathan-Turner to write the season opener, *Time and the Rani*, but Cartmel disliked their approach and found the development of the scripts problematic. To provide the other three stories required to make up the fourteen-episode run he commissioned new writers whose way of thinking was more in tune with his own. One of these, Stephen Wyatt, had contacted the production office and been recommended to him by Nathan-Turner (who had had some discussions with him the previous year when the series was temporarily without a script editor) but the other two, Malcolm Kohll and Ian Briggs, were contacts of his from his time at the Script Unit.

Cartmel was a big fan of contemporary comics, and was keen to bring that influence to *Doctor Who*. Collections of Alan Moore's *Halo Jones* stories from *2,000 AD* consequently became virtually required reading for prospective *Doctor Who* writers. 'Alan Moore's *Halo Jones* showed me you didn't have to write comics in a stylised way,' Cartmel told interviewer Tim Robins in 1991 for *The Frame* No. 19. 'You could actually explore interesting aspects of a character's personality.' Another suggestion the script editor frequently made to writers unfamiliar with the series was that they read the 1983 media studies book *Doctor Who – The Unfolding Text* by John Tulloch and Manuel Alvarado. Nathan-Turner meanwhile had decided that, with the series now reduced to only fourteen episodes per season on a permanent basis, a varied mix of stories should be maintained by subdividing each season into two four-parters and two three-parters in a 'traditional-bizarre-kooky-traditional' pattern, with writers selected to fit these styles according to their perceived strengths.

A significant constraint on the production team at this time was pressure from their superiors to avoid the inclusion of any overtly violent or adult content in the stories – a continuing legacy of the controversy that had surrounded the series during the sixth Doctor's era, when it had at one point been taken off the air for eighteen months. 'My basic idea was that I wanted the show to be quite dark and scary,' recalled Cartmel in a 1994 convention interview. 'When I went in to talk to the Head of

Drama one of the first things that he asked me was, "Who is *Doctor Who* for?" I said that it was for everyone – a diplomat's answer – but he said, "No, it's for children." I nodded, but thought, "No it isn't." I never thought that it should be a show that children shouldn't be able to watch, but I thought it should be an adult [show] that was accessible to children.'

Season 24 as it eventually reached the screen had a relatively light, whimsical quality. This, coupled with an avoidance of naturalism in the production and the casting of numerous well-known comedy and light-entertainment performers in guest roles, resulted in its coming under fire in sections of the fan press as a further move towards what some saw as a 'pantomime' style of drama in *Doctor Who*. Cartmel found these criticisms misplaced, as he explained to Bishop:

'If we could have just brought the lighting right down, and got really imaginative, moody lighting, I think the whole pantomime thing would have evaporated. That bright artificial lighting gives a brashness and a lack of depth. That's what made it look like a pantomime. Shooting on video really doesn't help.

'A lot of the problem with *Doctor Who* is that people will say that they don't like a story, the writing is crap, when what they actually mean is that the studio lighting is bad. Frequently the reasons that stories didn't work related to the costumes or the lighting, but fans don't analyse it that way.'

One aspect of the twenty-fourth season that came under particular fire from critics was Bonnie Langford's larger-than-life performance as Mel. Nathan-Turner, speaking to Peter Haining for his book *Doctor Who – 25 Glorious Years*, defended the actress's contribution: 'Bonnie helped bridge the change-over of Doctors very well. She established a very good relationship with Sylvester; they got on extremely well. Actually, they had worked together before on the stage in *The Pirates of Penzance*. I know there are those who love Bonnie or hate her, but to my mind that is the mark of somebody who is making an impact. I think she has been very good for *Doctor Who*.'

Langford had told Nathan-Turner at the start of 1987 that she would probably want to bow out of the series at some point during the course of the season. The production team decided in view of this to keep their options open by ensuring that the last two stories – the ones written by Kohll and Briggs – each featured a character who could if necessary succeed Mel as the Doctor's companion. There were practical considerations to this as well, as initially it was uncertain in which order the two stories would be transmitted. The potential companion character in Kohll's story, *Delta and the Bannermen*, was Ray, played by Sara Griffiths; in Briggs's, *Dragonfire*, it was Ace, played by Sophie Aldred. Cartmel was particularly keen to ensure that the new companion would be a strong and independent young woman: 'We were going for that sort of sisters-are-doing-it-for-themselves kind of thing, which was not Bonnie,' he told Bishop. 'We wanted a post-*Alien* teenage girl.' Ace was a refined version of just such a character, originally called Alf, for whom Nathan-Turner and Cartmel had drafted a rough description dated 26 January 1987, and it was she who was eventually kept on as a regular. A new character outline for Ace was prepared in August 1987 in view of her confirmed status as a companion, and a more detailed set of notes on her character and background were put together by Briggs two months later for inclusion in the guide supplied to prospective writers for the series. The latter read as follows:

> Notes on the character ACE
>
> Name: 'Ace' is her nickname. She's ashamed of her real name, and only told Mel in a moment of intimacy. (I feel that she would only ever tell another girl; not a man or a boy – probably not even the Doctor.) Her real name is Dorothy. I didn't specify a surname; it can be either the surname of Dorothy in *The Wizard of Oz*, or something that works in the context of the story it appears in – or, more likely, she'll just avoid the question and keep it secret.
>
> Age: At the point of her appearance in *Dragonfire*, she was meant to be 16 years and 11 months. In fact, she's based on three girls I know, all of whom are 14, so she has the

personality and maturity of a young (rather than middling) teenager.

Home: She comes from Perivale, which she regards as the pits of London. As far as she's concerned, the only good thing about Perivale is that it has two tube stations! (One of the girls she's based on actually said this while watching a recording.)

Family: She doesn't have any brothers or sisters. If she did, she'd have mentioned them in her intimate speech with Mel. Besides, she's too much of a loner inside. She didn't get on with her parents, and she gets angry simply at the mention of them. Sometimes she refuses to accept that she even has any parents; at other times she wants to believe that her 'real' parents – the kind, loving ones – are somewhere else, maybe on another planet. But however bad a picture she paints of them, the truth is that her parents are an ordinary middle-class couple who always kept their feelings hidden, and didn't know how to cope with their tearaway daughter.

School: She enjoyed chemistry and was taking it at A-level – although she would probably have failed because she isn't the academic type. She got suspended from school when she blew up the art room.

History: While she was at school she also had a boring evening job working in a fast-food cafeteria. She also used to do experiments with explosives in her bedroom, and it was an accident with one of these that triggered a time storm and carried her to Iceworld – where she again found work as a waitress.

Speech: She uses phrases typical of London teenagers: 'Wicked!', 'Well worth!', 'Naff!', and of course 'Ace!'. I don't care if, technically, she left Perivale in early 1987, and so ought still to be using the phrases of that period; the more current and realistic her speech, the better. She coins nicknames for everybody, such as 'Doughnut' for Mel, and 'Bilgebag' for Glitz. And even though it irritates the Doctor, she can't help calling him 'Professor'. The only time she reverts to using real names is when she's frightened, as when Kane was holding her hostage in *Dragonfire*.

Personality: Typical teenager really. Bright and full of life one moment, spiky and argumentative the next. Even though she likes the Doctor, she's bound to come over all moody and complaining with him from time to time. A particular characteristic is her heightened sense of excitement, which sometimes overrides her sense of danger: her immediate reaction on first seeing the Creature in *Dragonfire* was to yell with delight, and only later did she think to run like hell!

The urgency with which stories had been required to be commissioned for the twenty-fourth season had left Cartmel with little time for reflection. In preparing for the twenty-fifth, however, he was able to take a more considered approach. Acting on a fan's recommendation he viewed a number of highly regarded stories from *Doctor Who*'s past, including Season 13's *The Seeds of Doom* and Season 14's *The Talons of Weng-Chiang*, and formed the view that the essentially serious and dramatic style of earlier eras had been rather more effective than the relatively light-hearted and comedic one that had prevailed during McCoy's first season. He discussed this with Nathan-Turner and they decided that the departure of the somewhat lightweight Mel and the arrival of the strong, streetwise Ace should mark the start of a more general shift back towards that more serious and dramatic approach. There would also be a return to a more naturalistic style of production and an increased emphasis on social comment, both overt (such as in *Remembrance of the Daleks*, with its fascist characters in sixties London and a scene in which Ace discovers a NO COLOUREDS sign in the window of the guest house where she is staying) and allegorical (such as in *The Happiness Patrol*, with its thinly veiled attack on Thatcherism).

Another move that Cartmel was keen to make, in keeping with McCoy's own wishes, was to introduce a greater degree of mystery into the Doctor's character. He felt that over the years there had been too much revealed about the initially enigmatic time traveller's background, and that this had considerably lessened the appeal of the character. With Nathan-Turner's approval, he therefore briefed the writers of the twenty-fifth season to include in their stories some elements casting doubt on aspects of the Doctor's established history and on the true nature of his character. (See Chapter 2 for further details.)

Season 25 was also notable for the high degree of emphasis that it saw being placed on Ace. In the past it had often been the case that the companion characters had suffered from a lack of development after their initial introduction, but Ace by contrast came to take on an increasingly prominent role. McCoy, interviewed by Paul Travers in 1989 for *Doctor Who Magazine* No. 154, explained how this had come about:

'When we chatted between seasons, I thought it would be good for Ace to be educated between adventures. I would be educating her, pointing things out. Each time we got to a story she would arrive with new knowledge . . .

'It was a good idea, and the writers went further, and John Nathan-Turner too. They decided the Doctor was trying to make her get over her fears, her weaknesses. The Doctor, in a very back-handed and subtle way, is trying to put Ace straight, so that eventually, if he does leave her, she'll come back and be Prime Minister . . .!'

Cartmel continued for this season to pursue a policy of commissioning enthusiastic young writers who were new to the series and had little or no previous TV experience – something in which he again had Nathan-Turner's full support, as the producer told *Doctor Who Magazine*:

'I think that the new writers that we have encouraged, whether they're experienced or not, are bringing fresh ideas. They challenge the system, and by the system I include myself.

'We have a phrase here: *Who*ed out. Writers get *Who*ed out, they start going over the same territory. We really needed to get a new band of writers, and, as I've been here a long time, it's more challenging and stimulating to have people say "why not?" '

The newcomers this time were Ben Aaronovitch, who had come to Cartmel's attention when fellow BBC script editor Caroline Oulton had passed on to him a script that he had written; Graeme Curry, who contacted the production office after winning a screenplay competition with a play called *Over the Moon*, later adapted for BBC Radio 4; and Kevin Clarke, who was approached by Cartmel on the strength of a script he had written for a series called *Wish Me Luck*. The remaining story was provided by Stephen Wyatt.

Nathan-Turner had been content to remain as *Doctor Who*'s producer for the twenty-fifth anniversary season but had again asked his BBC superiors to make this his last year on the series. They refused this request and persuaded him to stay on for Season 26. Cartmel also remained on the series, for his third year as script editor.

This season continued to show the Doctor acting in an increasingly enigmatic light, manipulating events from the background rather than taking centre stage. Even his costume was changed to reflect the darker quality emerging in McCoy's characterisation: his previous light-coloured jacket was swapped for an identical dark-brown one and his tie and hat band were similarly exchanged for darker versions. Ace meanwhile was accorded an ever greater share of the action. She in fact turned out to be effectively the pivotal character in three of the season's four stories, and Sophie Aldred was given an early opportunity to talk to the writers about the development of the part. This was a consequence of Cartmel's preferred approach of working with his writers as a team and involving them more closely in the production than would normally have been the case in the past. Ben Aaronovitch was particularly heavily involved in the development of the season, acting almost as an unofficial assistant script editor, and in addition contributed its first story. Ian Briggs was also commissioned to provide a further story, but the other two writers for the season were again newcomers. Marc Platt had been a long-time fan of the series who had been submitting story ideas to the production office since Robert Holmes's time as script editor in the mid-seventies; Rona Munro was an up-and-coming writer who had met Cartmel when attending a training seminar at which he was a speaker and had been invited by him to send in some ideas.

The very positive reception given to Season 26 by fan critics suggests that the process of experimentation and development that had taken place during the McCoy years had resulted in the refinement of a highly effective new style for *Doctor Who*, and one that had just started to bear fruit at the point when the series was taken off the air by the BBC. How that achievement would have been capitalised upon in the planned twenty-seventh season, and what other developments would have lain in store, can only remain matters for speculation.

6: From Script to Screen – *Dragonfire*

Introduction

To try to analyse comprehensively the development of a *Doctor Who* adventure is not an easy matter. A television production is the result of many months' work by a large number of people, and what is ultimately seen on screen may have been affected and influenced in greater or lesser degrees by all of them.

Unless one is afforded a fly's eye view of every meeting and every aspect of the creative process, then any attempt to try to dissect the production is limited by the memories and personalities of those people to whom one speaks.

Bearing all this in mind, this chapter presents an in-depth look at just one of the seventh Doctor's stories – *Dragonfire*. In doing so it reveals the process of making *Doctor Who* at this point in the series' history and – a factor common to every story – some of the behind-the-scenes discussions and thought which go into a production.

The Scripts

Every *Doctor Who* adventure that appears on screen starts life as an idea. This may be in the mind of a writer; it may come from the producer or the script editor; or, as is more often the case, it may develop out of a discussion between two or more of these people. Once the initial contact has been made, a story outline or synopsis will generally be commissioned from the writer.

Assuming that all is well when that is delivered, one or more of the actual scripts themselves will then be commissioned. Depending on the status of the writer, these stages may be compacted or expanded accordingly.

In the case of *Dragonfire*, writer Ian Briggs was approached to contribute to the series by script editor Andrew Cartmel, whom he had met some months earlier at a writers' workshop at the BBC's Television Drama Script Unit. He had started his career in the theatre after studying drama at Manchester University, and had found work as a script reader – not only for the BBC but also for the Royal Court and some film companies – after several years spent as a theatre lighting and set designer and occasional actor.

Briggs's first idea, submitted in January 1987, was rejected by Cartmel, as the writer admitted to Paul Travers in a 1989 interview for *Doctor Who Magazine*: 'He read it, said it was rubbish, so I started again.' His second attempt – which had the working title *Absolute Zero* and then, when this was deemed too pretentious, *Pyramid in Space* – was judged more promising. 'The first one I'd written had been very old-fashioned, very clichéd SF. After Andrew rejected it, we'd sat down and talked about exactly what he was after, based on [the] new style he'd brought in. *Pyramid in Space* was close, but it went too far. It was too zany, too cartoonish . . . A disgusting fourteen year old boy who's a financial genius, running [a] huge business empire with an obsequious sidekick called Mr Spewey! Brilliant stuff, but perhaps not *Doctor Who* . . . But there were some good ideas in it; the idea of [a] creature living in the cold and itself being the treasure that everyone was hunting for. We hung on to that and constructed another story around it, which was much more serious.'

This more refined idea, which involved a huge pyramid floating through space with a strange creature roaming around its ventilation system, was developed into a detailed storyline bearing the revised working title *The Pyramid's Treasure*. This was commissioned on 9 March 1987, completed on 17 March, delivered on 23 March and formally accepted on 30 March.

The Pyramid's Treasure tells of a villain called Hess – 'whose body temperature is –250° C' – running a frozen-goods trading centre from a planet-sized pyramid in orbit around a larger planet. The Doctor and Mel arrive looking for refreshment and meet up with 'an intergalactic bounty hunter-cum-pirate called Razorback' who tells them about a treasure hidden in the pyramid, supposedly guarded by 'an ice monster'. The Doctor and Razorback go off to find the treasure, which turns out to be the monster itself, which 'is also the missing component in an opto-electronic circuit – a lens that will focus all the Pyramid's energy and give Hess immense power'. The Doctor realises that Hess's plans for galactic domination will be his downfall. This indeed proves to be the case as, when the pyramid moves out of the shadow of the larger planet, 'the crystalline circuitry . . . concentrates and focuses [the heat of the sun] on Hess . . . who melts away'. At the end of the story Ace, a young human waitress stranded at the trading centre, goes off with Razorback while Mel continues her travels with the Doctor.

On the strength of this storyline Briggs was quickly commissioned to write the three-part story that ultimately became *Dragonfire*. (Briggs's normal preference, as he confirmed in later interviews, was to prepare a scene breakdown between the storyline stage and the script stage, but this appears not to have happened in the case of *Dragonfire*.) The script for the first part was formally commissioned on 2 April 1987 with a target delivery date of 6 April, and those for the other two on 13 April with a target delivery date of 14 April – the closeness of these dates indicating that Briggs had already started working on the scripts, by informal agreement with Cartmel, prior to being formally commissioned. The three scripts were actually delivered by Briggs on 8 April, 16 April and 13 April and accepted by the BBC on 10 April, 22 April and 20 April respectively, Briggs having delivered the scripts out of order. A number of revisions were requested by Cartmel, in particular to remedy the fact that Briggs had overwritten, but these initial drafts were quickly turned into polished rehearsal scripts. Later, during the course of the rehearsal process, these were further refined into camera scripts for the studio recording.

In terms of content, the final scripts stuck quite closely to the original storyline. One of the few significant developments arose when Bonnie Langford, who played Mel, decided during the course of production to make this her last *Doctor Who* story. On 3 August 1987 Briggs submitted a new closing scene in which Mel is the one who goes off with the pirate – changed at producer John Nathan-Turner's request from Razorback to Glitz, played by Tony Selby, from the previous season's *The Trial of a Time Lord* – and Ace, played by Sophie Aldred, who leaves with the Doctor to become the new companion. Sylvester McCoy disliked this version, feeling that the Doctor seemed too unmoved by Mel's departure, and suggested that some lines of dialogue be incorporated from a short scene that Cartmel had originally written for the screen tests carried out in February 1987 for the role of the seventh Doctor. The objection he had raised was recognised to be a valid one, and further work was then carried out on the scene right up until the day of recording.

'Bonnie finally decided that she was going to leave after the first studio recording,' recalled Briggs, 'so that final scene was rewritten during rehearsals for the second studio work. We worked on it ten or twelve times and finally got it right at breakfast on the day it was [recorded]. It's a cliché, but it was genuinely written on a napkin at the breakfast bar in Television Centre.

'I feel it got there, but only by the skin of its teeth. The problem is not so much that it was written at the last minute, but that it could be no longer than three minutes, and it's very difficult to get all the stuff in, that needs to be there, in just three minutes. The biggest problem [was] that it followed straight on from the . . . death [of the villain] originally, so that it needed a minute – well, perhaps not even that, probably fifteen or twenty seconds – to wind down from the death to the farewell scene.'

Other, more minor changes made between storyline and final script included the alteration of the concept of the trading centre – called Iceworld in the final version – from a planet to a city-like spacecraft on the dark side of another planet; the renaming of the planet (between rehearsal script and camera script stage) from Tartros to Svartos; and the renaming of the villain from Hess to Kane.

'I [originally] wanted [a name for the villain] with lots of sibilants – "s" sounds – in it,' Briggs recalled in a 1989 interview conducted by Michael Proctor for the fanzine *Private Who*. 'I thought, "Hiss – what sounds like 'hiss'? Hass . . . Hess . . ." And I thought, "Hess – that sounds okay." A couple of minutes later, I realised it was the name of [a high ranking Nazi in World War Two], but I thought nobody would notice. [The first time we saw] the design of the [character's] helmet was the point at which we actually changed it. We'd been talking about changing it, because . . . something had happened – I think the real Hess had written some letters asking to be released or something. When we saw the costume design, we thought, "We can't do it," because it looked like a First World War German helmet and people would [have thought] there was a connection. I was also [conscious] that there were a lot of foreign names – all the baddies had foreign names, which felt uncomfortably racist. It's a cliché as well – something I wanted to avoid – so I was quite happy to change some of them to more English-sounding names like "Kane" and "McLuhan" . . . Three quarters of the stuff [in the scripts] had a reason for being there. Names had a reason, but I can't remember all of them now. Once you begin to piece together the big things, you forget about the small things.'

The name 'Kane' was in fact taken from Orson Welles' film *Citizen Kane*, and many of the other character names in the story also had cinematic connections. Belazs for example was named after Hungarian film theorist and critic Bela Belazs; Kracauer after German film critic Siegfried Kracauer; Bazin after French film critic André Bazin; McLuhan (originally to have been named Eisenstein after Russian director Sergei Eisenstein) after Canadian communication theorist and documentary maker Marshall McLuhan; Anderson (Ace's boss, unnamed in the final dialogue of the story) after British film maker Lindsay Anderson; Pudovkin after Russian film maker and theorist Vsevolod Pudovkin; Arnheim after German/American film and art critic Rudolph Arnheim; and Dorothy, alias Ace, after Dorothy Gale, the lead character in the film *The Wizard of Oz*.

One problem that Briggs encountered in writing the story was that he had only a vague idea of how McCoy was approaching the lead role. The sole example he had seen of the actor's work on the series was his initial screen test. He therefore had to rely on Cartmel telling him whenever he went wrong in his characterisation of the seventh Doctor. He later recalled Cartmel describing McCoy as a 'real-life animated cartoon', but admitted that he had not understood what this meant until he had actually seen the actor in rehearsals.

Of the writing out of Mel and the introduction of Ace, Briggs told *Private Who*: 'There was always the possibility that Bonnie might not want to continue for another season, and a stand-by companion had to be drawn up. The proposed character was a teenage girl called Alf from North London. Then the season was [reordered and *Delta and the Bannermen* was due to be] the final [story], so I was free to make some changes. I moved the character away from North London – because I had worrying visions of some trendy teenager from Islington! – and . . . changed the name because I never did like the idea of calling a woman "Alf". So Andrew [Cartmel] and John [Nathan-Turner] created the original idea for the character (so the BBC owns the copyright), I created the personality and Sophie brought the character to life. When my story was moved back to the end of the season and Bonnie decided to leave, Ace became the new companion.

'I fashioned the personality in a way that I found interesting – she's based on three teenage girls I know. I think it was always intended that she was going to be very contemporary. One of the themes of the story is loneliness . . . people who are lonely and don't have a home – a trait that struck me as fairly typical of teenagers. They feel as though they don't quite recognise themselves and everything isn't as it ought to be.'

Briggs was well satisfied with the story as it eventually reached the screen: 'The finished programme can never be as good as the original idea because what I saw in my mind was absolutely perfect. It took place in hundreds of places on different planets with different coloured skies . . . In that respect, every stage in the scripting and production process is a compromise between the vision and the possible. I don't think there's anything in that programme that anybody working on it need feel ashamed of. There are parts of it which are not the same as I envisaged them, but I don't claim a monopoly on creativity . . .'

'Briggs is a really skilled writer,' noted Cartmel in a 1994 interview with David Bishop for *TSV*, 'good on construction. I did have to keep hammering away about the thriller thing, because he came from a background of writing non-thriller material. But he's a really good writer because he gets passionately committed to things and he writes about people's emotions. When he invents characters, they've got something going for them emotionally.

'A problem was he hadn't written science-fiction before, as a lot of the writers hadn't, and I had to keep hammering that too. It's a thriller; it's a suspense story; it's got to have these punches at certain stages.

'I remember *Dragonfire* has got one of my favourite bits of Briggs's writing, where he has the Doctor trying to go into Glitz's spaceship and discussing philosophy with the guard . . .

'The thing I liked about *Dragonfire* was that there were a couple of nice revelations, like there's this monster but it's a synthetic monster and inside the monster is this jewel, which is the McGuffin they're looking for. Then that turns out to be the ignition key for the city, which turns out to be a whole spaceship.'

Direction

The director of *Dragonfire* was Chris Clough. Born in the Yorkshire town of Harrogate in 1951, he had started his working life as an accountant but then decided on a change of career and studied for a degree in English Literature at Leeds University, where he had also staged a number of student plays. In 1974 he had joined Granada TV as a researcher for current affairs programmes. His real interest lay in drama, however, and he had subsequently gained directing assignments on Channel 4's *Brookside* and on the BBC's *EastEnders*. It was on the strength of the latter that John Nathan-Turner had invited him to work on *Doctor Who*. He made his series debut on the last six episodes of Season Twenty-Three's *The Trial of a Time Lord* and then been invited back to handle Season Twenty-Four's last two stories, *Delta and the Bannermen* and *Dragonfire*, which were made effectively as two halves of a single production sharing mostly the same designers and behind-the-scenes crew.

The following description by Clough of his general approach to directing *Dragonfire*, and all the quotes attributed to him in later sections of this chapter, have been compiled from interviews that he gave to Richard Marson for *Doctor Who Magazine* (1988), Stephen Payne, David Richardson and Lee Matthews for *Starburst* (1988) and Rod Ulm for *Private Who* (1989), and from comments that he made during an on-stage interview at the PanoptiCon IX convention (1988).

'I leapt at the opportunity to return to *Doctor Who*, despite the fact that I didn't see the scripts beforehand. John Nathan-Turner just asks you whether or not you'd like to come back – you leave him and Andrew Cartmel to sort out the scripts. You certainly don't get approval. Basically, John decides which director will be right for which story and then allocates them accordingly.

'When scripts first arrive I read them very casually – almost just for enjoyment's sake – which allows me to gauge them as if I'm a viewer. Then I start to think about them more, reread them, tinker with a bit here, fiddle with a section there – just trying to get under the skin of the story really. It's a funny thing about any form of communication; the writer can write something with a certain emphasis in mind, and you can read that same piece and get something completely different out of it. So in those very early stages, I like to have conversations with the writers to discover what precisely their thinking is, and to debate whether there are any holes in the plot or whether I'm just being a bit thick and missing the point. From there it's a question of trying to inject some style into it – you have to consider what it's going to look like. Okay, the writers have given you some clue as to their ideas, but you have to consider not just that, but a whole range of other options.

'You have to have done your homework before you go into the rehearsal stage. You've got to know what you think the actors should be doing at any particular time in the story and where they should be in the set. Otherwise, all you can say is, "Let's just kick it around for a while."

'I start off with little drawings – he starts there and moves to here, the entrances are here, and so on – and I try to prepare my camera scripts – a very boring job – after I've rehearsed everything at least once. If you do your camera scripts too early, things don't work when you come to rehearsals and it restricts the actors.

'I like to keep the camera moving – there's an awful lot of boring television around, and I try to avoid the "wallpaper" effect.

'*Doctor Who* is the most difficult thing I've ever done! It is on its own; a mixture of action, adventure, fantasy and nightmare, and you are trying to amalgamate all these different areas to make the plausible out of the implausible. The concept of having a police box flying through space is obviously quite ludicrous, but the fun of it is to be able to turn the accepted form of logic on its head.'

Casting

The casting of any *Doctor Who* story is primarily the director's responsibility. Chris Clough recalled how he went about the task:

'Casting really is a long and complicated procedure. You have to begin by taking the decision to cast one particular part. Then if that person accepts, it affects who you can offer other roles to. It really is like a jigsaw puzzle – you're constantly trying to mesh together a well-balanced ensemble. After all, it's no good having a goodie and a baddie who share similar physical characteristics, because you're in danger of confusing the audience. You have to find a good mix of physical types, so that when any one character comes up on screen, that's that – the audience recognises immediately who it is. You cannot allow for creating shades of

"Is that him, or maybe him . . .?"; it has to be distinct.

'You have to consider what sort of characterisation an actor will bring to a role and what qualities they possess. Equally, you yourself have to establish what qualities you perceive within each character – it's no easy task. Whenever I get a script, I go through it and write out a list of casting ideas, which I discuss with John Nathan-Turner. We then see who is available – not everyone is free, and not everyone is willing to do it.'

Amongst the actors considered for the role of Kane were David Jason, who was sent copies of the scripts on 23 June 1987, and John Alderton, who was sent copies on 3 July. Eventually however it went to Edward Peel.

'Kane was a very difficult character to cast,' noted Clough, 'but I chose Edward because I thought the physical height would be good, and I liked the overall acting style. I had seen him in *Juliet Bravo*, and also many years before in Hull in a play called *What the Butler Saw*. I was pleased that he had already shaved off his usual moustache, as I would have asked him to take it off anyway. For one thing, you wouldn't have any surplus hair at –200° C; it would snap off. Also, I did think it made him look rather like a second-hand car salesman!'

Visual Effects

Dragonfire, in common with most other *Doctor Who* stories, had extensive visual effects requirements. The designer responsible for meeting these was Andy McVean of the BBC's own Visual Effects Department; but, as usual for this period of the series' history, he had the support of a number of the Department's assistants, including Mike Tucker, Lindsay McGowan, Paul Mann, Paul McGuinness and Jonathan Clarke, and contracted certain aspects of the work out to freelancers, including the team of Susan Moore and Stephen Mansfield. In the following section of this chapter, all quotes attributed to Tucker, Moore and Mansfield are taken from a 1988 interview conducted by David J. Howe, Mark Stammers and Stephen James Walker for *The Frame*.

One of the most important aspects of the effects team's work was the realisation of the dragon – the legendary beast hunted by the Doctor and Glitz. Tucker recalled how this had been achieved: 'The script initially said "a huge fire-breathing dragon". It turned out in Part Two to be a biomechanical creature with laser beam eyes, breathing smoke and fire. That was handled almost entirely by one guy in the Effects Department, Lindsay McGowan. Andy McVean came up with some initial design drawings for the head and Lindsay prepared a rough maquette of the creature – a small plasticine model about twelve inches tall – which was approved by John Nathan-Turner and Chris Clough. Then Lindsay sculpted a full-size version, which was a latex and polyurethane foam suit and a fibre-glass head. There was also a separate mechanical head, the mechanics of which were done by Paul Mann, which opened up to reveal the dragon's treasure. That suit was then painted up by Lindsay and Paul McGuinness, another effects assistant who in the previous season was inside Drathro. The head was sat on top of a helmet arrangement on top of the actor's head, and he looked out through the neck.'

'The original maquette of the creature was very beautiful, very menacing,' wrote McVean in *Ace! The Inside Story of the End of an Era*, 'but the actor that they cast was short and fat and we ended up making blocked up shoes for him, to try and get him to look taller. He really couldn't cope at all, because he had a complete rubber body suit on, which was uncomfortable, and because his hands needed to be free and he had to operate the smoke from the nostrils with a blow switch. This meant that when he blew into the mouthpiece it operated a solenoid, but it also meant that you had to have a battery and a gas canister in the head, so the entire thing was quite top heavy.'

Numerous other creatures were required for sequences set in Iceworld's refreshment bar, where Ace was seen working as a waitress. The intention was that these sequences should be reminiscent of *Star Wars*' famous cantina scene, with examples of a great many different alien life forms gathered together in one place. Moore explained how most of these had been created:

'The make-up designer asked us if we had any off-the-peg masks which had not been used in any other TV or film production. We had a number of bits and pieces that we'd made over the years – masks and puppets and so on – and I took along a whole collection, including a few masks made by another colleague. Make-up chose a selection and used them on the extras in the background. Luckily, the director was there at the same time and he spotted a half-mask I'd made for a party and thought that it would be perfect for the scene where the child wears a mask to frighten Mel. He also spotted Eric the puppet, and Eric became a legend in his own lunchtime! (For some obscure reason, every creature we make seems to end up being dubbed Eric – it's a silly name at the best of times, and it seems a suitably ridiculous name to give to anything that's an alien, and supposed to be taken seriously.)

'At one point, the producer called down from the gallery asking if it had a name. I just said "Eric". It was originally going to be in the background but then they decided to start the scene with Eric at the table with this fish creature that we provided, and they finished the scene off with him snapping at the Doctor as well. Eric was operated by the man in the green fish mask, and everyone was very pleased with it.'

Dragonfire also featured a certain amount of modelwork, all of which was shot on film rather than recorded on video owing to the greater controllability of the medium. A major aspect of this work was the realisation of Glitz's ship, the *Nosferatu*. 'Basically we knew it had to have an undocking scene, a take off scene, a flying away scene and an exploding scene,' noted Tucker, 'so two versions were made: one for all the flying work, and a breakable version for the scene where it explodes. The feel of *Dragonfire* was that Glitz's ship should be a rusty old tramp steamer, and that is basically what I used as an influence when we designed it. I had this rusty orange colour and a ship-like conning tower at the back and cargo pods. It just seemed to suit the character of Glitz, that this was the sort of ship he would have.' Another model required to feature prominently in the story was that of Iceworld itself. 'Initially what was wanted,' continued

Tucker, 'was a planet with an obvious hot side and an obvious cold side, and on that cold side . . . an icy, crystalline structure. This would be seen as simply a city, but in Part Three it would be revealed to be a spacecraft. So the initial shots had to disguise the fact that it was going to be a spacecraft, but at the same time it was designed around the fact that it would be taking off into space. Iceworld was designed by Andy and, because of lack of time, had to be made by outside contractors, Derek Hendon Associates.'

The shots in which icy vapour is seen to rise from Kane's hands and from a coin that he places on a desk were achieved, as Tucker explained, by a clever combination of effects: 'When we could, we ran smoke pipes through the costume and out through the cuffs. For the scene where the coin was put down on the desk, we used two chemical substances that, when mixed together, smoke slightly. We sprayed one on the coin, one on the desk top, and when the two were brought into contact they smoked.'

'The portrait on the coin was meant to be Kane's face,' pointed out Moore, 'so we modelled a likeness of Edward Peel on to it. I hope it looked like him, because originally we were told it was just going to be handed to people in long shot, and we were surprised when it was seen quite close up.'

One of the best-remembered aspects of *Dragonfire* is the horrific final sequence in which Kane's face melts away in the light of the sun – another effect achieved by Moore and Mansfield.

'While we were working on the Chimeron baby for *Delta and the Bannermen*,' recalled Mansfield, 'we were told that there was the possibility of a melting head sequence at the end of the final story. At that time it was not confirmed that we would be handling the sequence, but we were asked whether or not we thought it was feasible. We had to bear in mind the potential complexity of such a sequence and the limitations of a TV studio recording. There were two major stipulations. As the effect had to be done on a live recording day, it had to melt very quickly. In addition, there were to be no red colours on the under-skull or any liquid resembling blood.'

'We went off and did a lot of research,' added Moore, 'and

found out how the similar melting effect in *Raiders of the Lost Ark* was done. I spoke to some senior effects people in the film industry. Everyone said that it couldn't be done, not on video and certainly not that quickly. In spite of that, we felt the problems as we saw them could be overcome, and that it was certainly a project worth having a crack at. And, as it turned out, a month later we were offered the job.'

'Edward Peel apparently wasn't keen on the idea of having an alginate face cast made,' noted Mansfield, 'especially as it would have had to have been with his mouth open, which is doubly uncomfortable for the subject. There wasn't really the time, anyway. Andy McVean arranged for us to meet Edward Peel at Visual Effects during a break in rehearsals. We took instant photos of him in the facial position he would assume at the start of the melting scene. I then took caliper measurements of his face, while Sue took more detailed photographs. We set to modelling the head from the instant photos that same afternoon.'

'The head was sculpted in water based clay, from which a multi-piece plaster mould was taken,' explained Moore. 'From this mould six wax outer skins were eventually taken. As the mould was multi-piece, the original clay bust remained intact – just as the inflexible wax casts had to! Using the teeth and the top of the head as registering points, we started cutting away at the face, taking it back to what it would be if it had melted to the bone. A silicone mould was then taken of this new sculpture, and two fibre-glass skulls were cast. The skulls and the skins were then airbrushed.'

'As the melting had to be done very quickly,' continued Mansfield, 'the wax skins had to be very thin. Therefore when they melted, they tended to give off only a very thin dribble of wax and not much else. To overcome this problem we fitted the under-skulls with various pipes – in the mouth, in the nose and under the helmet – and through these pumped a liquid coloured to match the molten wax, thus creating a more authentic, head-sized volume of wastage.

'Selected areas of the glass-fibre skull were cast in latex and acted as bladders. These sections, when inflated, helped to distort the face, and generally accelerated the degeneration process by pushing wax away from the skull. The whole lot – six skins, two under-skulls, liquid and so on – was finally completed with hours to spare, at about 4 a.m. on the studio day, 29 July 1987.'

'The head had been fitted to a support post in the studio that was the same height as Edward Peel,' added Tucker, 'and Costume had provided a collar section to go around the neck – they couldn't use a real costume because all the wax and gunge would have ruined it.

'There were four of us operating it in the end. Steve provided the spit and gunge, while Sue, Paul Mann and I all wielded hot air guns and bladders. Cameras lined up on it and told us when we were in shot or out of shot. When we were all ready and out of shot we turned on the hot air guns and away we went.'

'There was a little bit of improvisation when the instruction came from the gallery to start dropping it out of shot,' admitted Moore. 'As the rig was mounted on a huge baseboard we couldn't literally drop it downwards – so we just tilted it backwards.'

'What they were trying to get,' explained Tucker, 'was the effect of a collapsing man; they wanted to see Kane shrivel and deflate as he melted, and they wanted to match this shot with one we had done of the body collapsing from behind.

'Then the electronic effects designer Dave Chapman, in post-production, actually managed to mix in Edward Peel's real mouth, so that it actually screamed as it melted.

'In the end we did only one take on it because it all seemed to go well and the gallery was happy with it.'

'Ultimately it turned out to be quite an unsettling effect in spite of the lack of red colours,' felt Moore. 'At one stage in the middle of shooting it, all this yellow gunge came out in a torrent because of a blockage in the air pipe. Also, one of the wax eyes that were underneath the skin popped and ran down the face. Not a pretty sight. Needless to say, none of this reached the final programme. We were flattered though to receive a round of applause from the assembled cast and crew.'

'What you saw on screen was a fraction of what was recorded,' reflected Tucker. 'It was shown at about thirty times normal speed, and the melting in real time took about ten minutes, from which they chose a suitable sequence to use.'

'I think on the whole it worked very well on screen,' concluded Moore, 'which is, of course, the ultimate consideration. Apparently it was the first time an effect of that type had been attempted on British television, so it was a first for *Doctor Who* – and of course for us.'

Chris Clough was well pleased with how this effect turned out, as he later confirmed:

'When it came to melting his head, I really did want to make it look realistic, otherwise it would have been awful. At one stage we considered, as an alternative, shooting it from behind Edward, having him pretend to melt and then cutting to a puddle on the floor. However, that might have looked very laughable, so we decided on going for it, and having the facial close-up, which is what I'd wanted to do from the start.

'For the body, we were going to do a reverse shot. Someone went and bought an inflatable doll from a sex shop, then we dressed it in Kane's clothes [and allowed it to deflate]. However, it ended up looking absolutely stupid. Still, there's a lovely photo of it somewhere with its trousers having fallen down, revealing these little [deflated] legs!

'In the end, rather than use the doll, we actually had a shot of Edward Peel sinking to his knees and used that instead, bleached out to give the impression of the blinding sunlight.'

In Studio

Rehearsals for *Dragonfire* took place in the then standard venue of the BBC's custom-built rehearsal block, sometimes referred to jokingly as the 'Acton Hilton', in Acton, West London. Camera rehearsal and recording then took place in two sessions, the first over 28 to 30 July 1987 in Television Centre Studio 1, the second over 12 and 13 August in Television Centre Studio 3.

'I think we had only one week between coming off the OB for *Delta and the Bannermen* and going back into rehearsals for

Dragonfire,' recalled Chris Clough, 'so everything had to be set up at the same time. I really needed to know that everything was already prepared, so that I could use that free week just to relax and to get my mind clear from the previous story.

'We did have a very tight recording schedule, and fortunately we didn't fall into the trap of letting things drift at the beginning, because if we had fallen behind then, by being too fussy or having things go wrong, it would have been very difficult to make up that time later. There's nothing easy about *Doctor Who* at all. Large chunks of dialogue are very easy to record, but we're dealing with SFX and also a great deal of action, which has to look convincing.

'We did a lot of rehearsal in costume for the scenes involving the dragon – it's unfair on actors to dump them in a costume at the last minute. The worst thing for them is the discomfort, because they sweat buckets.

'With the dragon, I think we had a good design. I tended to put it into half shadow and shoot it to avoid the legs, which never look terribly good on monsters.

'Kane had to be convincing too, without going over the top. That's always the problem with these ultimate foe-type characters – the temptation to go "Aargh!" and all that sort of stuff. And it usually works better if they do less. Then, when they're really angry, they can twitch their eyebrows or something. Edward Peel did that very well.

'And one of the things I enjoyed about *Dragonfire* was having the real cliffhanger with the Doctor and his umbrella at the end of Part One!'

Not everyone was pleased with how the latter scene turned out, however. 'The worst cliffhanger we ever had was the one at the end of *Dragonfire* Part One,' asserted Andrew Cartmel. 'In Ian Briggs's script, the Doctor climbs as far as he possibly can along a path in an ice cliff, then he is forced to climb down the face of the cliff itself. This all makes perfect sense in the script – he's on his way somewhere, the path runs out, he has no alternative, he has to start climbing downwards.

'But the way it's shot! He's walking along, then, for apparently no reason, suddenly he dangles himself over the edge. Someone rang me up and said, "Why does he do this?" The problem is, when you've got the script and you know what's supposed to be happening, when it's expressed on the screen like that, you don't question it. But if you're just a viewer watching this, there's no apparent reason for his actions.

'One of the things the director has to bear in mind is that the viewers don't know the script. Something to do with the essential visual grammar of that scene was missing.'

Ian Briggs himself felt that Clough's pacy, action-orientated style of direction was not entirely well suited to his scripts, which he saw as being very much driven by the characters and their motivations and interactions.

For Sophie Aldred, the recording of *Dragonfire* marked not only her debut as Ace but her first ever experience of acting in front of television cameras; before starting work on the production she had not even known where Television Centre was. The regular costume that she would wear in the role was inspired partly by some clothes of her own and partly by a couple of photographs of teenage girls wearing club gear that she recalled seeing in an issue (July 1987) of the style magazine *The Face*. She and costume designer Richard Croft went on a shopping trip to the King's Road in Chelsea to choose a collection of suitable items off-the-peg. Some of the many badges and patches that ultimately adorned the jacket were obtained on this trip; others were found by Croft in various Oxford Street shops; and the remainder were supplied by Aldred herself.

'I had every confidence in Sophie Aldred's Ace,' wrote John Nathan-Turner in 1996 in his memoirs for *Doctor Who Magazine*, 'but decided to wait and see her good work in the rehearsal room committed to tape before taking up the option on a full contract . . . The first studio day went well. Sophie was splendid. I took up the option and, in order to stave off any more leaks to the press, I swiftly organised a press call at TV Centre with Sophie, Sylvester and the TARDIS.'

An interesting contemporary view of the studio work for *Dragonfire* can be gleaned from the following report by *Doctor*

Who Magazine's Richard Marson, who visited the set for the final day's camera rehearsal and recording:

> To an outsider, watching the *Doctor Who* crew at work can be a very frustrating process. Just as a scene gets into its stride, it will either stop, so that [those responsible for] cameras and microphones can ensure their positions are exactly right (according to the director's detailed camera script), or simply because each scene doesn't tend to be longer than a couple of minutes . . . With all the stops for effects and added camera angles (which increase the pace and tension), as well as for the inevitable mistakes, one might be forgiven for thinking that the cast and crew would be slowly driven out of their minds.
>
> That this isn't so is generally down to the production manager. It is he or she who acts as the director's assistant on the studio floor and maintains the vital discipline that keeps the show on schedule, without the grind wearing down those who are involved. For *Dragonfire* . . . the production manager was Gary Downie . . . [who] has captured the ability to have jokes and keep smiling while at the same time letting everyone know what was what and that no slackness could be tolerated.
>
> This discipline showed itself when a confused actor walked off the set before he was cleared to go, and when the busy studio got too noisy . . .
>
> Making an ice planet convincing has been one of the principal challenges of this production, especially as it has all been taped in the studio, thus losing the added space that can be gained on location work . . . The sets were of necessity quite flimsy and, looking at them close up, it's a wonder that they look so good on screen. Very often television sets look absolutely dreadful and extremely tacky before they are lit, and this was definitely the case with those assembled for *Dragonfire*. However, on camera they looked fine; as convincing as it was possible to achieve and greatly helped by the acting of the cast.

> It was possible to view what was going to be seen on screen in the final stage by looking at one of the monitors carefully arranged around the studio. These are most important to all concerned, and everyone, from make-up and costume [staff] through to lighting men and production manager, [was] glued to what they showed during each run-through of a take. Woe betide anybody who got in the way!

The difficulties of creating a convincing frozen environment in a television studio, with expanded polystyrene 'snow' and sheets of plastic 'ice', were not lost on Chris Clough:

'There is always that problem with something of this nature, but there are no real alternatives to what we used. This was something we gave a lot of thought to in the planning stages, but without the money available you are always going to be limited to using the same old measures.

'John Asbridge's sets were highly original. We had wanted the cryogenic centre to be very big and very high – an example of pomposity gone berserk – and he did a splendid job. The swirling mists were an absolute nightmare to realise. We had dry ice machines everywhere, but the problem was that the stuff disperses very quickly. We got through literally hundreds of pounds' worth, but it was ultimately very effective. The one real problem though was that we couldn't show the actors' breath. Orson Welles got round this problem by building his sets in a cold storage unit, and Frank Capra put little boxes of dry ice inside the actors' mouths. Others have tried using cigarette smoke, but really, for us, it would have been virtually impossible to show.

'We just had to make sure that the actors kept in their heads the continuity of where they were supposed to be and didn't start wandering about as though it was the middle of summer. We rationalised it by saying, "Well, it's cold, but it's not *that* cold!" '

Andrew Cartmel also admired Asbridge's sets, but felt that they had been let down by over-bright lighting.

'That's always been a problem in television,' noted Clough.

'Don Babbage, who lit *Dragonfire*, worked with me on *East-Enders*, so we sorted our way through that. He calls me the Prince of Darkness, because I'm always after shadows everywhere and forever shouting, "Turn the bloody lights down!" '

Post-production

The recording of a *Doctor Who* adventure accounts for the raw material of what is eventually seen on screen, but the diary of a production does not end there. A period of many months can pass between the time a writer first submits his scripts and the time the story is eventually transmitted, and the proportion of that period which is spent in the studio – usually about one day per twenty-five-minute episode – is very low compared with that spent on work carried out both before and after the recording sessions.

'Once you've recorded it you go into editing,' noted Chris Clough, 'and you have to let the editor have his input, just like you let the actors have their input. One plays and discusses with the editor – I'll say, "I've shot it with this in mind," and he'll say, "Well that's a load of crap. Wouldn't it be better if . . ." and so on and so forth.

'Editing can be a frustrating process. You often find yourself saying, "Why the bloody hell didn't I shoot it from that angle, or go for a close-up there?"

'Boom shadows are very embarrassing, but if there was a choice between a take where the performance was better with the shadow and one where it was worse without it, I'd go for the better performance and try to edit round the shadow.

'In the case of *Dragonfire*, the main problem was that the episodes overran and had to be cut down to the right length. This meant, for example, that we trimmed a sequence where the Doctor gets trapped under a piece of falling ice and has to be freed by Glitz. In editing, you always have to trim the arty bits, which is very distressing.'

Ian Briggs recalled this trimming process in his interview for *Doctor Who Magazine*: 'Because we were trying to get so much in, we had to cut the "wind down" [between Kane's death scene and the start of Mel's farewell scene]. But when Chris had done a rough cut of the episode, we all agreed that there really was too much of a jump . . . Tony [Selby] had to come in and revoice something else, so I [took the opportunity to add an] extra linking scene between the [other] two – [specifically the one with Glitz making an announcement along the lines of] "This is your new captain speaking" – using some spare [visuals that had been recorded].'

'After the editing,' continued Clough, 'there's the sound dub. We have two days for location stuff and a day for studio stuff, which should be fairly simple. Dick Mills, the special sounds artist, adds his splits and splats and then there's the incidental music. For *Dragonfire*, the composer Dominic Glynn came down to both studios and we gave it a lot of thought.'

Interviewed by Philip Newman in 1990 for *Doctor Who Magazine*, Glynn recalled that his score for *Dragonfire* had represented a significant development in both style and quality of composition over the ones that he had provided for the previous season's *The Trial of a Time Lord*: 'The music for [those earlier episodes] was done purely on a synthesiser, which made it difficult to get certain "warm", "fat sounding" noises. I had to double track everything. But between seasons I bought a sampler, which made a huge difference to the range of sounds I could use. I could record a second, or a few seconds, of any instrument, sound or noise and then play it back, at any tone or pitch, on an electronic keyboard. So I was able to sample the jingle-bell sound from a baby's toy, and the biggest church organ in the South of England.'

Speaking to Austen Atkinson-Broadbelt in 1993, also for *Doctor Who Magazine*, Glynn elaborated on his intentions for *Dragonfire*: 'I was attempting to get a more orchestral feel in that story . . . I tried to give a feeling of being there on that freezing planet. It was a good story. I think I began to feel more relaxed by the time *Dragonfire* came along. I tried very hard to help build up the atmosphere on that one. I loved doing the music for the soldiers. That's all very metallic. Good stuff!'

Transmission

Dragonfire was transmitted over three consecutive Saturdays in November 1987 as the last story of *Doctor Who*'s twenty-fourth season. Its first episode captured an audience of 5.5 million viewers – the highest individual rating of the season – and it also received good audience reaction figures, reflecting a gradual upward trend during the course of the season. Ace proved to be an instant hit, gaining a higher approval rating than either the Doctor or – by some margin – Mel.

Ten viewers' phone calls about the story were logged at the BBC's duty office. One complained that the story was too childish; six thought that the scene of Kane's face melting was unsuitable for transmission so early in the evening; one considered that the series was great; one felt that the timeslot was wrong; and one was glad to see the back of Bonnie Langford. The production office also received one letter of complaint dated 2 December 1987 from a viewer named Dorothy Barrass, who was upset at a line of dialogue in which Ace had stated that the name 'Dorothy' was 'naff'. John Nathan-Turner replied on 11 December apologising for any offence that had been caused.

'There was something traditional about *Dragonfire* which made me feel it was the right story on which to end the season,' commented Nathan-Turner in his *Doctor Who Magazine* memoirs. 'It was studio-bound, of course, but it also somehow harked back to earlier days of the show while still using the latest technology. Sometimes innocent, sometimes simple, and yet advanced, moralistic and, hopefully, entertaining. Again, a story of "Hello, goodbye", but with a reasonable degree of optimism for the future.'

Credits

Director	Chris Clough
Producer	John Nathan-Turner
Script Editor	Andrew Cartmel
Production Associate	Ann Faggetter

Production Manager	Gary Downie
Assistant Floor Managers	Christopher Sandeman
	Kim Wilcocks
Production Assistants	Rosemary Parsons
	Karen King
Producer's Secretary	Kate Easteal
Designer	John Asbridge
Design Assistant	Hilda Liptrott
Costume Designer	Richard Croft
Costume Assistant	Leah Archer
Dressers	Bob Springett
	Lena Hansen
	Tom Reeve
	Kate Hirst
Make-Up Designer	Gillian Thomas
Make-Up Assistants	Petrona Winton
	Anabela Dellot-Seguro
	Jayne Buxton
Visual Effects Designer	Andy McVean
Visual Effects Assistants	Mike Tucker
	Paul Mann
	Paul McGuinness
	Lindsay McGowan
	Jonathan Clarke
Properties Buyer	Cathy Cosgrove
Sound	Brian Clark
Deputy Sound Supervisor	Mike Weaver
Lighting	Don Babbage
Technical Co-ordinator	Richard Wilson
Senior Cameraman	Alec Wheal
Video Effects	Dave Chapman
Vision Mixer	Shirley Coward
Videotape Editor	Hugh Parson
Film Cameraman	William Dudman
Floor Assistant	Jes Nightingale
Production Operatives	Arthur Stacey
	Dicky Wickes

	Dave Rogers
	Barry Du Pille
Title Music	Ron Grainer, arranged by Keff McCulloch
Incidental Music	Dominic Glynn
Special Sound	Dick Mills
Writer	Ian Briggs

7: The Wilderness Years

After the completion of work on its twenty-sixth season, *Doctor Who* was effectively cancelled as a BBC production. Unlike when it had been taken off the air for eighteen months in 1984, however, there was no official announcement made to this effect. Consequently there was no press coverage of the series' demise and, at least initially, no concerted attempt by fans to get the BBC to change their minds.

Although *Survival* was the last story to be screened in the ongoing series, *Ghost Light* was the last to go before the cameras, the season having been made out of transmission order. Following its completion, there were just two pieces of additional recording undertaken. The first was of a voice-over by actor David Bingham for Part One of *Battlefield*. This was done on 13 August 1989. The second was of a voice-over by Sylvester McCoy consisting of the Doctor's final monologue for the end of Part Three of *Survival*. Whether by accident or design, this was done on a very appropriate date, 23 November 1989 – the twenty-sixth anniversary of *Doctor Who*'s debut transmission.

The BBC's *Doctor Who* production office had already begun to wind down a couple of months before this, and Sylvester McCoy was reported as telling a convention audience: 'The BBC don't want to make *Doctor Who*. They aren't interested in a series that's lasted twenty-six years.'

There had for some time been rumours circulating that the BBC wanted to farm *Doctor Who* out to be made by an independent production company. (At this point in the BBC's history there was a general move towards outsourcing as many productions as possible; *Doctor Who* was one of the last drama series to be made in house, and John Nathan-Turner was the last producer on the staff of the Series and Serials Department, all his former colleagues having been obliged to go freelance.) Bids were rumoured to have been made to the BBC by a number of interested companies, including Cinema Verity (run by former series producer Verity Lambert), Saffron Productions (run by former series story editor and writer Victor Pemberton) and Coast-to-Coast Productions Ltd (who were in fact looking to make a feature film based on the series – a subject covered in a later section of this chapter).

In November 1989, prompted by numerous enquiries from concerned fans and a certain amount of press speculation about the series' future, the BBC's new Head of Serials, Peter Cregeen, issued a statement in which he claimed that *Doctor Who* could easily continue for a further twenty-six years but added that the BBC was considering the best way to 'take *Doctor Who* through the 90s'. These words were to ring ever more hollow as variations on the same statement continued to be issued by the BBC to anyone who enquired about the future of *Doctor Who* in the years that followed. Another notable occurrence in November 1989 was that Nathan-Turner officially stood down as *Doctor Who*'s producer after some ten years in that post. He remained on the BBC's payroll, however, and would continue to take an active role as the series' 'guardian'.

The following month, former story editor and writer Gerry Davis and writer Terry Nation confirmed in the fanzine *DWB* that they were interested in making a joint bid to produce the series. This, along with approaches from other sources, apparently forced the BBC to reconsider its attitude to the series to the extent that the senior press officer, Kevin O'Shea (who had handled much of *Doctor Who*'s press promotion in the past), made a statement that an announcement on its future was likely to be made soon. Nothing came of this, although two months later, in February 1990, Cregeen was back with another pronouncement, commenting cryptically: 'There will be more changes than people think . . .'

1990

The only new *Doctor Who*-related production to be transmitted during 1990 was the edition of the BBC schools series *Search Out Science*, in which Sylvester McCoy's Doctor and Sophie Aldred's Ace were joined by a John Leeson-voiced K-9 to educate viewers in the wonders of space (as described in detail in Chapter 3). There was plenty of old *Doctor Who* to be seen, however, as it became one of the flagship shows on the new satellite channel BSB (which was also available through many cable television suppliers). This began in April, repeating selected stories from the William Hartnell era onwards, and on 22 and 23 September had an entire '*Doctor Who* weekend', otherwise known as '31 Who'. This consisted of special screenings, guest appearances and other items put together largely by Nathan-Turner, who had finally left the BBC at the end of the previous month (although he had immediately gained work with BBC Enterprises, producing *Doctor Who* video projects – see Chapter 9). Nathan-Turner also acted as on-screen co-presenter with Shyama Perera and Debbie Flint.

The stories and individual episodes shown on the Saturday were: *100,000 BC*, *The Mutants*, *Inside the Spaceship* (with the second episode accidentally preceding the first), *The Abominable Snowmen* Episode Two, *The Web of Fear* Episode One, *The Space Museum*, *The Keys of Marinus* and *The Aztecs*. Also shown was the sixties cinema film *Dr. Who and the Daleks*. Interspersed between these screenings were short interviews with: William Russell ('Ian'), Carole Ann Ford ('Susan'), Verity Lambert (producer), Waris Hussein (director), Elisabeth Sladen ('Sarah Jane Smith'), Terry Nation (writer), Raymond P. Cusick (designer), Mervyn Haisman (writer), Nicholas Courtney ('the Brigadier'), Sylvester McCoy ('the Doctor'), Andrew Beech (fan), Peter Purves ('Steven'), John Freeman (editor, *Doctor Who Magazine*), Terrance Dicks (script editor and writer), Gerry Davis (story editor and writer), Deborah Watling ('Victoria') and Jennie Linden ('Barbara' from the cinema films). Also presented during the course of the day were a *Doctor Who* 'expert' quiz, a piece on American *Doctor Who* conventions, vox pops of people doing Dalek impressions, an interview with a Cyberman and the video for the 'Doctor in Distress' single record from 1984.

The stories and individual episodes shown on the Sunday were: *The War Games*, *The Dominators*, *The Mind Robber*, *The Three Doctors*, *The Abominable Snowmen* Episode Two, *The Web of Fear* Episode One and *Inside the Spaceship* (with the episodes screened the correct way round). Also shown, between *The Three Doctors* and *The Abominable Snowmen* Episode Two, was the cinema film *Daleks Invasion Earth 2150* AD. The interviews this time were with Wendy Padbury ('Zoe'), Frazer Hines ('Jamie'), Pat Godfrey (costume designer), Brian Hodgson (special sound effects), Dick Mills (special sound effects), Sylvester McCoy ('the Doctor'), Stephen Mansfield (visual effects), Susan Moore (visual effects), Raymond P. Cusick (designer), Barry Newbery (designer), Peter Hawkins (voice artiste), Terrance Dicks (script editor and writer), Nicholas Courtney ('the Brigadier'), Bob Baker (writer), Dave Martin (writer), David J. Howe (collector), Verity Lambert (producer) and Terry Nation (writer). Additional features this time were a special-effects demonstration and a top ten *Doctor Who* monsters compilation.

BSB spent a great deal of time and effort promoting *Doctor Who* generally, but all this came to an end in November 1990 when it merged with the rival Sky and the *Doctor Who* repeats stopped.

Also in November, one year on from the end of the twenty-sixth season and with no signs of the BBC taking any specific action to revive the series, a 'day of protest' was organised by the fanzine *DWB*. The idea was that on this particular day, Sunday 2 November, fans would bombard the BBC with at least twenty phone calls each in protest at the delay in returning the series to production. In the event, however, only 973 *Doctor Who*-related calls were logged at the duty offices of BBC television and radio. This was certainly far more than on an average day (on the Saturday immediately beforehand, for instance, 23 such calls had been logged), but it still fell well below the organisers' hopes; and while the great majority of callers were no doubt sincere individuals genuinely concerned about the series' future, the fact that some gave names very similar to those of well-known *Doctor Who* characters and production personnel – 'Mr T. Jovka', 'John Turner' and 'Alistair Gordon' among them – does raise questions about the motives of a minority. A further problem with this well-intentioned initiative is that, far from increasing the chance of new *Doctor Who* being made, it reportedly had the opposite effect of turning some senior BBC executives against the series altogether, leaving them determined not to let the fans dictate their policy in relation to a show that they considered dead.

The following month, the BBC stated that a final decision on the series' future would be made in 1991.

The year did end on a relatively high note, however, when *Doctor Who* was the subject of a *Cult Heroes* documentary on BBC Radio 5 on Christmas Eve. This was produced by Anne Hinds, written by Ed Thomason and presented by comedian Tony Slattery and featured contributions from John Nathan-Turner (producer), Sylvester McCoy ('the Doctor'), John Collins (DWAS Coordinator), Verity Lambert (producer), Dick Mills (special sound effects), Jon Pertwee ('the Doctor') and Elisabeth Sladen ('Sarah Jane Smith'). Also included were interview clips of Tom Baker taken from the 1977 *Lively Arts* documentary *Whose Doctor Who*.

1991

February 1991 saw BBC Chairman Marmaduke Hussey, in response to an enquiry from Sir Hugh Rossi MP, stating that the Corporation was looking 'at all possible avenues before making any long-term decisions' on *Doctor Who*'s future. Other senior BBC figures responded to public enquiries with standard letters along similar lines.

There was no further movement until May when, following questions from the national press, the BBC finally confirmed that any future series would be made by an independent production company rather than in house. No particular company was named, however, and nothing of substance seemed to be happening. Some magazines picked up the fact that a new science fiction show was about to be made at Shepperton Studios and leapt to the conclusion that it must be *Doctor Who*. It was actually a completely different production.

Arguably the biggest development during 1991 was the launching by Virgin books of their New Adventures range of original novels featuring the seventh Doctor and Ace. (See Chapter 12.) Visitors to London's Museum of the Moving Image (MOMI) were meanwhile able to see 'Behind the Sofa', a major exhibition devoted to *Doctor Who*. This opened on 5 July following a press launch at which three concept models of creatures from the supposed forthcoming Green Light feature film were on show. Jointly arranged by MOMI, BBC Worldwide and Lorne Martin's company Experience (who were hired by BBC Worldwide to manage all the *Doctor Who*-related exhibitions), it proved massively popular and was extended several times, finally running until 23 February 1992 before going on tour to regional venues until November 1992.

Tying in with the exhibition, a company called Teynham Productions, the directors of which were John Nathan-Turner, Gary Downie, Fiona Cumming and Ian Fraser, staged a series of two-day events at MOMI. These involved people associated with *Doctor Who* giving lectures about their work to a group of paying attendees. The dates and speakers were as follows: 6/7 July 1991: Jeremy Bentham (history of *Doctor Who*), Bernard Wilkie and Jack Kine (visual effects), Colin Baker ('the Doctor'), Carole Todd (director, *The Ultimate Adventure* stage play), June Hudson (costumes), Nicholas Courtney ('the Brigadier'), Fiona Cumming (director), Sophie Aldred ('Ace'), John Freeman (editor, *Doctor Who Magazine*), Dick Mills (sound effects), Sylvester McCoy ('the Doctor'); 2/3 November 1991: David J. Howe (collecting), Barry Newbery (designer), Sue Anstruther (production assistant), Ken Trew (costumes), Mitch Mitchell (video effects), Barry Letts (producer), Tony Selby ('Glitz'), Ian Dow (lighting), Kevin O'Shea (publicity), Nicola Bryant ('Peri'),

Shirley Coward (vision mixer), Elisabeth Sladen ('Sarah Jane Smith'), Ian Fraser (production manager), Jon Pertwee ('the Doctor'); 15/16 February 1992: Andrew Beech (appreciating *Doctor Who*), Gary Downie (choreographer, production assistant), Keff McCulloch (music), June Collins (production manager), Henry Barber (lighting), Jane Wellesley (production assistant), Tom Baker ('the Doctor'), Stuart Fell (stuntman), Lorne Martin and Martin Wilkie (exhibitions), Janet Fielding ('Tegan'), Graeme Smith ('Jason' in *The Ultimate Adventure*), Christopher Barry (director), Denise Baron (make-up), Terry Molloy ('Davros'). Teynham subsequently organised a number of similar events, some of them lasting only one day, in different locations around the UK.

On 26 August 1991 the series' pilot episode had its first ever transmission, some 28 years after it was made, as part of BBC2's tribute to Lime Grove Studios, which were shortly to be demolished. The same month, Peter Cregeen issued another statement to *Doctor Who Magazine* about the series' future:

'There is no question of *Doctor Who* being abandoned. It is still an important programme and when the time is right it should return. However, the show's popularity over the years has waned in the United Kingdom, with an average audience of four million. In a competitive market environment, where BBC TV Drama is required to produce a wide range of programmes at an economically viable price, one cannot continue to support a programme that is not able to achieve a substantial audience.

'A decision was taken to rest the programme for an extended period so that when it returns it will be seen as a fresh, inventive and vibrant addition to the schedule – rather than a battle-weary Time Lord languishing in the backwaters of audience popularity.

'*Doctor Who* is too valuable a property for us to relaunch until we are absolutely confident of it as a major success once again.'

Confused and angered by what they saw as yet another bland statement from the BBC, a group of fans announced plans in October to take the BBC to court for failing to make *Doctor Who* in the face of massive public demand. The consortium included chairman and legal adviser John Giacobbi, Andrew Beech, Steve

Wickham, Colin Griffiths and Jonathan Way from the DWAS, Gary Leigh from *DWB* and historian Jeremy Bentham. This well-intentioned but perhaps misguided campaign ultimately came to nothing as a prize competition intended to raise money received only a lukewarm response and insufficient funds were raised to pursue the matter further.

1992

3 January 1992 saw the transmission on BBC2 of a half-hour overview of *Doctor Who* entitled *Resistance is Useless*. This was put together by the production team of the arts programme *The Late Show* (who had also been responsible for the previous August's screening of the pilot episode) and directed by Archie Lauchlan. It consisted mainly of clips from *Doctor Who* compiled into a number of categories and linked by a mysterious character who appeared to be nothing more than literally a talking anorak – the voice for which was provided by comedian Steve Steen. The clips were selected on the basis of responses to a questionnaire sent to a number of fans and on the advice of John Nathan-Turner, who had been engaged as a consultant. Other contributors to the programme included Steve Roberts (a fan who worked in the telecine department at the BBC) and Ian Levine, who along with Nathan-Turner supplied Lauchlan with lists of what was available to be included. The list of categories was: Resistance Is Useless; Thoughts Of An Anorak; Time And Relative Dimensions In Space; Fab Gadgets; Fashion Victims; Leave It To Me, Dear; The Brigadier's Finest Moments; Doc Fax; Behind The Sofa; Doc Fax (again); Effects (Special); Death By Special Effect; Give It All You've Got; Surreal; and Doctor In Charge.

Transmission of *Resistance is Useless* led on to a season of BBC2 repeats, starting with *The Time Meddler*, *The Mind Robber*, *The Sea Devils* and, in a specially restored recolourised version (combining images from a broadcast-standard black-and-white print with those from a poorer-quality colour home video recorded off-air in the USA), *The Dæmons*. This was the first time that the BBC had screened any complete repeats of *Doctor Who* since *The Five Doctors* in 1984. The satellite and cable channel UK Gold also began transmitting regular repeats of the series, following the demise of BSB.

In February, Dark Light Productions was reported by *Doctor Who Magazine* to be the latest independent company bidding to produce a new series. The producer, Alan Jonns, eventually made a statement in the May edition of the magazine, indicating that no episodes had been filmed, no actor had been cast and no contracts with the BBC had been signed. He revealed that his company had simply been carrying out test work to see if their ideas were suitable. Although this work ultimately came to nothing, some of the monster designs created for the company by the Henson Creature Shop were later seen in relation both to the aborted thirtieth anniversary special *The Dark Dimension* (see below), one test photograph even appearing on the proposed cover of an ultimately unpublished Adrian Rigelsford book about that production, and to a potential Bill Baggs video drama featuring Cybermen and Ice Warriors.

Other notable events during 1992 included as part of the BBC's ongoing programme of *Doctor Who* video releases the cancelled Season 17 story *Shada*, with the missing scenes bridged by narration from Tom Baker, and in May the Season 5 story *The Tomb of the Cybermen*, all four episodes of which had been among a consignment of film prints recently recovered from Hong Kong after being missing for many years from the BBC archives. In Virgin's New Adventures novels, meanwhile, a new – and ultimately highly popular – companion named Bernice Summerfield made her debut.

1993

The run of BBC2 repeats continued into the early part of 1993 with *Genesis of the Daleks*, *The Caves of Androzani*, *Revelation of the Daleks* (in the edited four-part version originally created for overseas sales purposes) and *Battlefield*.

In April the BBC held a press launch, with Jon Pertwee, Peter

Davison, Colin Baker, Sylvester McCoy and Nicholas Courtney in attendance, promoting the package of video and audio releases planned for that autumn to tie in with *Doctor Who*'s thirtieth anniversary. Tony Greenwood, Director of Home Entertainment at BBC Enterprises, also mentioned that, as had been rumoured since the previous December, a script had been written for a special anniversary production – although he added that it might not actually reach fruition as the necessary agreements had yet to be concluded. (The original aim of BBC Enterprises in holding this press launch had in fact been to announce the making of the special, but they had had to backtrack as it had yet to be given the go-ahead.)

The following month it was confirmed that the special, entitled *The Dark Dimension* and intended to feature all the surviving Doctors, would be directed by Graeme Harper (who had made his mark on the series with *The Caves of Androzani* and *Revelation of the Daleks*). Then in June there came the only official announcement that the BBC ever made on the subject when a 96-minute 16 mm film special, referred to as *Doctor Who: Lost in the Dark Dimension*, was listed in its forthcoming drama publicity press release. The special was written by Adrian Rigelsford and Jo McCaul and a production office was set up with Penny Mills (from BBC Enterprises) and the newly resigned Head of Drama, Peter Cregeen, acting as co-producers.

On 9 July the special was abruptly cancelled. No official reason was ever given as the BBC denied that it was ever a finalised project. The Managing Director of Network Television, Will Wyatt, blamed overeager fans for taking it beyond the ideas stage. BBC Video's David Jackson broke the news by saying: 'Due to the constrictions of our budget and the time available the production has been cancelled.' It is believed that internal BBC politics and objections raised by Philip Segal, the American-based producer bidding for the rights to make a new series (see Part Four), also contributed to the decision not to go ahead with the project. Rigelsford, who had been trying to get his script produced for two years, was reported by *Doctor Who Magazine* to be 'deeply disappointed'. It was also revealed by *Doctor*

Who Magazine that Nick Jagels had been brought on board as production associate and that Rigelsford, Harper and Jagels, together with Alan Jonns, had been the 'guiding force' behind Dark Light's earlier attempts to get *Doctor Who* back on air.

Despite future rumours to the contrary, Tom Baker was the only actor ever contracted to appear in the special (and hence the only one to be paid); no other casting was ever agreed (although the other surviving Doctors – who, with the exception of Sylvester McCoy, would have had much smaller roles – were sent copies of the script); no filming or location work was ever carried out; and, aside from Rigelsford writing a draft rehearsal script (of which there appear to have been several different versions, none of them bearing a co-writing credit for McCaul), the only other production work ever carried out consisted of one or two early 'ideas' meetings drawing together interested parties – including production designer Nigel Jones, visual-effects designer Tony Harding and first assistant director Kevan van Thompson – who may or may not have ended up working on the project had it gone ahead. Kevin Davies had also been approached with a view to designing the title sequence and Mark Russell and Alan Hawkshawe had been under consideration to provide the music.

In August, BBC Radio 5 transmitted a new *Doctor Who* radio serial entitled *Paradise of Death*, written by Barry Letts and featuring Jon Pertwee, Elisabeth Sladen and Nicholas Courtney reprising their roles as the third Doctor, Sarah Jane Smith and Brigadier Lethbridge-Stewart respectively. This had been recorded in May. (See *The Handbook – The Third Doctor* for further details.) The serial's producer, Phil Clarke, was also responsible for a documentary, *Doctor Who – 30 Years*, which was broadcast on BBC Radio 2 on 20 November and ran for 55 minutes, 44 seconds. This was narrated by Nicholas Courtney and featured interviews with: Gary Russell (editor, *Doctor Who Magazine*), Katy Manning ('Jo'), John Scott Martin (Dalek operator), Jon Pertwee ('the Doctor'), William Russell ('Ian'), Peter Purves ('Steven'), Louise Jameson ('Leela'), Barry Letts (director, producer and writer), Terrance Dicks (script editor and writer), Terry Nation (writer), Frazer Hines ('Jamie'), Jessica Carney (William Hartnell's granddaughter), John Nathan-Turner (producer), Verity Lambert (producer), Sylvester McCoy ('the Doctor') and Brian Hodgson (special sound effects). Also recorded but unused in the final programme were interviews with Anneke Wills ('Polly'), Elisabeth Sladen ('Sarah Jane Smith'), David J. Howe (historian) and Roberta Tovey ('Susan' from the cinema films).

The Season 10 story *Planet of the Daleks* was meanwhile repeated on BBC1 in November and December, with a five-minute 'mini-documentary' preceding each episode. The themes of these mini-documentaries were as follows: *Bigger Inside Than Out* (Colin Baker narrating a piece on the history of the TARDIS and the police box upon which its external appearance was based); *The Antique Doctor Who Show* (a pastiche of the BBC's *The Antiques Road Show* in which presenter Justin Pressland and collector David J. Howe spoke to several fans about their *Doctor Who* collections); *Missing in Action* (a look at the junking of *Doctor Who* episodes and the efforts to retrieve them); *I Was That Monster* (interviews with people who had played monsters); *Crimefile – The Master* (a pastiche of the crime prevention show *Police 5* in which presenter Shaw Taylor warned the public to be on the lookout for the Master); and *UNIT Recruiting Film* (in which Nicholas Courtney encouraged people to join up). At the end of the last of these mini-documentaries was given a telephone number, callers to which could hear Courtney telling them that *The Green Death* was due to be repeated the following year.

Although plans for a proper anniversary story had come to nothing, there was a minor consolation for fans as the two-part skit *Dimensions in Time* was transmitted as part of BBC1's annual Children in Need telethon on 26 and 27 November. (See Chapter 3.)

On 29 November BBC1 also transmitted a more substantial fifty-minute documentary entitled *30 Years in the TARDIS* (which was released on video the following year with additional material under the title *More than 30 Years in the TARDIS*). This had suddenly been given the green light in September by the team responsible for the previous year's *Resistance is Useless*. Recorded during October and November, it brought together clips, interviews and dramatic interludes to provide a well-balanced overview of the series. Interviews were conducted with: Mat Irvine (visual effects), Mike Tucker (visual effects), Colin Baker ('the Doctor'), Nicola Bryant ('Peri'), Carole Ann Ford ('Susan'), Verity Lambert (producer), Roberta Tovey ('Susan' from the cinema films), Sophie Aldred ('Ace'), Sylvester McCoy ('the Doctor'), Barry Letts (director, producer and writer), Terrance Dicks (script editor and writer), Elisabeth Sladen ('Sarah Jane Smith'), Delia Derbyshire (theme music arranger), Brian Hodgson (special sound effects), Dick Mills (special sound effects), Jessica Carney (William Hartnell's granddaughter), Jennie Linden ('Barbara' from the cinema films), Deborah Watling ('Victoria'), Frazer Hines ('Jamie'), John Nathan-Turner (producer), Ian Levine (fan), Gary Russell (editor, *Doctor Who Magazine*), Jon Pertwee ('the Doctor'), Eric Saward (script editor and writer), Mary Whitehouse (retired head of the National Viewers' and Listeners' Association), Ben Aaronovitch (writer), Philip Hinchcliffe (producer); Stephen Bayley (academic), Professor Steve Jones (academic); Lowrey Turner (fashion editor); Mike Gatting (England cricketer/celebrity fan), Ken Livingstone (politician/celebrity fan), Toyah Wilcox (pop singer and presenter/celebrity fan) and Gerry Anderson (puppet series producer/celebrity fan). Several of those interviewed were not seen in the broadcast programme, although Davies was able to include some of the unused material in the later video release.

1994

Further repeats – this time of *The Green Death* and *Pyramids of Mars* – were transmitted on BBC2 at the start of 1994. Then, in July, Virgin launched a new range of Missing Adventures books to complement their New Adventures. (See Chapter 12.)

On 9 July listeners to BBC Radio 4 were able to hear *Whatever Happened to . . . Susan?*, the fifth in a series of humorous programmes looking at the lives of popular fictional characters, the subject in this case being the Doctor's granddaughter Susan Foreman, played here by Jane Asher after the original actress, Carole Ann Ford, apparently failed to return the BBC's calls. The programme was produced by Brian King, written by Adrian Mourby and in addition to Asher featured James Grout (playing Ian Chesterton), June Barne (Barbara Wright), Eva Haddon (Jo Jones, née Grant), Andrew Sachs (Temmosus Skyedron), Peter Woodthorpe (Joey Oxford), Barry Harrison (researcher) and Claire Rayner (as herself).

Following the success of *Paradise of Death*, a further *Doctor Who* radio serial, *Doctor Who and the Ghosts of N Space*, was recorded in November, although its transmission was ultimately delayed until March 1996, when it went out on BBC Radio 2 (Radio 5 having by this point become an all-news station). Like *The Paradise of Death* it was produced by Phil Clarke, written by Barry Letts and featured Jon Pertwee, Elisabeth Sladen, Nicholas Courtney and new regular Richard Pearce playing Sarah's young assistant Jeremy. (Again, for further details see *The Handbook – The Third Doctor*.)

1995

This was a relatively quiet year for *Doctor Who*, although UK Gold continued to transmit repeats and there was still a steady stream of new tie-in merchandise being issued, including the first in a range of BBC audio books featuring abridged versions of the Target novelisations of televised stories read by their respective Doctors. By this point, however, the series' followers were becoming increasingly excited by news reports that seemed to suggest that there might, at long last, be a real prospect of new *Doctor Who* being seen on television for the first time in over six years . . .

MOVIE HELL

Omitted from the preceding sections of this chapter has been any mention of the numerous unsuccessful attempts to get a *Doctor*

Who feature film off the ground during the late eighties and nineties – a subject that merits a section all of its own.

There had been serious talk of a *Doctor Who* movie from as early as 1976, when Tom Baker, actor Ian Marter (who played companion Harry Sullivan) and producer James Hill developed an idea with the working titles *Doctor Who and the Big Game* and *Doctor Who Meets Scratchman* featuring 'Scratchman', another name for the devil, as the villain. After much negotiation, BBC Enterprises granted James Hill Productions with effect from 1 November 1978 a one-year option to make the film, with no commitment on their part to renew. The project eventually fell through, however, due to difficulties in raising the necessary finance.

In the meantime, numerous other overtures were made to the BBC by parties interested in pursuing *Doctor Who* film projects. On 4 April 1978 Jill Foster Ltd made contact regarding a Douglas Adams film treatment based on the series. An approach came on 12 May 1980 from producer Brian Eastman of Paramount; another on 23 August 1982 from Anthony Williams of Sandfire Productions, based at Pinewood Studios; and another in May 1984 from American producer Norman Rubenstein, who remained in contact with the BBC until October of that year. These all came to nothing. Milton Subotsky, co-producer of the two sixties *Doctor Who* films, contacted the Head of Series and Serials, Jonathan Powell, in April 1984 to indicate that he would like to do a third. This had the working title *Doctor Who's Greatest Adventure* and would have involved two Doctors teaming up to combat some giant monsters. Powell turned the idea down, and confirmed with the Head of Copyright, Brian Turner, that there was nothing in Subotsky's original contracts with the BBC that gave him any rights in this regard. A proposal that progressed a little further was put forward on 15 October 1984 by Edward Joffe of Multivision Communications Ltd. The BBC stipulated as conditions for granting the film rights to Multivision that John Nathan-Turner would have to be involved in the project; that one of the television Doctors would have to be given the lead role; and that a fee of around £50,000 would have to be paid. Peter Davison was subsequently contacted to see if he would be interested in starring in the film, and Christopher H. Bidmead was earmarked as a possible writer. In the end, however, this also fell through. On 7 May 1985 Nathan-Turner suggested that *Doctor Who*'s first producer Verity Lambert might be a good candidate to make a film based on the series. Then, on 21 June 1985, producer Michael Bond put forward a film treatment entitled *The Crossroads in Time*. This too came to nothing.

It was in March 1985 that Coast-to-Coast Productions Ltd – run by co-directors Peter Litten, George Dugdale and John Humphreys – first entered into negotiations with BBC Enterprises with a view to acquiring the rights to make a *Doctor Who* feature film, having apparently started discussing the idea the previous month. In November of the same year, Litten wrote an undated letter to BBC Enterprises' Director of Business Administration, John Keeble, setting out the company's latest proposals for the film and indicating that the budget and scope had recently been increased in all departments. He stated that: actors Denholm Elliott, Steven Berkoff, Caroline Munro, Tim Curry and Laurence Olivier had all agreed to be involved; composer Mike Oldfield had been approached to adapt the series' theme tune and provide the incidental music; make-up artist Christopher Tucker, whose credits included *The Elephant Man* and *The Company of Wolves*, would be creating the creatures and monsters; John Stears, who had won an Oscar for his work on *Star Wars*, would be in charge of visual effects; Rodney Matthews and Anton Furst would be teaming up to design the sets and costumes; Douglas Adams would be acting as script consultant; Robert Holmes would be providing the screenplay; and Richard Lester, the man at the helm of *Superman 2* and *Superman 3* among many other projects, was being considered as director. He also stated that Sun Alliance had undertaken to provide financial backing for the film, and that only the BBC's agreement was now required.

Jonathan Powell, when shown Litten's letter, expressed considerable scepticism. In an internal memo to Keeble he wrote: 'With respect, this strikes me as slightly full of baloney. *No* actors would agree without a script. The technicians mentioned would never agree without production dates. Robert Holmes is not an adventurous choice to write the screenplay. Anyone can *consider* Richard Lester. The statement means absolutely nothing in practice.'

Powell went on to state that he believed that the BBC should keep the project for themselves, and that if they did decide to allow it to go ahead outside then there should be 'some known factor involved'. He concluded by stating that he was unimpressed by Litten's letter, which made many promises and listed many prospective contributors when 'clearly their statements are absolutely meaningless'. He also asked if anyone had any idea as to what Litten had done in the past, or what his production company had actually achieved.

Despite this unfavourable reception from Powell, negotiations with Coast-to-Coast continued and were eventually concluded around July 1987, when the company was finally granted the rights to make a *Doctor Who* feature film in return for a substantial fee, reported to be £46,000. It was apparently envisaged that the company would need to raise some £1.6 million in backing in order to proceed with the project.

During the latter half of 1987, rumours regarding the film's casting, content and production started to appear with increasing frequency in newspapers and magazines. It was reported that actress Caroline Munro would be featuring in the film as the villain; that £5 million was being spent on the effects alone; that Sylvester McCoy was the hot favourite for the role of the Doctor; that the budget was around £9 million; that Tom Conti and Tim Curry had turned down the starring role; and that Tom Baker was the hot favourite to take the lead.

Stage and Television Today carried a short piece on the film on 8 October 1987 headed by a mocked-up image of Munro as the computerised television host Max Headroom (Coast-to-Coast having previously been involved in the production of Chrysalis's *Max Headroom* show). John Humphreys was quoted as saying: 'We intend to make it a big budget film with extensive and advanced special effects – I can promise you we won't be using the BBC's infamous quarry.' The report went on to suggest that the film involved Munro cast 'in the title role' as a robot who operates a pirate radio spaceship to beam pop videos down to Earth. However, as this sounds suspiciously like a description of *Max Headroom*, it is possible that the reporter had his or her wires crossed.

Early in 1988, John Cleese was tipped to play the Doctor and Dudley Moore was also mentioned as a strong contender for the part. Munro was now apparently in line to play the companion rather than the villain, and it was reported that the film's directors would be Litten and Dugdale. Fourteen million pounds was the latest figure quoted for the budget, and a script was said to have been commissioned from writer Mark Ezra. In March, another writer, Johnny Byrne, was reported to be under contract to work on the scripts and a release date of Easter 1989 was mooted.

In May 1988, fan Ian Levine was confirmed as a consultant on the project. Then, the following month, it was predicted that shooting would commence in January 1989. John Cleese was at this time still being tipped to play the Doctor and, in a new twist, it was suggested that there would be no fewer than four companion characters. In November 1988, the *Daily Mail* gave over part of the front page of one of its editions to the news that Dudley Moore was to star as the Doctor in a film with a budget of £19 million – the highest figure yet suggested. The following month, however, Moore was reported to be only one of a number of contenders for the title role, others being Donald Sutherland, Ian Holm and Peter Firth. Filming was still reported to be due to start in January, the chosen locations being London and the Canary Islands, but Munro had now apparently reverted to playing the villain.

In April 1989, with no shooting having actually taken place, it was reported that the film had been postponed indefinitely due to lack of finance. In August of that year, however, it was apparently back on again, with filming due to start in March 1990 in Yugoslavia. On 23 October 1989 a number of newspapers reported that Donald Sutherland was to take the lead role, having been cast in preference to Dudley Moore, Michael Caine, John Cleese and Sylvester Stallone, and that – scandalously – the film would show the Doctor boozing, having bar-room brawls, carrying a gun and making love to his assistant. The budget at this time was claimed to be £20 million, and the makers of the Johnny Byrne-scripted film were said to be Pathé.

By the end of 1989, *Doctor Who* fans who had eagerly followed all these reports were understandably totally confused, and many were starting to become highly sceptical that the film would ever see the light of day. Philip Newman, a fan who wrote regularly for several genre magazines and who had apparently been in regular contact with Litten since December 1987, tried to clear the air by explaining in the fanzine *Proteus* what had been really happening. 'Firstly,' he wrote, 'I think it is most important to get one particular message across: *Doctor Who – The Movie* is *definitely* going ahead, and will go into production once all the financial, distribution and other arrangements have been finalised – probably sometime early in 1990.' On the subject of why it had taken so long to get to this stage, Newman indicated that Coast-to-Coast wanted to keep the film as authentic as possible to the original television series and that, with much of the financial backing coming from America, it had 'been hard to keep control of all aspects of the film's production and, moreover, to keep it British'.

As for the scripting of the film, Newman recounted that Mark Ezra had written a first 'rough framework' in 1987 and that this had since been totally reworked by Byrne into a full-length script, which had subsequently been through as many as sixteen rewrites. Levine had checked the script for accuracy in terms of the series' mythology, but otherwise had had no involvement in the project. According to Newman, only twelve actors had ever been seriously considered for the role of the Doctor and just four of these were still seen as possible contenders. At no point had any of the television Doctors ever been under consideration. Newman went on to add: 'Pre-production work is well underway, with twelve conceptual artists, working from different parts of the country, now engaged on producing preliminary designs and plans for all the sets, lighting rigs, creatures and costumes.

Several storyboard artists are currently at work on realising the large volume of special effects sequences that the film requires.'

Jean-Marc Lofficier's book *The Nth Doctor*, published by Virgin Publishing in 1997, also gives a description of Coast-to-Coast's abortive attempts to get their *Doctor Who* film off the ground, and in some respects this is at odds with the account presented by Newman. According to Lofficier, Ezra had by August 1987 completed not only a 'rough framework' but a full draft script entitled *Doctor Who – The Movie*. Byrne then worked on several different treatments and drafts during 1988 and 1989, and the story gradually evolved away from Ezra's original. The resultant scripts were retitled *Doctor Who – [The] Last of the Time Lords*. The project was sufficiently advanced for the Coast-to-Coast team, now calling themselves Green Light, to prepare an advertising flier for the Moving Pictures International film conference in Milan in October 1990. This showed a re-worked *Doctor Who* logo along with the tag line: 'The Man – The Myth – The Movie'.

As *The Nth Doctor* tells it, Byrne completely rewrote his script in 1991 while Litten and Dugdale brought to fruition another project: a low-budget horror feature called *Living Doll*. Green Light, meanwhile, obtained from the BBC another extension of the time period available to them to make the film. This would now expire on 6 April 1994, at which point, if shooting had not commenced, all rights would revert to the BBC.

In 1992, in a further attempt to gain the required finance, Green Light joined forces with Lumiere Pictures and apparently sold on the *Doctor Who* rights to them. One of Lumiere's first acts was to abandon Byrne's work on the project, and instead to commission a totally new script, first from Nicholas Meyer and then, when this did not work out, from a writing partner of Meyer's, Denny Martin Flinn. Lumiere also approached actor and director Leonard Nimoy (famous for his role as Spock in *Star Trek*) and, after reading Flinn's script, he agreed to produce and direct the film. The actor strongly wanted to play the part of the Doctor at this time was Pierce Brosnan. In the event, however, Green Light/Lumiere were unable to commence filming by the deadline date, at which point Lumiere decided to withdraw from the project.

There is one final development to report in this saga. On 10 January 1996, just as news of the Philip Segal/Universal/BBC Worldwide television movie was breaking (see Chapter 8), the London *Evening Standard* carried a two-page exposé on the problems that had beset the earlier feature film project. The report by Keith Dovkants stated that Litten, Dugdale and Humpreys were all 'special effects experts' who had worked on *Doctor Who* (it is indeed the case that Litten and Dugdale once worked in the BBC's Visual Effects Department, and it is known that the Morlox creature seen in Season 22's *Timelash* was built by one or other of them, although neither ever received a credit on the series) and had decided to obtain the rights to make a *Doctor Who* film in the late eighties (*sic*) as they 'deplored the fact that no one was tapping the enormous cinema potential'. The report went on to explain that the three men had obtained finance from a consortium of about twenty individuals (including singer Bryan Ferry and, from the band Dire Straits, John Illsley) and formed a company called Daltenreys to take the project forward, pouring in additional money from second mortgages on their homes in the process. Their deal with the BBC was reported to have been with Keeble, and it was stated that Daltenreys had had meetings with Warner Brothers in America, who had suggested Jack Nicholson as a suitable actor to play the villain – this was at the time when Tim Burton's *Batman*, featuring Nicholson as the Joker, was flavour of the month – and Bill Cosby, Denholm Elliot, Donald Sutherland and Alan Rickman as potential Doctors.

The problem had come, according to the report, when Keeble had resigned from the BBC and BBC Enterprises had become BBC Worldwide with a remit from the new BBC Director General John Birt to maximise profits. Humphreys was quoted as saying that Daltenreys had signed a deal with Lumiere in 1993; that Lumiere had wanted to make three *Doctor Who* films with a budget of more than $30 million; that Leonard Nimoy had been engaged as director and Alan Rickman 'courted' to play the

Doctor; and that after they had heard Stephen Spielberg's name linked to a *Doctor Who* film project (as it had been in the press) they had contacted the BBC and been fobbed off: 'We got the run around.'

The report went on to note that Daltenreys had spent the next few months trying to work out what their position was and that on 4 March, a month before the filming deadline, the BBC's senior lawyer Rowan Vevers had written to them querying their arrangement with Lumiere on what Humphreys described as a 'technicality'. This had apparently been too much for Lumiere, who according to the report had already spent over a million pounds on the project, and they had withdrawn. This had left Daltenreys high and dry and with no other option but to speak to their own lawyers regarding the legality of the BBC's actions.

The resultant legal action was reported by Joanna Bale in *The Times* a year later, on 15 February 1997. Daltenreys were said to be seeking a million pounds in compensation and £21 million in damages against the potential profits from the three film versions of *Doctor Who* that they had planned to make. They were also said to have paid £440,000 for the rights to make the films. In an interesting aside, Bale reported that the BBC claimed to know nothing about any legal action, but that if it was pursued they would 'vigorously contest it'.

As of writing, nothing more has been reported about the prospective legal action. Nor have any further proposals for *Doctor Who* feature films been made public, although this remains a distinct possibility for the future . . .

PART FOUR – THE TELEVISION MOVIE

8: Paul McGann: In His Own Words

ON PUBLICITY:

'We've never been Mr and Mrs Showbiz.'

Interviewed by Garry Jenkins for *TV Times* dated 25–31 May 1996.

'I'm fairly private, you know. I don't live in London. I don't do that "showbiz" stuff. I've got family. There's times when I don't want to get involved, and there's times when it's great to be associated with something . . . Fame is a double-edged sword.'

Speaking in Birmingham after a screening of *Withnail and I* on 22 March 1996.

ON TAKING OVER THE ROLE OF THE DOCTOR:

'When I saw the casting agent in Los Angeles I kept saying, "You've got the wrong fella." Other actors seemed to fit the image better, so I turned it down. I said, "This is daft, I can't do it." There was no pressure, it's easy to say no.'

Interviewed by Garry Jenkins for *TV Times* dated 25–31 May 1996.

'Taking on such a key role hasn't really sunk in yet. It is just beginning to dawn on me what all this means. Sylvester McCoy is a friend so he's told me everything I need to know. I loved *Doctor Who* as a kid. William Hartnell used to terrify me. My favourite villain was the Yeti but the Daleks never did it for me – they couldn't run upstairs.

'This film will be loyal to the spirit of past series, but will find fresh appeal too.'

Speaking at a press launch on 10 January 1996.

'I was on the *News at 10*! My mum was ringing me up saying, "You're on tonight!" It's like being an ambassador. That's what it feels like for a Brit. It's an honour, but a responsibility as well, which is the part that's beginning to dawn on me.'

Interviewed by Frank Garcia for *Starlog* dated June 1996.

'There was a style to the Doctor that, quite honestly, I didn't think I could live up to. Some of the skills were almost vaudevillian. It was sort of that indoor scarf-wearing, eccentric kind of thing. It wasn't me.'

Interviewed by Mark Nollinger for *TV Guide* dated May 11–17 1996.

'In the past, the Doctors have been rather kooky, manic and zany. I am not a kooky person. When Philip [Segal] initially offered me the role, I said to myself, "What is this person thinking! I'm all wrong for this part." '

Interviewed by Lou Anders for *Sci-Fi Universe* dated December 1996.

'I've signed a contract. I can't go anywhere. I am him. I am Who. He is me.'

Interviewed by Christy Slewinski for the *New York Daily News* dated 14 May 1996.

'I knew I'd have an effect on lots of people, and especially on children. It is a responsibility. But I thought that if I was going to do telly, I may as well do the biggest telly. And there's no doubt the biggest telly is *Doctor Who*.'

Interviewed by Gary Gillatt in 1996 for *Doctor Who Magazine* No. 238.

'It's like a top posting. It's like being the ambassador to the US or something. It's like getting a mega-top job. The Beeb's equivalent of "our man overseas" or something. I'm just realising the size of the job.'

Speaking on the video *Bidding Adieu* produced by BBV and released in 1996.

ON THE EIGHTH DOCTOR'S CHARACTER:

'He's a bit clean, isn't he, old Doctor Who? There's gonna be some changes . . . I might put that out on the internet – "There's gonna be some changes . . ." '

Speaking in Birmingham after a screening of *Withnail and I* on 22 March 1996.

'There are elements like the jelly babies. There are little bits that have been carried over that have survived. I can't help thinking of Patrick Troughton or Bill Hartnell, but certainly, I'm doing it *my* way. That's easy. It's the only way I *can* do it.'

Interviewed by Frank Garcia for *Starlog* dated June 1996.

'I have been looking for something more edgy. It's like the vampire. You can't have hung around for three hundred years and not feel kind of bitter. There are darker elements to it.'

Interviewed by Garry Jenkins for *The Times Magazine* dated 25 May 1996.

'Playing the Doctor has been strange, trying to find the right level. I spend half of the film not knowing who I am, so the character's not even there. It's a learning process for me. I'd like to do more so I can get my teeth into it, and work with the Doctor.'

Interviewed by Gary Gillatt in 1996 for *Doctor Who Magazine* No. 237.

'Being British and having grown up in Britain you couldn't see past . . . the character as he's been represented – that collective popular understanding of what the Doctor is like. So not only was I not convinced that I could hack it, I also couldn't see how they could make it seem remotely interesting for me. I think it was because the names that were being bandied round, pop stars and celebrities rather than actors, created a certain impression about the type of person who would be playing the Doctor. I didn't see that I could fit in with the expectation that a known eccentric should play the part. Much as I loved *Doctor Who* as a kid, I felt I could no sooner play him than I could play, say, Prince Charles. As I said, it's just not what I do.'

Interviewed by Gary Gillatt in 1996 for *Doctor Who Magazine* No. 238.

'What'll I bring to the part? Youth. Glamour. I was going to say "Scouseness", but I'm following in a long line of Scouse Doctor Whos, because Tom Baker's one, isn't he? I shall bring my usual thing. I just do my thing, whatever it is I do.'

Interviewed by Mark Gatiss in 1996 for *Starburst* Special #28.

ON KISSING GRACE:

'There are kisses and kisses. There are kisses that are innocently meant. He doesn't kiss her by mistake. But it is not licentiousness.'

Interviewed by Garry Jenkins in 1996 for *TV Zone* Issue 78.

'I kept my lips together when I kissed Daphne [Ashbrook] because I didn't want the love scenes to be too sexy. It is the first time the Doctor has been seen kissing and I didn't want to do anything that might upset a family audience.'

Interviewed by Shoba Vazirani for the *Sun* dated 25 May 1996.

'All innocently meant, though, you see . . . It's an American kiss, it's not a European one . . . no tonsil-tickling.'

Speaking on the video *Bidding Adieu* produced by BBV and released in 1996.

'It's a magic moment.'

Interviewed by Garry Jenkins for *Inside TV* dated 25–31 May 1996.

'This has been a sore point, hasn't it? I wasn't aware actually that there had never been a . . . that there was never a . . . I mean . . . has the Doctor never had a snog? . . . So is it going to get the fans' backs up?'

Interviewed by Gary Gillatt in 1996 for *Doctor Who Magazine* No. 238.

ON THE AMERICANISATION OF *DOCTOR WHO*:

'We have got mad chases on police bikes – why not? We have had gunfights at the OK Corral in *Doctor Who* before. Who says we can't have *The Streets of San Francisco*?'

Interviewed by Garry Jenkins for *The Times Magazine* dated 25 May 1996.

'This is going off in a new direction. If it goes to a series, I don't know what I'll do, really. It depends whether I've got the bottle to just go with it, embrace it. . . . Given that it's pitched deliberately as North American, the remnants of the quintessential Britishness of it will have to remain because they regard that as commercial.'

Interviewed by Mark Gatiss in 1996 for *Starburst* Issue 214.

ON FANDOM AND ATTENDING CONVENTIONS:

'The thought of me going anywhere near a convention at the moment makes my flesh creep! I know I'm going to have to. I'm going to get collared at some point, but I want to die when I think about it. Obviously it comes with the job. I can't run and hide forever. Mind you, I can always send one of my brothers . . .'

Interviewed by Mark Gatiss in 1996 for *Starburst* Special #28.

'It fills me *with absolute dread*, to be honest with you. I know I'll do it. I just know I'll end up doing it at least once, because I like to scare myself. That's very Catholic. I know McCoy does the circuit. But he's very gifted. He can simply stand on a stage and entertain two thousand people for an hour. I'm nervous – the thought of standing there – I won't even do the theatre for the same reason. I'm too scared. I suggested to McCoy that I go along with him in disguise, incognito, to see what it's like and he said there's no such thing anymore. He said, "You would be eaten alive! They can smell you! You don't stand a chance!" '

Interviewed by Frank Garcia for *Starlog* dated June 1996.

'The fans are very understanding. I've been very pleased and surprised to find that the real fans, the people from the magazine and stuff, have the right amount of "tongue-in-cheekness" about it. It's great 'cause they love it and they're into it, but it's only a game – they're not going to put someone's nose out of joint! They seem to realise that if I don't want to do something, I won't do it. And recognising that is generally the best way to deal with me. I'm the kid that says "no" to something for ages then eventually knocks on the door and says, "Well actually, can I join in?" – y'know? I'll do it in my own time though.'

Interviewed by Simon J. Gerard in 1996 for *Doctor Who Magazine* No. 246.

ON FAN REACTION:

'Sylvester McCoy put it well when he told me that I was basically on a hiding to nothing. He said that some people would love me and some people would hate me, but everyone has their own views of what the Doctor should be like and you can't please all of them. He told me I can't really win but I can't really fail either.'

Interviewed by Gary Gillatt in 1996 for *Doctor Who Magazine* No. 238.

'There's a lot of people that care a lot – for quite a big group I'm suddenly the star, there are thousands of people I'm suddenly really important to. But feelings do seem to run very high. People take it all deadly seriously, which is strange because it's actually quite a light and witty programme.'

Interviewed by Gary Gillatt in 1996 for *Doctor Who Magazine* No. 238.

ON THE FINISHED PRODUCT:

'I have a good feeling about it. But who knows, who knows?'

Interviewed by Garry Jenkins in 1996 for *TV Zone* Issue 78.

'When I saw the finished film, I thought it looked amazing. It looks like a major movie.'

Interviewed by John Millar for the *Daily Record* dated 25 May 1996.

'The ratings will be what we're judged by, but the future of the series also seems to be contingent on whether the "big cheeses" like it – that's the impression I get. We've been getting good feedback, though; we've been receiving flowers from Hollywood every day, so we must be doing something right. We're getting a good vibe, and we're having a laugh doing it.'

Interviewed by Gary Gillatt in 1996 for *Doctor Who Magazine* No. 237.

ON THE FUTURE:

'I'll stay with it. I've got to. I've signed a piece of paper that says I will'

Interviewed by Frank Garcia for *Starlog* dated June 1996.

'Even if it doesn't go any further and I end up being the George Lazenby of the Time Lords, I'll have had a good time. And I'll still get asked to the *Doctor Who* conventions.'

Interviewed by John Millar for the *Daily Record* dated 25 May 1996.

'Well, frankly, it'll be great if it takes off, because I'll be offered more work. That's the first consideration – I won't be sitting on my arse as much as I used to. As for the type of work . . . I don't know, it's hard to say . . . I'm not conditioned to think that far ahead. I go out of my mind if I try to do that.'

Interviewed by Gary Gillatt in 1996 for *Doctor Who Magazine* No. 238.

'The situation is that we're doing a TV movie but putatively it's a pilot and it might go to a series. But the fact is that the people who run the series are another department altogether. So who knows? If it was all under the same roof then probably they'd know by now that it was going to go [to a series] and things would be a lot clearer. What's going to be happening in twelve months . . . who knows? It might not go at all. The chances are dead against it, in fact.'

Speaking on the video *Bidding Adieu* produced by BBV and released in 1996.

9: The Eighth Doctor

It was always the intention of executive producer Philip David Segal to introduce an eighth Doctor in the television movie; no serious consideration was ever given to featuring the seventh Doctor in anything other than a brief appearance leading up to a regeneration. Interviewed exclusively for this book, Segal recalled the qualities that he had been looking for in the new Doctor:

'I don't think my perception ever really changed. I knew the qualities that he had to have. Looking at the series itself, and even at the information gleaned from the books that have been written about it, you can see that a good proportion of what was established with the previous Doctors was stuff that the actors themselves brought to the role. So all we could really do to influence that was to find someone whose appearance and demeanour gave us indications that externally they had the stuff to give us what they might have internally.

'Obviously humour and a dark side and a sort of childlike behaviour along with some alien-like qualities are all important parts of the mixture.

'It influenced the casting in a certain way. I wasn't trying to do anything that I thought was so brilliant that everyone would say it was a work of genius. All I wanted to do was to find somebody who fitted the shoes, so to speak, because whether you like it or not, if you try to go in a direction that moves a long way away from the spirit of who this character is then I think you're actually damaging the fabric of the franchise. So it wasn't so much that I could bring a unique perspective to this; that wasn't my intention at all. I never felt that I was doing this because I was the one who understood *Doctor Who* better than anyone else in the world. I never felt that way at all. But I was the one who was the keeper of the keys, so I had the opportunity to keep it going, and given that that was an enormous task I tried to do things that were aesthetically pleasing to me and creatively responsible for the franchise.

'The casting was my responsibility, but I had bosses. I couldn't just wave my wand and have whoever I wanted. Paul McGann was always my first choice, but he joined the project late and there was a reason for that; it was my responsibility to go out into the field, as it were.'

McGann himself was reluctant to become associated with the project, and in fact initially declined, unable to see himself in the role as it was popularly presented in the media as an outrageously costumed eccentric. In the end, however, he was won over.

Also instrumental in shaping the eighth Doctor's character was writer Matthew Jacobs. 'He had very strong opinions about what the Doctor should and should not be,' acknowledged Segal. 'There was a lot of Matthew's influence in the material . . . I specified areas that I felt were very important for us to touch on and that I felt were central to the Doctor's world, and Matthew really ran with it. We had numerous conversations about things that we could and could not touch on. He was terrific in that he was like a sponge: once he got an idea of the direction I wanted to go, he was very good at picking up the ball and taking it on to the next step. There's very much his imprint on the material. I think he did quite a good job, all things considered.

'When Paul was cast, the thing took on a life of its own. Paul brought his own unique qualities to the role. The first time I saw him on set in his costume it was pretty uncanny. There was one moment where I didn't think he ever wasn't the Doctor. Once he settled down, I think he felt the same way. I don't know what the general perception was from the audience, but I believe it was fairly positive.'

Any attempt to evaluate the eighth Doctor's character on the basis of just a single adventure is inevitably fraught with difficulty. (To realise this, one need only consider how skewed an assessment would be gained from considering in isolation the debut story of each of the other Doctors.) Some fan commentators have attempted to do so, however, and a particularly perceptive summation was made by Lance Parkin in *Matrix* Issue 53 dated autumn 1996: 'The eighth Doctor acts impulsively, without planning. He lacks arrogance, instead demonstrating child-like qualities of wonder and boundless energy. Everything is done in earnest, with a passion. He fixes on things and is capable of brilliant improvisation.'

As the Doctor himself says to Grace in the movie: 'I can't make your dream come true for ever, but I can make it come true today.'

10: Production Development

It was in 1994 that Philip David Segal, an Englishman working as head of television production at Stephen Spielberg's Amblin company in the USA, was granted by BBC Enterprises the rights to make a new series of *Doctor Who*. This was an ambition that he had been pursuing ever since the BBC stopped producing the series in 1989, as he explained:

'I wanted *Doctor Who* back. And that took a long time. Simply put, my aim was to rebuild the franchise; that was the object of the exercise, to bring it back. There was a period of time at the BBC where there was a real willingness to do that, so I took advantage of that, and that's essentially how we got *Doctor Who* back.

'That intensified and really became real in 1993; that was when it really became real in terms of actually negotiating a deal with the BBC and wanting to move forward.'

Segal's intention was always to make a television series rather than a feature film, so the fact that the BBC had already granted the *Doctor Who* film rights to the group now known as Daltenreys (see Chapter 7) presented no obstacle. 'We had no interest in making a feature film,' he confirmed. 'That was always the case. I made it very clear from the very beginning that I didn't think that it should be relaunched as a feature film; that there was still a lot of work that had to be done in terms of television; but that ultimately one day it could become the basis of a film . . . We had some dialogue with Daltenreys but nothing that really meant anything significant to me. The sad thing about it is that you don't like to see anyone spend the kind of money they did and not get anywhere, which they did. I feel bad for them in that regard. But it had no bearing on what I was doing.'

The project was initially envisaged as a three-way co-production between BBC Enterprises, Amblin and Universal Television in the USA. Writer John Leekley was commissioned by Segal to put together a 'series bible' – a detailed document outlining, partly for the benefit of potential purchasers, the concept and its intended treatment – and the script for a movie-length pilot episode. The bible turned out to be a lavish affair. Printed on parchment paper and bound in a real-leather cover embossed with the Seal of Rassilon, it purported to be written by Lord Borusa and charted the history and activities of a Time Lord known as the Doctor. By way of illustration, several new pieces of black-and-white artwork were used (including a sequence of drawings showing some redesigned 'spider' Daleks) along with more familiar (to *Doctor Who* fans) images intended to give an idea of what the characters and settings might look like. To illustrate the section on the Master, for example, Segal used a photograph of Michael Jayston as the Valeyard from *The Trial of a Time Lord*, simply because his flowing robes and dramatic appearance matched the style and vision he and Leekley had of the Master. Similarly, to depict an effective alien being, an image was taken from the cover of one of Virgin Publishing's New Adventures novels, *Birthright* by Nigel Robinson.

Leekley's script for the pilot movie featured the Daleks, Davros and the Master in a story set partly on the Doctor's home planet Gallifrey. Entitled simply *Doctor Who* (although the writer later suggested that *Fathers and Brothers* would have made a good subtitle), it was completed in September 1994 but ultimately failed to find favour. Robert de Laurentis was then commissioned to provide a replacement; his attempt, entitled *Dr Who?*, was completed in December 1994. Segal was at this time attempting to sell the series in the US to the Fox television network, although when problems arose in his negotiations with them he also entered into discussions with a number of other networks. 'Fox didn't decline it,' he explains. 'There was a situation that happened where there was a distinct split between Amblin and Universal that caused a derailment of the project. It wasn't Fox's fault. But the situation sort of reorganised itself when an executive called Trevor Walton, who is English, came to Fox. We had had serious offers from CBS at that time as well, although they ultimately declined.'

Walton was in Fox's made-for-television movie division, which meant that the project was now seen primarily in that light. 'In our eyes it was still a pilot for a series,' commented Segal, 'but it was produced through the movie division of Fox and not the TV division. It's not unusual, though, for a two-hour movie to be made by the movie division and still end up being treated as a pilot; it's standard in the States. In this situation you would be canny enough to produce it to look like and feel like and smell like a pilot, so that it had enough story to satisfy a two-hour movie audience but at the same time had enough strings so that you could see the character returning. So there were deliberate attempts on our part to package the movie in that way, to give us the basis for hopefully a good series.'

At the Gallifrey convention in Los Angeles in February 1995, Segal showed attendees a video featuring some test images of a new computer-generated title sequence (very similar in style to the one used during the fourth Doctor's era) and of the redesigned spider-like Daleks. He also gave a short slide show displaying some early set and prop ideas prepared by one of the movie's production artists.

Segal had always been keen that his version of *Doctor Who* should be true to the spirit of the original, and he found that Walton was much more sympathetic towards this idea than had been his colleagues in Fox's TV division. Walton, for instance, agreed with him that the movie should if possible be explicitly linked to the continuity of the BBC series by opening with Sylvester McCoy's Doctor and leading up to a regeneration, whereas the TV division executives had wanted it to stand completely apart from what had gone before, to the extent that Segal had considered having dialogue included in the script indicating that it took place in a parallel universe (drawing inspiration from an idea presented in the third Doctor story *Inferno*). A new script was thus required and, although the established series writer Terrance Dicks was on the short list of potential writers, it was eventually commissioned from Matthew Jacobs, another Englishman who already had experience of working in American as well as UK network television.

'It was actually Trevor Walton who had worked with Matthew and asked us to consider him and meet him,' noted Segal. 'The networks rarely make demands over things like that. Usually they will allow you to make a case for a particular writer. However, there were reasons why Matthew made sense to me. When I sat and talked with him at Amblin it turned out that his grandfather had been an actor in the Wyatt Earp episode of *Doctor Who* [Season 3's *The Gunfighters*, in which Anthony Jacobs played Doc Holliday]. His relationship with his father had been an incredibly rocky one, and when his father had eventually died they had not been reconciled, so there was this real emotional kind of bridge that this script was going to build for him. And I liked his writing style. He's a very colourful individual and brought a lot of colour and passion to the project, so I was very pleased indeed with the choice.'

Jacobs started working on his script around April 1995, and the first complete draft was dated 18 July. Segal recalled the factors that had influenced its development:

'It was a pretty fast track once we got going. There were a couple of glitches in the story as we went, though. Some that I thought were good changes and some that I was disappointed with. Ultimately there was more than one voice in that script, so that's the struggle that I had.

'We knew that the Doctor had to have a companion, simply from the mechanics of the franchise. The problem with the Doctor is that unless he has someone to ask what he's doing or thinking, the audience never gets to know what he's doing or thinking. That's just the flaw of the process.

'I think we first set about trying to think where the location should be. We knew it had to be in the United States for identification reasons, but we also wanted it to be a place that had some universal awareness of it. Most people know of San Francisco and it's my favourite city in America. The last place I wanted it to be was Los Angeles; it would have felt just so clichéd for some reason. San Francisco didn't seem clichéd. It had a sort of mystique to it that Los Angeles didn't have. It didn't hurt that Matthew lived in San Francisco. We started to formulate the story out of this and it changed dramatically as we went along. Matthew's first impressions had a lot more emotionality for Chang Lee than we ultimately ended up with.

'The hospital thing was something that we were also playing around with. We didn't get all the mileage out of that really.

'There were several companies that needed specific things, and there was definitely a distinct difference between Fox's need for something with an adult appeal and the familiar perception of *Doctor Who* as a family or children's show. The end product was not necessarily what the BBC wanted, but how far they were prepared to go. They were extremely collaborative with me at various points. Alan Yentob was, and is in my opinion today, this project's best friend. That's just a reality from my eyes. This is the man who, through thick and thin, has supported this project and who still believes in *Doctor Who* as a franchise. He's in a very difficult position. One's philosophy has to be to let management manage, so if you hire someone to do a job you have to stay out of their way and let them do it; he can make suggestions, but he really has to let people manage.'

Amblin (where Segal had earlier been given a co-executive producer in the person of fellow Englishman Peter Wagg) dropped out of the picture in 1995 after Spielberg joined forces with former Disney executive Jeffrey Katzenberg and music mogul David Geffen in a new company called Dreamworks SKG. Segal left the company in September and went on to produce the movie independently as a joint venture between the BBC (80 per cent of whose financial input came from BBC Worldwide, as BBC Enterprises had now been renamed, and 20 per cent from BBC television) and Universal. Fox also had a financial input into the movie.

'The production office was located in the Spelling complex. We leased out some space in Barnerby, just outside Vancouver. That was where the stages were. Locations were in and around Vancouver proper. The production itself was housed in Burnaby, and I had an office there. During preproduction I was moving backwards and forwards between Los Angeles, Vancouver and London. I also spent some time in New York doing casting. But I worked out of my office on the Paramount lot.

'Universal gave me a boss by the name of Alex Beaton. This was because I was somewhat alienated from the studio – I wasn't somebody they had a tremendous love affair with, let's put it that way – and they wanted to make sure their interests were protected. But Alex and I got on very well. His job was basically to manage the money. He never interfered creatively at all with the production – nobody did: I had the final say in all creative matters – but when it came to the financial side of things, and I fought for what I wanted, I won some battles and I lost some battles.

'Then there was a producer by the name of Peter Ware, who basically managed the physical production. There was also a unit production manager called Fran Rosati. He was a fabulous guy. It was his below-the-line crew that worked on the movie.

'Richard Hudolin was the production designer, and was first-class. He and I got on like a house on fire. I told him exactly what I wanted to do and it was done.

'The amazing thing about a lot of these people is that they immediately went out and got every *Doctor Who* book that existed and looked at everything that had been done in the past. So many of them were fans. There was a real passion to get everything right, and sometimes they'd go overboard. The funny thing about it of course is that as you dip into *Doctor Who* you're taking from thirty years of mythology. It's interesting to see people's reactions when you take material from different eras, mixing them up and putting them all in one thing. Some fans look at you and say, "You can't do that!" I thought it was wonderful to take from the cupboard of mythology and just paint a new picture. That's what we did with this production to a certain extent. We painted details throughout it that gave you a taste of the traditions of the show.

'Jo Wright from the BBC was ultimately given the title of executive producer in the end credits; she was the BBC's person.

'Each of the organisations involved had to have its own person; that's the reality of life. Trevor from Fox never got a credit; American network executives don't get credits on movies. He was the big boss. He was the one looking over scripts. I must say he was very supportive of me in the process. What happens is that once a network commits to a project, it goes into a slot and the clock ticks. The pressure is to deliver that project for that timeslot, because there's nothing else to fill it; they don't double develop and double produce. So once *Doctor Who* had been given a firm airdate, which we knew at the start was 14 May 1996, we were on a runaway train. Five months to make it with no excuses. Trevor's job became much more difficult, because the studio wanted to cut corners to save money, it had other agendas; the BBC had its own agenda; and BBC Worldwide had its own agenda – although the truth of the matter is that it was not managing anything.'

The completed movie was delivered to Fox about a week before it premiered. It was promoted with the tag line 'He's Back

– And It's About Time' and US newspaper critics gave it an almost universally positive reception. In ratings terms, however, the movie ultimately underperformed. This was partly due to the fact that it was up against some very strong competition from the other networks, including a much-anticipated episode of the comedy series *Roseanne* in which the title character's husband, played by John Goodman, suffers a heart attack. In Segal's view, however, there were other underlying political reasons why it did less well than it might have:

'When you really go into the mechanics of why *Doctor Who* didn't get a bigger audience, that would require a two-hour dissertation on who the Fox network actually are, who their station groups are, what their demographic audience is . . .

'If you had put that same movie on a different network, at a different time, with different promotion, away from the sweeps – which is programming designed to hype the network – you may or may not have had a different result. I can't sit here and say to you, "Oh my show would have done a twenty share anywhere else." I don't know that. There may truly have been some problems with the female appeal of the show, the audience awareness of *Doctor Who*, the story itself. There may have been a lot of things working against us.'

In the UK the movie did much better, winning very good ratings and generally enthusiastic audience feedback. (See Chapter 12 for further details.) There were over 100,000 copies sold of the BBC's video release of the production, some 55,000 copies of Gary Russell's novelisation and even some 15,000 copies of the script book. Total worldwide sales of the video release were in excess of 150,000 copies. Universal retained an option on *Doctor Who* until the end of 1997, but in the event did not take it up.

'Several things happened that made it very clear that it wasn't going to be a series,' reflected Segal, 'least of which was the fact that it underperformed. I was also very tired – eighteen hour days, not seeing your family, the stress and the politics, it does take it out of you. There was another regime change at Fox; there were regime changes all the time at the BBC. The movie itself happened for very specific reasons; it wasn't just because I pushed hard enough, there were other reasons, and we got caught up in the tidal wave. All the fans could really see was that it was coming back, but the truth on the inside was that it was a limited-time offer – get it now while it's available. But that's another story.'

Even though the movie did not, in the end, lead on to the hoped-for series, Segal was well satisfied with the end product:

'My job as producer is to bring all the elements together. I think it's ultimately a mistake to try to impose your will on people. That's a dangerous thing to do. I think the object of the exercise is to bring together the best people you can get hold of and give them the room and the opportunity to be the best that they can be. That's something that I take a lot of pride in. I'm very strong when it comes to what I want and don't want, but I also feel that once I've had my two cents' worth, it's very important to take two giant steps back and let people do their jobs. If I feel that the wheels are coming off, then I'm quite happy to jump in and to try and fix that.

'I feel that what you saw there was a chorus of very talented people who came together and made something very special, in my opinion. For all its faults and for all the problems and things like that I think we did a damn good job given the rules that we had to play by. I feel that everyone did the best that they could do and I'm certainly very proud of it.'

As for the future, Segal asserts: 'I really believe that *Doctor Who* will be back again. I really do. Whether it's me or someone else who makes it. You can't kill *Doctor Who*. It will never die.'

11: Rewriting the Myth

Throughout *Doctor Who*'s history, each successive change in the series' behind-the-scenes team led to a development of its style and content – and of its mythology. Never was this more true than of the 1996 television movie.

The action opens with a seventh Doctor who is visibly older than when last seen. He also seems to have dramatically reconfigured his TARDIS interior, which now has a very Gothic,

'Wellsian' look to it – appropriately enough, given that he is seen reading a copy of Wells's *The Time Machine*. The possibility of such reconfiguration had been well established in earlier stories – some of which, including Season 15's *The Invasion of Time* and Season 19's *Castrovalva*, had made explicit reference to it – but the change seen here is the most radical to date. Even more novel is the revelation that the ship contains in its cloister room an Eye of Harmony. Season 14's *The Deadly Assassin* had suggested that there was just a single Eye of Harmony, the source of all the Time Lords' power, located on Gallifrey; now it seems that every TARDIS must contain a fragment of the Eye. This does make some sort of sense, as it is difficult to see how otherwise the power from a central source could reach the ships, given that they can go anywhere in space and time.

The Eye as seen in the television movie appears to have many properties and functions aside from simply powering the TARDIS. It is somehow connected to the Doctor himself, and can 'see' what he sees. It can also project images of his earlier incarnations and, when correctly set up, can actually transfer one Time Lord's remaining lives to another (as the Master attempts to do here). Perhaps the strangest idea is that it can actually swallow the Master whole, a process that apparently gives the TARDIS 'indigestion'. Also remarkable is the fact that it is able to restore life to both Grace and Chang Lee after the Master has killed them. This could perhaps be viewed as a result of the TARDIS moving back in time to the point before the Eye destroyed the Earth, although an alternative explanation might be that it stored the life essence of the Doctors' two friends when they died and then returned it to them once time had resumed its normal course. The Doctor's own observation is that the TARDIS is sentimental.

The Doctor's regeneration on this occasion is a delayed reaction to his being shot and actually dying on the operating table, his alien metabolism adversely affected by the anaesthetic and by Grace's manipulation of a heart probe. Following the regeneration, the new Doctor goes through the customary period of confusion before recovering fully.

One of the most talked-about aspects of the television movie is its revelation that the Doctor is half human. This, however, ties in quite well with what has gone before. For one thing, it helps to explain why the Doctor has always seemed to have such an affinity for the Earth and its indigenous people (the Doctor talks of seeing Gallifreyan skies with his father, which perhaps suggests that it was his mother who was human, although this is never explicitly stated). It could also explain why his granddaughter Susan wanted to attend school in England. In addition, it provides possible answers to the questions raised about the Doctor's identity in the series' twenty-fifth and twenty-sixth seasons – including the suggestion that he was more than just a Time Lord – and how he managed to return to Earth at the end of *Survival* (as discussed in Chapter 4).

Another fact revealed in the movie is that when a Time Lord reaches the end of his regenerative cycle he can apparently change species. The Master has become (whether or not by his own choice is left unclear) a reptilian snakelike creature. With this change he has acquired the power to change form; to spit a burning venom that can immobilise the victim; and to possess those 'marked' with the venom.

There is arguably only one major aspect of the movie's plot that it is difficult to reconcile with what has gone before. This is the aforementioned idea of the TARDIS travelling back in time to a point before the Eye of Harmony was opened so as to prevent the disaster precipitated by the Master. This flies in the face of many previous assertions made by the Doctor about his being unable to change the course of history – as, for example, when his companion Adric was killed at the end of Season 18's *Earthshock* – and undermines the whole basis of the series' format by raising the question why he does not always simply travel back in time to thwart all his adversaries' schemes before they have even got off the drawing board.

It is a pity that this one less than satisfactory aspect marred what was otherwise an admirable production from the point of view of the use and development of *Doctor Who* mythology.

PART FIVE – SELLING THE DOCTOR

12: Selling the Doctor

Media

by Ian Wheeler

Doctor Who has always been considered newsworthy by the British media, who over the years have expressed both love and hatred for the series – often according to the whims or prejudices of the particular journalist responsible. The Sylvester McCoy era was no exception, and in fact proved to be perhaps the most controversial period of *Doctor Who*'s history as far as press reaction was concerned. In 1985, during Colin Baker's time as the Doctor, the tabloid newspapers had campaigned to save the series when it appeared that it was going to be axed. By 1987, it was clear that things had changed and that the seventh Doctor was going to get a somewhat rockier ride.

On 28 February 1987, the *Sun* was the first to report the identity of the seventh Doctor. Under the headline NEW DOCTOR WHO IS THE UNKNOWN McCOY, Charles Catchpole wrote: 'A zany Scot who used to make a living by stuffing ferrets down his trousers is the new Doctor Who.' The paper referred to McCoy as 'a shock choice', adding that other hopefuls had included former companion actor Frazer Hines (who had, in fact, never been under consideration).

The *Sun*'s exclusive was followed by reports in other papers on 3 March (an announcement of the new Doctor's identity having been made on the television news the day before). A number were quick to point out McCoy's lack of celebrity status but, more positively, some also reported that the actor had been awarded a three-year contract. In *Today*, McCoy was quoted as saying: 'I might not be all that well-known but that's going to change. People have been telling me for years that I'd be perfect to play Doctor Who and I'm going to prove them right.'

The launch of the new Doctor was somewhat overshadowed by the news at the end of March that one of his predecessors, Patrick Troughton, had died following a heart attack at a *Doctor Who* convention in the USA.

The first reports of the new season came at the beginning of April, when a modest number of papers featured the new Doctor in costume on location for *Time and the Rani*. Details were sparse, with particular emphasis being given to the fact that Kate O'Mara was also appearing in the story. A more informative item on the making of the story was however to be seen on the BBC's *Breakfast Time* programme on 5 May. Other TV coverage of the series during this period included items about the location recording of *Delta and the Bannermen* on BBC Wales on 31 July and on BBC1's *But First This . . .* on 31 August.

It was in September, with the 24th season now beginning on BBC1, that the new Doctor really began to make his presence felt. The *Star* promised that the new-look show would be 'the glossiest ever', going 'flat out for fun' with stars such as popular comedy actor Richard Briers. Meanwhile, the 5–11 September edition of the BBC's listings magazine *Radio Times* featured the seventh Doctor in full colour on page three with an additional article included as part of the 'John Craven's Back Pages' feature.

The reviews for *Time and the Rani* proved to be less enthusiastic than the pre-publicity. McCoy was nominated 'Wally of the Week' in the *Daily Express* and described as being 'bland' and 'a joke' in the *Sunday Post*. Paul Mount, television reviewer for the monthly science-fiction magazine *Starburst*, also expressed dislike for the new series but at least admitted to McCoy being 'convincing in a way that neither Peter Davison or Colin Baker ever were'.

October began with the *Sun* reporting that the BBC had axed *Doctor Who* after 24 years. This 'exclusive' went on to say that the show was losing viewers every week and that the current series would be the last. Days later, the *Sun* was claiming to have saved the show, adding that a new movie produced by Coast-to-Coast was set to appear in November 1988.

At the end of October, a more encouraging piece appeared in the *Daily Mirror*. The article focused on the appearance of comedian Ken Dodd and actor Don Henderson in Malcolm Kohll's *Delta and the Bannermen*. According to the report, *Coronation Street* had failed to kill off the Doctor with the Time Lord attracting 'an audience of more than five million'.

The floodgates really opened in November, the month of the series' twenty-fourth anniversary. McCoy gave an interview to the *Daily Express* during which he was quoted as saying: 'I believe the Doctor is still valid in the *Star Wars* generation.' The week after, the *Star* printed a disturbing article with the headline WHO'S A LOAD OF RUBBISH? Fans were said to be dissatisfied with the series and were calling for producer John Nathan-Turner to be sacked. This was prompted by campaigning reports in the fanzine *DWB*, a source to which several newspapers turned for their more sensationalist coverage of the series.

Later the same month, the *Daily Telegraph*'s Charles Spencer reviewed *Dragonfire* Part One, and was generally supportive, referring to McCoy as 'an appealing Doctor with a genuine sense of wonder and a nice line in irony'. He was, however, not entirely without reservations and felt that the new Doctor could do with 'a little less whimsy and a shade more authority'.

Following *Dragonfire*'s spectacular climax in which the villain Kane melted on screen, the *Star* reported that angry mothers had phoned the BBC to complain about the sequence. The editor of *DWB*, Gary Levy, was quoted as saying that 'This new controversy will prove more damaging'.

'The Daleks are back!' was the very clear message carried by most of the national newspapers in the spring of 1988. 'Doctor

Who has defeated his greatest enemy – former BBC1 chief Michael Grade,' reported the *Daily Express*, 'and when he returns to BBC screens in the autumn, Doctor Who will take on his other deadly foe – the Daleks'. And according to the *Sun* on the same day, 'The Daleks are as evil as ever, but they have swapped their dull grey metal jackets for a gold and white livery.'

A colour article in the *Radio Times* heralded the return of the Daleks as part of BBC1's autumn season: 'Those evil, heartless, cruel, diabolical Daleks are back – and the latest Doctor Who is rather pleased about it!' John Davies's full-page feature included comments from Sylvester McCoy, John Nathan-Turner and writer Ben Aaronovitch. Each had his own opinion on the secret of the Daleks' appeal, with Aaronovitch commenting that 'They are beings within machines rather than just machines. If they were just robots, they'd be boring.'

Following some glowing reviews of *Remembrance of the Daleks* Part One, *Doctor Who* was the subject of an in-depth critique in the *Listener* magazine. 'Sylvester McCoy, the new and promising Doctor,' wrote Mark Ball, 'faces the uphill grind of a series hopelessly locked in repetition, unable any longer to break out of its past.' A letter from Dr David M. Duckels in the 10 November edition suggested that 'Sylvester McCoy seems set to establish himself as a vintage Doctor.'

A more controversial piece appeared in the *News of the World* on 13 November. BERTIE BASSETT TAKES ON DOCTOR WHO was the headline following a protest from Bev Stokes, chairman of the confectionery manufacturers Bassett's, about the alleged similarity between the Kandy Man from *The Happiness Patrol* and the company's famous marketing character, Bertie. 'We would like the programme to do something to restore Bertie's honour,' Stokes commented. The Kandy Man's 'death' in Part Three of the story brought the matter to a quiet close.

The week of *Doctor Who*'s twenty-fifth anniversary saw the beginning in the *Radio Times* of a new feature called 'My Kind of Day'. McCoy was the subject of the first piece and was shown sitting in a tree house. As the year drew to a close, the *Weekend*

Guardian's reference to McCoy as 'one of the best Doctors yet' boded well for the venerable Time Lord in 1989.

In May 1989, the *News of the World* asked WHO'S THAT EVIL PARSON? referring to Nicholas Parsons's guest appearance in *The Curse of Fenric*. The actor commented that McCoy had 'been a joy to work with' and that he had 'never had so much fun in [his] life'. Rather less fun was had by Sophie Aldred in June when, as reported by the press, she was nearly killed in a water tank accident during studio recording for *Battlefield*.

The beginning of the twenty-sixth season in September was met with minimal press coverage and even the *Radio Times*, once the show's greatest supporter, let the side down by running only a brief black-and-white article about Ace on the children's page. *TV Guide* was far more generous, featuring McCoy on its front cover and a two-page report, WHAT'S UP DOC?, from the location of *Survival*.

Ever a creature of habit, the *Sun* again claimed that *Doctor Who* had been axed on 21 October. Unfortunately, this time, it was true. 1989 came to a close with the series' future uncertain but, according to the BBC, at least safe.

1990 began with the news, on 5 February in the *Daily Express*, that Sylvester McCoy and Sophie Aldred had had their contracts withdrawn, and that the odds were firmly against their returning to play the Doctor and Ace. The paper claimed that independent companies were bidding to produce the twenty-seventh season and that Dalek creator Terry Nation and Gerry Davis, co-creator of the Cybermen, were the favourites. Again these stories appear to have been inspired by reports in the fanzine *DWB*.

'Doctor Who could be in for a sex change,' suggested the *News of the World* on 26 August. Ex-companion Mary Tamm, who had been the first Romana during the Tom Baker years, was quoted as saying that she would 'love to play the Doctor'.

An interview with McCoy was published by the *Daily Express* on 9 October under the heading DOCTOR WHO'S THE REAL McCOY – BY SYLVESTER. John Munro reported that McCoy had 'fought his way back to the top in theatre' after his 'high-flying career was brought down to Earth when the BBC axed the show' and added that 'when the BBC mandarins finally get round to launching a new series it's odds on that the flamboyant McCoy will be playing the good Doctor'.

As the years rolled by, there were to be a great number of speculative newspaper articles about *Doctor Who*'s future, many of them bizarre and almost all of them inaccurate. Actors David Hasselhoff, Eric Idle, Pamela Anderson and director Steven Spielberg were just some of the names that were linked with a mooted *Doctor Who* TV series or movie. Fans had to wait many years before concrete news about the series' future was finally to emerge.

The TV Movie

by Ian Wheeler

After years of speculation and many disappointments, the identity of the eighth Doctor was finally revealed to the world on 11 January 1996. All the major newspapers covered the story and reported that a television movie was in production. OUR MAN McGANN BEATS THE STARS TO BECOME NEW DOCTOR WHO declared the *Daily Express*, obviously delighted that the role had gone to a British actor rather than an American. Among the celebrities who it claimed had been considered for the part were Bill Cosby, Jack Nicholson and Alan Rickman, while the *Daily Star* reported that Simon Callow and the pop star Sting had both been in the running.

As the first new *Doctor Who* to be broadcast in over six years, the TV movie itself was understandably the subject of considerable media attention. For the first time in its history, *Doctor Who* had the honour of being featured on the front cover of the IPC-published listings magazine *TV Times* (which had at one time covered only ITV programmes). The magazine described McGann as 'the unlikeliest Time Lord – EVER!' and quoted him as saying that he wanted the Doctor to be 'a bit more edgy . . . a bit darker. It's also important to me that I have a hoot – and this *is* a hoot. I've got a good feeling about it now.' *Radio Times* also ran a *Doctor Who* cover and rewarded its readers with a free, sixteen-page *Doctor Who* souvenir booklet. In addition, there was the promise of a new comic strip based on the series, which would begin in the following issue. This was written by Gary Russell and drawn by Lee Sullivan.

Initial press excitement about the Doctor's return was counterbalanced by a distinct lack of enthusiasm once the movie had actually been transmitted. Reviews were mixed, to say the least. Max Davidson of the *Daily Mail* commented that the movie 'was like a bad memory of childhood. I thought this absurdly inflated character had achieved his final resting place as a line in a knock-knock joke. Seeing the TARDIS again, in a vulgar American reincarnation, was too depressing for words. Do we never grow up?' Others were more positive, and the *Daily Express*'s review by Maureen Paton was fairly typical: 'At last we have a grown up hi-tech *Doctor Who* in Paul McGann . . . Only a low-tech Luddite would miss the endearing amateurism of the old teatime serial format . . . The makers would be mad not to pursue the option of a series.' Matthew Bond of *The Times* would probably have shared this sentiment but felt that 'If the series is to return, it will need stronger scripts than this simplistic offering, which struggled to fill eighty-five minutes and laboured somewhat in its search for wit.'

The general public were also determined to have their say on the movie, and the letters page of *Radio Times* for the week beginning 15 June 1996 was packed with viewers' comments. 'Paul McGann's performance in the new *Doctor Who* film delighted me,' wrote Simon Harries of Dartford. 'He brought an exciting new intensity and intelligence to the character, while still reminding me of Tom Baker at his most "other-worldly" and Patrick Troughton at his most mixed up.' Georgina Scott of Derby was also taken by the new Doctor and claimed that the BBC had given her a 'universally acceptable new sex symbol' in the form of McGann. Sean Coleman of Scunthorpe was more critical. 'The BBC should be exterminated!' he wrote, concluding that the Corporation had 'sold our dear old Time Lord down the Mississippi'.

In the pages of the *Doctor Who* fan press, there was an equally wide range of comments. *Doctor Who* Appreciation Society (DWAS) member Peter Lewis was 'pleasantly surprised and impressed' by the movie, whereas *Doctor Who Magazine* reader Michael Dax found it to be 'a god-awful mess'. Perhaps the best summary was offered in the DWAS's *Celestial Toyroom* newsletter by editor Keith Hopkins, who considered the project to be 'a success . . . a qualified success perhaps, but a success nonetheless'. One way or another, the new movie had generated a huge amount of media and public interest and *Doctor Who* had once again demonstrated its unique ability to make an impact and refuse to go unnoticed.

Personal Appearances

by Ian Wheeler

Of all the actors to have played the Doctor, Sylvester McCoy was one of the keenest to promote and publicise the series. Many people received their first glimpse of the new Doctor on 2 March 1987, when he emerged from the TARDIS on the Monday edition of the children's magazine show *Blue Peter* and chatted with presenter Janet Ellis about his hopes for the role. He also appeared on BBC1's Saturday morning children's show *It's Wicked* on 30 May. When Season 24 began transmission, *Doctor Who* was featured on *Open Air*, the BBC's daytime television discussion programme. McCoy was present, along with companion actress Bonnie Langford and producer John Nathan-Turner, and early viewer reaction to the seventh Doctor seemed to be positive. As his tenure progressed, McCoy was also to be seen on the youngsters' Saturday morning show *Going Live* (in 1987, and again in 1988 for *Doctor Who*'s twenty-fifth anniversary), the *Children's Royal Variety Performance* and the 1988 *Tomorrow's World Christmas Quiz*. In 1989, he joined TV presenter Noel Edmonds and comedy actor Jeffrey Holland on *The Noel Edmonds Saturday Roadshow* and in November participated in the Children in Need telethon.

From late 1989 onward, with *Doctor Who* no longer in production, McCoy tended to avoid wearing his seventh Doctor costume for personal appearances. He did, however, relate a *Doctor Who* anecdote or two to presenter Bruce Forsyth on the ITV game show *You Bet!* in 1990, and briefly stepped back into character for a BBC schools programme, *Search Out Science*, which also saw the return of Sophie Aldred as Ace. (See Chapter 3 for further details.)

When the ill-fated satellite broadcaster BSB ran a whole weekend of *Doctor Who* episodes and other related material – another first for the series – McCoy was one of the large number of stars to be interviewed about his involvement with it. (See Chapter 7 for further details.)

In 1993, McCoy joined sixth Doctor Colin Baker and a Tractator (from the fifth Doctor story *Frontios*) on *This Morning*, and the following year he appeared with Baker, fifth Doctor Peter Davison and actors Tim Brooke-Taylor, Bill Oddie and Graeme Garden (otherwise known as the Goodies from the eponymous cult BBC series of the seventies), for an item on animals on *Good Morning with Anne and Nick*. McCoy was invariably happy to be seen on screen with his fellow Doctors, and good fun and humour were always evident on such occasions.

Perhaps the most unusual appearance for McCoy's Doctor was not on television, but in the pages of one of the nation's favourite children's comics. In the spring of 1988, he was featured in the 'Strange Hill School' comic strip in *The Dandy*, being pursued, rather appropriately, by hideous monsters.

Advertisers were also among those eager to utilise McCoy's talents. He played the Doctor in a television commercial for the *Radio Times* in which he claimed to like the travel section of the magazine. On the radio, meanwhile, he participated in a commercial for batteries, which saw the Doctor up against his old enemies, the Cybermen.

This brief summary has highlighted those personal appearances by McCoy that were primarily intended to publicise *Doctor Who* or had an interesting *Doctor Who* connection. It should be noted that throughout his time as the Doctor, and beyond, McCoy was much in demand as a celebrity in his own right. He was frequently to be seen on a variety of light-entertainment shows, his contributions ranging from being a mystery guest on the children's programme *Knock Knock* to appearing as a panellist on *The Holiday Quiz*.

Things changed dramatically when Paul McGann inherited the mantle of the Doctor in 1996. McGann was clearly a much more private person than McCoy and was unwilling to be associated with the role in terms of public appearances. In interviews, he expressed a reluctance to attend any kind of *Doctor Who* convention, claiming that he lacked McCoy's ability to get up and entertain an audience. Consequently the only appearance of the eighth Doctor in costume was in the television movie itself and in related press photocalls, and the only on-camera interviews McGann gave about the role were for the movie's 'electronic press kit', used by the Sci-Fi Channel among others to compile behind-the-scenes reports on the production, and the Bill Baggs-produced video documentary *Bidding Adieu*. It was the end of an era in more ways than one.

The Twenty-fifth Anniversary

by Ian Wheeler

Nineteen eighty-eight was a year of growing optimism for *Doctor Who* fans, and the series' twenty-fifth anniversary was celebrated in a quiet but enthusiastic manner. There was no special story reuniting old Doctors, as there had been for the tenth and twentieth anniversaries, but the Cybermen were brought back in the three-parter *Silver Nemesis* and, as the Cyber Leader actor and sometime writer David Banks remarked in his book *Cybermen*, 'It was thought . . . that the Cybermen would make it an appropriately Silver Anniversary.' The season opener *Remembrance of the Daleks* also contained nostalgic elements and included a return to the junkyard in Totter's Lane where the Doctor had begun his travels in the winter of 1963.

Production of *Silver Nemesis* was covered by a crew from the US television station New Jersey Network for a programme entitled *The Making of Doctor Who* (one of a series of documentaries that NJN had made about the series). This was not transmitted in the UK but would eventually be made available in edited form as part of the BBC's *Silver Nemesis* video release.

The British press were also keen to publicise the story and chose to focus on the appearance of actress Mary Reynolds in a cameo as the Queen. Under the headline HER ROYAL WHO-NESS!, the *Star*'s TV editor Michael Burke reported on 29 June 1988 that 'new locations and a record budget of £1.5 million mean that the autumn anniversary series will be the best ever for fans all over the world'.

Sylvester McCoy, Sophie Aldred and third Doctor Jon Pertwee appeared on *Daytime Live*, a popular BBC interview show, to publicise the anniversary. The three actors stepped out of the TARDIS and answered questions from the audience (a group of *Doctor Who* fans who had been specially invited). McCoy was asked if he had been approached to take the lead role in the mooted *Doctor Who* feature film. He and Pertwee both seemed keen to be involved and expressed the view that all the surviving Doctors should appear in the film. Aldred meanwhile seemed delighted to be taking on the Daleks and the Cybermen in stories during the anniversary season. Clips of each of the seven Doctors were also shown on the programme.

Radio Times celebrated the milestone by running a retrospective article on the Doctor's many companions. There were also a modest number of merchandise items issued to commemorate the anniversary. These included an album featuring various versions of the theme tune and a selection of Keff McCulloch's incidental music from stories such as *Paradise Towers* and *Remembrance of the Daleks*; *Doctor Who – 25 Glorious Years*, a W. H. Allen hardback book by Peter Haining; a special *Doctor Who* playset from Dapol; a badge from the BBC; and two different 'first-day covers' featuring the signature of one of the actors to have played the Doctor.

The first episode of *Silver Nemesis* was transmitted in the UK on the actual date of the anniversary. The night before, Noel Edmonds had mentioned the Doctor's birthday on an edition of his *Telly Addicts* quiz show. A trailer had also been extensively shown, utilising scenes from the new story and old footage of William Hartnell from Season 2's *The Web Planet*, to emphasise the series' longevity.

There was also a press call to publicise *Silver Nemesis*. This was held at Space Adventure, a new 'theme ride' located in London's Tooley Street, which boasted an exhibition of *Doctor Who* costumes and props. A photograph from this event of Sylvester McCoy and Sophie Aldred cutting a TARDIS cake appeared in the national press. Shortly after the anniversary, producer John Nathan-Turner was a guest on the afternoon show *Behind the Screen*, talking about the Doctor's past and future. A clip from the forthcoming adventure *The Greatest Show in the Galaxy* was shown and when asked if there were any plans for a new Doctor, Nathan-Turner replied that he was perfectly happy with McCoy's portrayal.

The Thirtieth Anniversary

by Ian Wheeler

Doctor Who's thirtieth anniversary in 1993 was a time of surprises and disappointments. The main event planned for the year was *The Dark Dimension*. (See Chapter 7.) When this was cancelled, press coverage focused on the fact that Adrian Rigelsford's story had given the fourth and seventh Doctors by far the biggest slices of the action, with the third, fifth and sixth relegated virtually to 'guest appearances' – something that had greatly displeased actors Jon Pertwee, Peter Davison and Colin Baker when they had received copies of the script prior to any formal contract discussions taking place. A number of reports even suggested, incorrectly, that this was the reason why the special had been abandoned.

The two-part skit *Dimensions in Time*, involving characters both from *Doctor Who* and from the popular BBC soap opera *EastEnders*, was transmitted in November as part of the BBC's Children in Need telethon. (See Chapter 3.) This was featured on the front cover of the *Radio Times*, making it the first *Doctor Who*-related production to be accorded this accolade since *The*

Five Doctors exactly ten years earlier. The BBC's popular science programme *Tomorrow's World* ran a report on the new 3-D process and also acknowledged *Doctor Who*'s anniversary by examining the concept of time travel as part of a special feature.

In addition to the Children in Need special, BBC1 broadcast the new *Doctor Who* documentary *30 Years in the TARDIS* and repeated the Season 10 story *Planet of the Daleks*, each episode of which was preceded by a five-minute mini-documentary examining one aspect of the series. BBC Radio 2 meanwhile had its own retrospective, *Doctor Who – 30 Years*, produced by Phil Clarke and narrated by Nicholas Courtney. (See Chapter 7 for further details.)

On the merchandise front, two commemorative video tins were released by BBC Enterprises. The first featured the Daleks and contained videos of Season Two's *The Chase* and Season 25's *Remembrance of the Daleks* together with a booklet about the Daleks. The other was a TARDIS-shaped tin containing all fourteen episodes of Season 23's *The Trial of a Time Lord*. Both tins came in a variety of 'editions' featuring different photographs on their bases. Videos of *Resurrection of the Daleks* and *The Two Doctors* also arrived in the shops, having been designated the 'Fan's Choice' following a *Doctor Who Magazine* poll. Virgin released David J. Howe's *Timeframe*, a lavish and colourful collection of photographs and artwork from the series' thirty-year history, which went on to become one of Virgin Publishing's best-selling *Doctor Who* titles. Marvel Comics meanwhile produced a special magazine stylistically based on the *Radio Times* publication in 1973 to celebrate the series' tenth anniversary, with Sylvester McCoy replacing Jon Pertwee in a similar cover photograph. The DWAS published their own glossy booklet with contributions from many of the series' stars, and Dominitemporal Services Ltd organised for them a huge convention in Hammersmith, London, with Doctors Jon Pertwee, Tom Baker, Peter Davison, Colin Baker and Sylvester McCoy attending. All but Tom Baker appeared on stage together in front of a delighted audience. Despite the absence of a new series of

Doctor Who on television, the thirtieth anniversary was, all things considered, celebrated in fine style.

Merchandise

by Ian Wheeler and David J. Howe

During the McCoy years, the range of *Doctor Who* merchandise available continued to grow at an incredible ratc. One notable development was the launching by a company called Dapol of a collection of poseable plastic figures, similar in scale to a famous *Star Wars* range. Early examples included models of the seventh Doctor, his companion Melanie, a Tetrap, K-9 and the TARDIS. They would later be joined by Daleks, Cybermen and an assortment of monsters and other characters. Dapol also manufactured children's versions of the costumes worn by the seventh Doctor and Melanie and an adult-sized replica of the former's pullover, complete with question marks.

Of the other new items that became available during McCoy's time as the Doctor, the most noteworthy included: a TARDIS telephone (manufactured by Holdcourt Ltd and costing nearly £100), which had the rare distinction of appearing on the popular singer and television presenter Cilla Black's *Surprise Surprise* programme; *Doctor Who* bubble bath (also in the shape of the TARDIS); slippers; the initial volumes of a *Doctor Who* encyclopedia (written by former *Doctor Who* Appreciation Society Coordinator David Saunders and published by Piccadilly Press); and a set of *Doctor Who* logo badges, cloth patches and magazine binders (commissioned by John Fitton Books and Magazines). Not strictly a *Doctor Who* item in itself, but still worthy of mention, is a single record entitled 'Doctorin' the Tardis'. This was based on and sampled 'Rock and Roll Part One' by Gary Glitter and was released in 1988 by a group calling themselves the Timelords, later revealed to be an incarnation of cult band the KLF. It eventually topped the UK music charts for one week in June and also appeared in various remixed forms, including most notably 'Gary in the TARDIS', featuring new vocals by Glitter himself.

The discontinuation of *Doctor Who* as an ongoing series in 1989 did little to decrease its popularity, and new merchandise continued to appear. The BBC video releases of old stories were one of the main growth areas. The number of new titles made available each year increased dramatically in the early nineties before decreasing again towards the end of the decade. In addition to 'standard' stories, special extended editions of *The Curse of Fenric*, *Silver Nemesis*, *The Five Doctors* and *Battlefield* were released. The BBC also produced and marketed a series of video documentaries, commonly referred to as 'the Years tapes', each of which featured themed clips and episodes and was introduced by one of the actors who had played the Doctor. The titles issued were: *The Hartnell Years*, *The Troughton Years*, *The Pertwee Years*, *The Tom Baker Years*, *The Colin Baker Years*, *Daleks – The Early Years* and *Cybermen – The Early Years*. Other special BBC video projects included: a completed version of *Shada*, the Season 17 story that had been abandoned due to industrial action, with the missing scenes bridged by narration from Tom Baker and a facsimile edition of the original scripts included in the package as a special bonus; and *More Than 30 Years in the TARDIS*, an extended and re-edited version of the *30 Years in the TARDIS* documentary.

The nineties also saw major developments occurring in the world of *Doctor Who* publishing. With the appearance of John Peel's *The Power of the Daleks* and *The Evil of the Daleks*, the long-running series of licensed novelisations of the televised stories came to an end. (There remained four transmitted stories – *The Pirate Planet, City of Death*, *Resurrection of the Daleks* and *Revelation of the Daleks* – that had not been novelised, but these could not be done because the original scriptwriters had withheld their permission.) In their place Virgin Publishing launched a range of original seventh Doctor novels known collectively as the New Adventures.

The publishers, at that time W. H. Allen, had first approached the BBC with the idea of presenting 'further adventures' of the Doctor in a letter dated 18 October 1985 from Nigel Robinson, the then editor of the novelisations, but John Nathan-Turner had replied that he was unwilling to consider such a move until January 1987 at the earliest. The idea had then been reactivated in a letter dated 6 February 1989 from new editor Jo Thurm, and again in one dated 30 August 1989 from her successor Peter Darvill-Evans. Following these approaches, Nathan-Turner had eventually agreed to the principle of the original novels being done. Darvill-Evans then prepared a detailed proposal, which was sent to the BBC on 1 February 1990. It was at this point that W. H. Allen was bought by Virgin Publishing. A large number of W. H. Allen staff were made redundant and existing book ranges sold off to other publishers. The Target range of *Doctor Who* novelisations remained, however, and Darvill-Evans continued working towards his aim of publishing original *Doctor Who* fiction.

On 27 June 1990, Darvill-Evans sent out a press release inviting submissions from authors. One of the first to send in ideas was John Peel, whose work was liked by Darvill-Evans. His *Timewyrm: Genesys* consequently became the lead title in the initial four-book 'season' featuring a creature called the Timewyrm. The second book, *Exodus*, was commissioned from experienced *Doctor Who* author Terrance Dicks, while the third and fourth came from ideas submitted by Nigel Robinson and new author Paul Cornell respectively. Robinson's had the working title *The God-Machine* but was renamed *Apocalypse* to follow the Biblical theme now decided upon for the titles of the Timewyrm books. Cornell's, which had the working title *Total Eclipse Rewrite* and was later retitled *Revelation*, was based on a short story that he had previously written for the fanzine *Space Rat*. Nathan-Turner disliked Cornell's submission but, as the television series was by this point no longer in production and the *Doctor Who* office had been closed down, Darvill-Evans decided to publish it anyway. The New Adventures were launched to the public on 20 June 1991. They were initially published at the rate of one every two months but eventually moved to a monthly schedule starting with Gareth Roberts's *The Highest Science* in February 1993.

In July 1994, Virgin launched a complementary range of

Missing Adventures – original novels featuring previous incarnations of the Doctor. The first entry in this range was *Goth Opera* by Paul Cornell, published on 21 July. Further titles followed, again on a bimonthly basis initially but quickly moving to a monthly schedule in September.

Virgin also continued to produce a range of factual *Doctor Who* books. Titles such as *The Sixties*, *The Seventies* and *The Eighties* and the series of Handbooks (of which you are reading the final one!) by David J. Howe, Mark Stammers and Stephen James Walker won widespread critical acclaim. *Ace! The Inside Story Of The End Of An Era* by Sophie Aldred and Mike Tucker, which took an in-depth look at many of the seventh Doctor's adventures from the point of view of the authors (Aldred had played Ace and Tucker was one of the BBC's visual effects assistants), was also very popular. Other titles in the range included *The Gallifrey Chronicles* by John Peel, *Monsters* by Adrian Rigelsford, *Companions* by David J. Howe and Mark Stammers, *Timeframe* by David J. Howe and *Blacklight*, an extensive portfolio of Andrew Skilleter's *Doctor Who* artwork. Jean-Marc Lofficier updated his *Doctor Who Programme Guide* for the final time and also produced two further books, *The Terrestrial Index* (which included a chronology of the Doctor's adventures) and *The Universal Databank* (an A-to-Z of characters and terms from the series). Lofficier also wrote *The Nth Doctor*, a study of several aborted *Doctor Who* film projects; Lance Parkin was responsible for a more comprehensive chronology in *A History of the Universe*; and, for those eager to see the funny side of *Doctor Who*, Paul Cornell, Martin Day and Keith Topping unleashed *The Discontinuity Guide* and Chris Howarth and Steve Lyons came up with *The Completely Useless Encyclopedia*. Virgin also published one unlicensed *Doctor Who* title called, appropriately enough, *Licence Denied*, a compilation of fanzine material edited by Paul Cornell.

In the spirit of the World Distributors *Doctor Who* annuals, which ceased publication in 1986, Marvel began publishing a series of Yearbooks. This ran from 1991 to 1995. They also launched a *Doctor Who Classic Comics* magazine, which over its 27 issue run reprinted many of the Doctor's comic-strip escapades from the sixties and seventies (in some cases with added colour) along with related interview and feature material, and a short-lived *Doctor Who* poster magazine.

Virgin's domination of *Doctor Who* book publishing was unsuccessfully challenged by Boxtree, who brought out a number of titles. The *Doctor Who Poster Book* and the *Doctor Who Postcard Book* were straightforward collections of photographs from the series. More ambitious was Adrian Rigelsford's *The Doctors – 30 Years of Time Travel*, which was unlicensed by the BBC and heavily criticised by reviewers for its many factual inaccuracies and major omissions and its quoting of much interview material from unidentified sources. Boxtree also published Rigelsford's *Classic Who: The Hinchcliffe Years*, a look at the *Doctor Who* work of producer Philip Hinchcliffe. The 'Classic Who' appellation was adopted in order to avoid the use of the BBC's own *Doctor Who* logo. The BBC was nevertheless displeased that such books were appearing and brought its weight to bear on the publishers. Consequently Rigelsford's final Boxtree book – *Classic Who: The Harper Classics*, featuring the *Doctor Who* work of director Graeme Harper – although originally intended to be unlicensed, was in fact licensed and the appropriate credit given to the BBC. After this, Boxtree decided not to continue with further *Doctor Who* titles (four others – *The 500 Year Diary*, *The Making of 'The Dark Dimension'* and similar *Classic Who* books covering the *Doctor Who* work of director David Maloney and producer Barry Letts respectively – having been mooted by Rigelsford).

With no prospect of new *Doctor Who* appearing on television, groups of fans took matters into their own hands by producing on a professional basis a number of independent spin-off dramas designed for video release (although some were subsequently also transmitted on the Sci-Fi Channel, as were various different versions of a video documentary that took its title and cover image from Adrian Rigelsford's book *The Doctors – 30 Years of Time Travel*). The first such project – *Wartime*, starring John Levene as Benton, a character from the third and fourth Doctors' eras – was masterminded by Keith Barnfather and released in 1988 by Reeltime Pictures. Dreamwatch Media followed this up in 1994 with *Shakedown*, featuring established *Doctor Who* monsters the Sontarans and the Rutans. This was scripted by Terrance Dicks and directed by Kevin Davies and starred, albeit not in their familiar television roles, *Doctor Who* regulars Sophie Aldred and Carole Ann Ford and *Blake's 7* regulars Jan Chappell and Brian Croucher. The following year, Reeltime Pictures released *Downtime*, directed by *Doctor Who* veteran Christopher Barry and written by Marc Platt, who had scripted *Ghost Light* for *Doctor Who*'s twenty-sixth season. *Doctor Who* characters featured in this production included the Brigadier (Nicholas Courtney), Sarah Jane Smith (Elisabeth Sladen), Victoria Waterfield (Deborah Watling) and, providing the opposition, the Great Intelligence and its Yeti robots (as seen in the fifth season stories *The Abominable Snowmen* and *The Web of Fear*). 1997 saw the release of *Auton*, written and directed by Nick Briggs and featuring the return of the Nestene Consciousness and its killer plastic Auton mannequins from Season 7's *Spearhead from Space* and Season 8's *Terror of the Autons*. This was produced by Bill Baggs and released commercially by Reeltime Pictures, who have also continued throughout the nineties to add to their range of Myth Makers video interviews with former *Doctor Who* cast and crew members.

Other video releases with looser *Doctor Who* connections included, as well as some one-off projects, the *Stranger* series featuring Colin Baker as 'the Stranger' and Nicola Bryant as 'Miss Brown' and several titles about an investigative organisation called PROBE, headed by the third Doctor's companion Liz Shaw (Caroline John), now elevated to the status of a professor. These dramas were produced by Baggs and also starred, in new roles, other well-known *Doctor Who* actors including Peter Davison, Jon Pertwee, Colin Baker and Sylvester McCoy.

On the audio front, cassettes and CDs related to *Doctor Who* became more popular. It was possible to buy selected incidental music soundtracks (for *The Greatest Show in the Galaxy*, *Ghost Light* and *The Curse of Fenric* among others), talking-book versions of certain novelisations, tapes taken from old off-air recordings of television stories otherwise missing from the BBC archives and even audio equivalents of the spin-off drama videos.

When the *Doctor Who* television movie finally came to fruition in 1996 its transmission precipitated a minor flood of related items. The BBC themselves released a video of the movie (which was actually available to buy about a week before the UK transmission), a novelisation by Gary Russell and a script book. Other items included posters, a record bag, a watch, a set of postcards and, in 1997, a CD of the soundtrack. This last item was available only through specialist dealers as it was privately released by one of the composers, John Debney, as a promotional item.

A significant change in *Doctor Who* licensing came in 1996 when, as a direct result of their involvement with the television movie, the BBC declined to renew Virgin Publishing's long-standing fiction licence so that they could take over publication of the range of original *Doctor Who* novels themselves. The switch came in May 1997, which saw publication of the final novels in the Virgin range, Lance Parkin's eighth Doctor New Adventure *The Dying Days* and Gareth Roberts's fourth Doctor Missing Adventure *The Well-Mannered War*. The following month, the BBC's range began with *The Eight Doctors* by Terrance Dicks and *The Devil Goblins from Neptune* by Martin Day and Keith Topping. The BBC also released at this time a Paul McGann-narrated talking book of Gary Russell's novelisation and a postcard book of images from the movie. Further original novels then followed at the rate of two per month, one featuring the eighth Doctor and his new companion Sam, the other featuring a past-Doctor-and-companion team. Virgin, meanwhile, continued their range of New Adventures minus the *Doctor Who* logo (which they had actually dropped some months beforehand in order to help ensure a smooth transition) and with no BBC-owned characters, concentrating instead on the exploits of the Doctor's erstwhile companion Bernice Summerfield, who had been created for the range by author Paul Cornell some years earlier. From June 1998 these Doctor-less New Adventures moved from a monthly to a bimonthly schedule.

While Virgin retained an interest in factual *Doctor Who* publishing, the BBC also embarked on a programme of such books. The first titles to see print were *The Book of Lists* by Justin Richards and Andrew Martin and *A Book of Monsters* by David J. Howe. These have been followed up by *The Television Companion* by David J. Howe and Stephen James Walker and *From A to Z* by *Doctor Who Magazine* editor Gary Gillatt.

Doctor Who merchandise continues to sell well and at the time of writing there is no sign of the series' popularity waning. There have been many other items released in addition to those mentioned here – everything from calendars, posters and graphic novels to trading cards, playing cards and model kits. *Who's There?*, a biography of William Hartnell written by his granddaughter, Jessica Carney, has been published; Tom Baker's autobiography, *Who on Earth is Tom Baker?*, was launched with a nationwide book-signing tour by the actor and has sold very well (as has a talking-book version); and *I Am The Doctor*, a memoir co-written by the late Jon Pertwee and David J. Howe, has been much sought after. Other products released in the wake of the television movie include a BBC CD-ROM game called *Destiny of the Doctors*.

There may be no new *Doctor Who* on television but the series and its characters and creations live on in many different media, ensuring that the good Doctor will be around in one form or another for years to come.

The Virgin Doctor

by David Robinson and Richard Prekodravac

The 61 New Adventures novels published by Virgin took the characters and concepts of the television series and used them as the basis for stories, as they put it, 'too broad and too deep for the small screen'. The seventh Doctor as presented in the first 60 of these novels is a complex individual who is defined by his actions, by his relationships with his companions and by his place in the societies he touches. He is a dark Doctor, a clown, a horrifying alien. He is also someone who changes and matures, evolving from an apparently uncaring manipulator of events to a somewhat redeemed and responsible humanitarian. The novels' numerous authors created and developed not only a multifaceted seventh Doctor but also, along the way, a rich tapestry of new *Doctor Who* mythology, adding to that of the televised adventures.

Mythology and Time's Champion

The first layer of mythology to be introduced was generically termed 'the Cartmel master plan'. Set out in a format document dated 9 November 1990, this was developed for Virgin by Andrew Cartmel, Ben Aaronovitch and Marc Platt based on ideas devised by them while working on the series' twenty-fifth and twenty-sixth seasons. It postulated the Doctor's origins and his connection with the Hand of Omega and the Other (a character from Aaronovitch's novelisation of *Remembrance of the Daleks*) and described Time Lord society as developing out of an era of superstition dominated by the powerful matriarchal Pythia (as subsequently featured in the fifth novel, Platt's *Time's Crucible*), whose rule fell with the establishment of a lasting curse that transformed Gallifrey into the society as seen in the televised stories.

The second layer of mythology established here was that of the Gallifreyan gods. These are Eternals who exist only as representations of archetypal ideas stemming from the Gallifreyan collective consciousness. Time, Death and Pain are the main gods used by the Gallifreyans as an aid to understanding the ideas they represent; Pain, for example, acts as a reminder of the sacrifice made by betraying friends (*The Left-Handed Hummingbird*, *Set Piece*, *Sleepy*). In order to prevent himself becoming his potential evil incarnation the Valeyard (as seen in Season 23's *The Trial of a Time Lord*), the Doctor became Time's champion in a deal with the Gallifreyan god (*Love and War*, *Millennial Rites*). This idea followed a Western literary tradition established by the classical Greeks: the hero as a champion to one of the gods. In this case it was essentially about the Doctor becoming responsible for the actions of his present and past incarnations. It was this acceptance of responsibility that caused him to become a much darker character. The Doctor would use the role of Time's champion as a technique to rationalise his thoughts and actions. Hence he would take up the mantle of someone who not only interceded in the problems of others but was also responsible for the consequences of his actions.

The Dark Doctor

The seventh Doctor in the novels was initially the character as presented on television. This had been firmly established in Season 25's *Remembrance of the Daleks* and perhaps best demonstrated in Season 26's *The Curse of Fenric*, where the Doctor defeats Fenric by betraying the trust of his companion, Ace. The first 23 New Adventures novels concentrated on this dark aspect of his character. He was someone who made deals with Death, Time and Pain and would ride roughshod over the feelings of his companions and friends in order to win the greater battles. Often unemotional and distant, he would sacrifice lives to win. He was described as being 'what monsters have nightmares about'.

The Pit presented perhaps the lowest point of this dark characterisation. In this, the twelfth novel in the series, the villain is a Gallifreyan named Kopyion who has been responsible for the deaths of millions of people on seven planets. The Doctor, controversially, makes no attempt to stop or even condemn his actions; it seems he is unable to take the high moral ground because Kopyion is a reflection of what he himself could become if his character were taken to extremes. The Doctor's development from *Remembrance of the Daleks* to *The Pit* was born out of the culture of the antihero such as in the *Terminator* and *Alien* films; the authors now realised that his character was ultimately self-destructive. This was highlighted in the twenty-first novel, *The Left-Handed Hummingbird*. Then in the twenty-third, *No Future*, the Doctor finally becomes aware that his actions are not only self-destructive but also hurtful to his companions Ace and Bernice.

The Human Alien

Even after the events of *No Future* the Doctor remains aloof, carrying the dark legacy with him. He becomes distant and detached, his alien nature being emphasised as something incomprehensible (*Sky Pirates!*). After Ace departs at the end of the thirty-fifth novel, *Set Piece*, he discovers a need to develop a sense of empathy and humanity. In the thirty-eighth novel, *Human Nature*, he strips all aspects of his Time Lord self away, including his physiology and memories, and becomes the human Dr John Smith. While this allowed author Paul Cornell to set up the Doctor's discovery of human values it also, more importantly, enabled him to explore what it meant to be the Doctor. It firmly established a broader conceptualisation of the Doctor as a whole person composed of seven distinct personalities: he was not only the seventh Doctor but also *the* Doctor. This idea had been foreshadowed in the earlier novel *Transit*, the tenth in the series, when Ben Aaronovitch had poetically described him as 'all things to all cultures'.

With the arrival of the eighth Doctor on television and imminent loss of Virgin's *Doctor Who* fiction licence, plans were made to bring the New Adventures to a conclusion. The last few novels in the series emphasise the Doctor's redemption. He has carried the burden of blaming himself for the tragedy of his lifetime; he has sacrificed friends and companions, manipulated lives, betrayed friendships and trust, all in the cause of fighting and winning. He is conscious that he looks at the big picture at the expense of the important details (*Bad Therapy*) and knows that he cannot regenerate until he has faced up to the mistakes he has made.

The House of Lungbarrow

In the penultimate novel, *Lungbarrow*, which picks up on events in *Time's Crucible,* the Doctor is forced to return to Gallifrey and rediscover his neglected family, the people of the strange House of Lungbarrow. *Lungbarrow* sees the Doctor learning of the power of the Hand of Omega and the nature of his identity. He has to accept and come to terms with his past and his family in order to move on. The truth is frightening but it defines the Doctor and, in doing so, heals him.

Commenting on *Lungbarrow* in Issue 14 of the fanzine *Broadsword*, Jonathan Blum wrote: 'Care as he does about what he believes in, fight as he does to do what he sees as right, he is never a tyrant, never in love with his own power, never out of touch with the small beauties and disappointments of life.'

Throughout the course of the New Adventures, the Doctor underwent a far more radical process of change and development than had ever been attempted on television. The novels also bequeathed a legacy of myth and theme that authors and readers alike have delighted in picking up and developing further. The seventh Doctor became an essentially tragic figure imbued with the compassion and eccentricity that can be found only in *Doctor Who*.

Overseas

AMERICA

by Robert D. Franks

Doctor Who's popularity in the United States was on the wane by the mid-eighties, having hit its peak earlier in the decade with frequent airings of the Tom Baker episodes by PBS stations. John Nathan-Turner, realising the potential of the American market, was keen to reverse this trend and actively sought out publicity opportunities. On 28 February 1987, a mobile *Doctor Who* trailer exhibition that had been touring the country for nearly a year made a scheduled stop at Mercer University in Georgia. Here Nathan-Turner, accompanied by Jon Pertwee and Sylvester McCoy, joined it to announce that McCoy had been cast as the new Doctor. This occurred three days before the official BBC announcement in the UK.

Lionheart commenced distributing the McCoy serials towards the end of 1987 as television 'movies' – the episodes of each story being edited together into single 'feature length' adventures. *Doctor Who* was now saturating the American market, with over one hundred PBS stations carrying the series. Around this time, the newly formed Friends of *Doctor Who* group held several 'Day with the Doctor' mini-conventions which, although not on the same scale as the earlier Chicago events presented by the commercial Spirit of Light organisation, still attracted a large turnout.

In 1992, with *Doctor Who* no longer in production and its future up in the air, the fledgling cable Sci-Fi Channel tried to negotiate with BBC Worldwide for exclusive American rights to transmit the series. It ultimately managed to secure a set of Tom Baker episodes. This, however, had an adverse effect on the PBS stations: when they found that they were no longer able to bill the series as 'exclusive', many started dropping it from their schedules.

Coinciding with this decline in the series' coverage of the American market there was, paradoxically, a revival of the large-scale conventions both on the East coast and on the West. Two of these annual events – the Visions convention in Chicago and the Gallifrey gathering in Los Angeles – continue to attract a large number of fans each year.

CANADA

by Michael J. Doran

The McCoy era marked a change in the way *Doctor Who* was seen in Canada. From 1976 until 1988, the provincial Ontario-only network TVOntario (TVO) had aired selected Jon Pertwee episodes (several of which, including *The Claws of Axos*, *The Curse of Peladon*, *The Mutants* and *The Time Monster*, were returned to the BBC as 525-line two-inch recordings in the early 1980s as the only broadcast-quality colour versions in existence), all but a couple of Tom Baker stories, and all Peter Davison and Colin Baker stories. With a Saturday evening timeslot, the show had been able to develop a following similar to the one it enjoyed in the UK. The first local fan clubs had started up in 1978 and this activity had formed the basis for the *Doctor Who* Information Network (DWIN), established in 1980 and now the longest running *Doctor Who* fan club in North America. The twenty-fourth season was aired on TVO in the usual way, on Saturday evenings with a repeat the following Thursday evening. The run started with *Time and the Rani* Part One on 9 January 1989 and concluded with *Dragonfire* Part Three on 10 April 1989. In July 1989, however, it was announced that TVO had lost the *Doctor Who* rights to the recently launched nationwide youth-orientated cable network YTV. For the first time since 1965 (when the Canadian Broadcasting Corporation had aired the first five William Hartnell serials), *Doctor Who* would be available right across the country for Seasons 25 and 26.

One TVO insider put this development down to the network simply forgetting to renew the rights in time and YTV snatching them up. Nevertheless, it is unlikely that TVO would have been able to continue much longer as a broadcaster of *Doctor Who*, as it had been showing the series in blocks of approximately 26 episodes, its 'seasons' bearing no relation to the originals, and with the BBC now producing only 14 episodes per year this would soon have become impracticable. As it was, the twenty-third and twenty-fourth seasons were linked together for broadcast in Canada and the latter was aired only seventeen months after its UK transmission, whereas the gap in the past had generally been more than two years.

The twenty-fifth season premiered on YTV on 3 September 1989, in a 7 p.m. Sunday timeslot, with *The Happiness Patrol* Part One, the stories being shown out of their UK transmission sequence. Due to a programming error (transmission of *The Greatest Show in the Galaxy* Part Four was delayed by a week as *Remembrance of the Daleks* Part Four was mistakenly rerun in its place), the run lasted fifteen weeks and finished on 10 December. Viewers had only a short time to wait for more new episodes, as the twenty-sixth season went out during the spring of 1990, in a 5.30 p.m. Saturday timeslot. Again the stories were shown out of their UK sequence.

Between September 1989 and August 1994 YTV also aired, in a variety of afternoon, evening, and late-night timeslots, all the other complete stories that still existed in the BBC archives at the time. Fan reaction to YTV was often negative, particularly in

Ontario, where many viewers disliked the fact that – unlike on TVO in the past – the episodes were interrupted by commercials. The station nevertheless managed to bring *Doctor Who* to many Canadians who had never seen it before or who had previously had to depend on American PBS border stations. Their screenings were also the first opportunity that Canadian viewers had to see most Hartnell, any Troughton and many Pertwee serials.

CITV, the TV station in Edmonton, Alberta, was the first broadcaster anywhere in the world to air the Fox/BBC/Universal *Doctor Who* television movie (which had been filmed in British Columbia, Canada). This was transmitted on Sunday 12 May 1996 at 10 p.m. Canadian Mountain Time. The movie was also aired by CHCH Hamilton on 14 May at 9 p.m. Canadian Eastern Time. Both stations are available on a variety of cable systems across Canada.

In 1998, *Doctor Who* has once again been on cable in Canada. SPACE: The Imagination Station has purchased a run of episodes and aired the series commercial-free from Monday to Friday. The McCoy episodes should roll around on the schedule in due course.

AUSTRALIA

by Damian Shanahan and Dallas Jones

The arrival of Sylvester McCoy as the Doctor coincided with a change in the way that *Doctor Who* was handled by the Australian Broadcasting Company (ABC). Instead of being dealt with by the Drama Department and screened in a 6.30 p.m. timeslot, as had traditionally been the case, the series now formed part of *The Afternoon Show*, run by the Children's and Education Department, and went out an hour earlier. This change was made for two reasons. First, the ABC under the helm of Controller David Hill now had a policy of competing with the commercial networks, and *Doctor Who* was seen as lacking in audience-pulling power in an early evening slot dominated by the networks' current-affairs programmes. Secondly, many viewers had actually requested such a change.

The new season was announced in September 1988 and commenced with *Time and the Rani* on Monday 31 October at 5.30 p.m., running five nights a week. An ABC spokesperson indicated that the series would receive no publicity and would be cancelled if acceptable ratings were not achieved – a decision that shocked but did not entirely surprise Australian fans, given the new policy that had been adopted. The ABC declined to indicate what it would consider to be acceptable ratings, but there is no doubt that *Doctor Who* had never been particularly popular with the general viewing public in Australia. Its previous best performance had been an 8 per cent share of the viewing audience for the twentieth anniversary special *The Five Doctors*. Repeats of Tom Baker's stories, as movie-length compilations on Saturdays at 1 p.m. during this period, had received only between 3 per cent and 5 per cent – although this may have understated the series' true popularity judging by an article in the *Sydney Morning Herald* on 27 February 1988 in which a spokesperson for the ratings company AGB McNair was quoted as saying of the new 'people meter' assessment devices: 'Some mothers tended to conceal the fact that their children were watching *Neighbours* or *Doctor Who*.'

Unknown technical difficulties resulted in a loss of vision for the opening titles of one episode of *Delta and the Bannermen*, but otherwise the transmission of the twenty-fourth season proceeded uneventfully, concluding with *Dragonfire* Part Three on Thursday 17 November. Surprisingly, however, the run then continued with the following season's opening story, *Remembrance of the Daleks*, which aired from Friday 18 to Wednesday 23 November. This was a one-off advance screening arranged – apparently at the behest of *The Afternoon Show*'s host James Valentine – so that the ABC could properly celebrate *Doctor Who*'s silver anniversary. The remainder of the twenty-fifth season was not purchased at this stage, even though the twenty-fourth had won a significant increase on the poor ratings for the Saturday afternoon repeats and the previous 6.30 p.m. weekday transmissions – *Time and the Rani*, for instance, had gained a 6–7 per cent share of the viewing audience.

As in the UK, the anniversary period saw the release of the Timelords' 'Doctorin' the TARDIS' single, which entered the Australian music charts on 21 August at No. 8, rose the following week to No. 4, spent the next four weeks at No. 3 and then on 2 October peaked at No. 2. The later 'Gary in the TARDIS' remix failed to enter the Australian charts.

After *Remembrance of the Daleks*, the ABC recommenced screening repeats of the Tom Baker stories. It was not until August 1989 that premiere dates were confirmed for the remainder of the twenty-fifth season, which was to be preceded by a second run of all the earlier McCoy episodes. Originally the ABC planned to start this run on Tuesday 24 October so that the first episode of *Silver Nemesis* would be transmitted on 23 November – enabling Australian viewers to see the start of the series' twenty-fifth anniversary story on the twenty-sixth anniversary! It was then realised, however, that a screening of cricket and golf would interfere with this (sporting events routinely being given priority over Children's and Education Department programmes) so, following consultation with the Australasian *Doctor Who* Fan Club, the ABC brought the start date forward to Friday 20 October and screened the stories in production order rather than UK transmission order. In this way the first episode of *Silver Nemesis* still went out on the anniversary date, and the season eventually ended with *The Happiness Patrol* Part Three on Monday 4 December 1989. Some regional viewers had the last five episodes of the season delayed by the screening of a cricket match, but only by a few days.

The last three stories of Season 25 were repeated in a run that began on Tuesday 16 October 1990 and led directly on to the premiere screening of Season 26, publicity for which had been planned at a special meeting as the ABC had viewed all the episodes and been very impressed with their quality. The season began with *Battlefield* Part One on 29 October and ran, as before, five nights a week, Monday to Friday at 5.30 p.m., as part of *The Afternoon Show*. It concluded with the final episode of *Survival* on Friday 16 November.

NEW ZEALAND

by Paul Scoones

In September 1987, while Sylvester McCoy was making his debut in the UK, New Zealanders were watching the Tom Baker story *Horror of Fang Rock* – the latest in a chronological run of *Doctor Who* repeats and first-time screenings that had commenced in April 1985 and continued virtually uninterrupted since then.

Part Three of *Horror of Fang Rock* was watched by 15 per cent of the potential viewing audience, placing it 49th on the top 50 most watched programmes chart for the third week of September and making it the second most watched *Doctor Who* episode since 1983 (bettered only by *The Hand of Fear* Part Four, which, with a rating of 18.5 per cent, had charted 45th in the first week of July 1987). These pleasing ratings most probably caused Television New Zealand (TVNZ) programmers to consider something special to celebrate the series' impending twenty-fifth anniversary, and the result was a week-long series of screenings dubbed '*Doctor Who* Silver Jubilee Week'.

The week's viewing began on Saturday 19 November 1988 on Television Two with *The Dalek Invasion of Earth* and *The Seeds of Death*. It continued the following day with *The Five Doctors* and the Peter Cushing movie *Dr Who and the Daleks*. A four-episode version of *Revelation of the Daleks* was screened between Monday and Thursday and an omnibus edition of *Silver Nemesis* on Friday. This made New Zealand the first country in the world to see Parts Two and Three of the latter story (Part One having been transmitted in the UK just two days earlier, on 23 November) – a distinction unmentioned in the otherwise extensive publicity for the 'Silver Jubilee Week'. The compilation was scheduled in a 90-minute slot from 4.30 p.m. to 6 p.m., with commercial breaks and, between Parts Two and Three, a five-minute news headlines break. Part One's opening titles (complete with 'Part One' caption) were used at the beginning and Part Three's closing credits at the end, and although the other opening and closing titles were removed, Parts Two and Three retained their opening reprises and episode-number captions. Part One was further cut, with about a minute missing at the point at which a commercial break occurred, although it is unknown whether this was due to a mistake in the editing in of the break or was considered to be a convenient point at which to make a timing edit. The missing material was that of the Doctor and Ace discussing the arrival of the Nemesis and Ace finding the empty bow case, and then Lady Peinforte and Richard observing the arrival of the police at the crash site. Ratings for the story averaged 6.0 per cent, falling from 6.5 per cent for Part One to 5.5 per cent for Part Three.

New Zealand viewers subsequently had to wait more than a year to see further McCoy stories. The regular screenings (which had got up to *Time-Flight* by the time of the 'Silver Jubilee Week') finally reached the seventh Doctor's era when *Time and the Rani* Part One debuted on Television Two on 23 January 1990. At this point, episodes were being transmitted every week-day at 4.30 p.m. From *Remembrance of the Daleks* Part One onward, however, *Doctor Who* was moved to a Sunday morning slot, beginning on 18 February 1990. *Remembrance of the Daleks* Parts Two and Three were screened a fortnight apart to accommodate repeats of the 1990 Commonwealth Games, but there were no other breaks in the run. The stories of Season 25, although not those of Season 26, were screened in production order rather than UK transmission order (with *Silver Nemesis* this time in its original three-part form). *The Curse of Fenric* Part One strangely lacked the on-screen subtitles for the Russian soldiers' lines in the opening scenes, but otherwise the episodes were unedited.

TVNZ's six-and-a-half-year screening of *Doctor Who* finally reached its conclusion with *Survival* Part Three on 16 September 1990. This was coincidentally the same weekend that New Zealand's first national *Doctor Who* convention with guests from the series took place in Christchurch. WhoCon 1990 was organised by the New Zealand *Doctor Who* Fan Club and featured personal appearances by Jon Pertwee and Mark Strickson. The timing of this event was fitting as the birth of organised *Doctor Who* fandom in New Zealand had coincided with the mid-1987 announcement of Sylvester McCoy being cast as the seventh Doctor. The Club and its highly regarded fanzine *TSV* (*Time/Space Visualiser*) continue to this day.

The 1996 television movie made its New Zealand debut on Wednesday 30 October 1996 at 8.30 p.m. on Television Two. TVNZ was offered both the uncut US version and the edited UK version of the movie, and opted to screen the former. It was watched by 13.2 per cent of the potential viewing audience – an officially estimated total of 412,682 viewers, placing it higher than the programmes screening on the other two channels and eighth in the top ten television movies and mini series screened on New Zealand television in 1996.

Fandom

by Ian Wheeler

The *Doctor Who* Appreciation Society (DWAS) had been at the centre of fan activity in the UK since its formation in 1976 and was still going strong when the seventh Doctor arrived in 1987. Its long-running newsletter *Celestial Toyroom*, now edited by Neil Hutchings, was a lively and well-presented mixture of news, comment and rather overt humour. Hutchings was succeeded by Brian J. Robb in 1988, and although the layout became somewhat untidy the contents still made for a satisfying read. The next permanent editor, following a short stint by Andy Lane and Andrew Martin in 1989, was Michael Proctor, who arguably inherited the newsletter at the worst possible time as *Doctor Who* was no longer in production, news stories were hard to find and the Society's membership seemed reluctant to contribute articles or features. Although Proctor made a brave attempt it was not until Martin Kennaugh took over in 1990 that things began to improve and *Celestial Toyroom* once again became essential reading. Kennaugh remained as editor for four successful years. His assistant Keith Hopkins then took over and the newsletter continued to go from strength to strength. Eventually, however, Hopkins left and a succession of short-term editors then followed before Steve Haywood took over on a permanent basis in 1997. The DWAS's flagship magazine, *TARDIS,* also returned to regular publication in 1997, having made only sporadic appearances during the late eighties, but somehow lacked the professional and authoritative edge that it had once enjoyed.

The DWAS had been irregularly beset throughout this period by problems in the running of its Membership Department, which had a knock-on impact on the distribution of *Celestial Toyroom* – members frequently received issues late and occasionally even in the wrong order. Another difficulty faced by the Society in the late eighties was increasing competition in the form of glossy, independent fanzines. *The Frame* was one of the best examples and contained a lively mix of rare photographs, interviews, features, fiction, artwork, humour and behind-the-scenes articles. Created and published by David J. Howe, Mark Stammers and Stephen James Walker, it began in 1987 and ran until 1993, when the editorial team reluctantly decided that they could no longer produce the fanzine at the same time as writing their two series of nonfiction *Doctor Who* books for Virgin Publishing. *The Frame* took a balanced approach towards criticism of *Doctor Who*, not least because all three editors had a great affection for the series. *Doctor Who Bulletin*, on the other hand, was probably the most opinionated *Doctor Who* fanzine ever to be produced. Edited and published by Gary Levy (who later changed his name to Gary Leigh), it had been launched in 1983 but became increasingly critical of the series during the Sylvester McCoy years and was particularly negative about the work of producer John Nathan-Turner.

While the opinions expressed by Levy and his contributors were often extremely harsh, they were not entirely unrepresentative; fandom was deeply split over McCoy's first season in particular. There were indeed some fans who had doubts about McCoy's suitability for the role of the Doctor right from the very beginning, and it was not only in the pages of *Doctor Who Bulletin* that negative comments appeared. After *Time and the Rani* Part One was broadcast, DWAS Coordinator Andrew Beech wrote an article for the *Daily Mail* in which he expressed the view that McCoy 'showed the glimmerings of a believable performance [but] the sight of the Doctor grinning inanely, prancing about and doing pratfalls over non-existent obstacles, uttering lines such as "absence makes the nose grow longer" and making a cheap joke of the role does not inspire confidence'. As McCoy settled into the role, however, he gradually began to win over his critics, and by 1989 his popularity was such that he was able to romp to victory in the 'favourite Doctor' category of the *Doctor Who Magazine* readers poll for that year.

Doctor Who Bulletin, or *DWB* as it was called on its masthead, was to remain highly outspoken throughout its long run. In 1989 it transformed into *Dreamwatch Bulletin* (which conveniently also abbreviated to *DWB*) and broadened its coverage to include a whole range of fantasy films and television programmes; then in 1994 it evolved into *Dreamwatch*, a successful, professionally published news-stand magazine.

While *The Frame* and most other glossy fanzines, including *Private Who*, *Proteus* and *NWE* (*New Whovical Express*), slowly faded away in the early nineties, a handful – most notably *Skaro* and *Matrix* – continued. There was also something of a revival of more modest, photocopied fanzines produced on a tiny budget and supported by a small readership and lots of enthusiasm.

Conventions and other special events remained an important part of the fan scene during the late eighties and nineties. Dominitemporal Services Ltd, on behalf of the DWAS, continued to hold its large-scale PanoptiCon gatherings, generally on an annual basis, but here too faced increasing competition from independent fan groups organising their own successful events. Smaller-scale gatherings took place under the auspices of an ever-growing network of DWAS and independent *Doctor Who* local groups.

Other fan activities during this period included a number of campaigns to try to persuade the BBC to put *Doctor Who* back into production. These included the 'Target Who' letter-writing campaign directed at *Radio Times* and *Points of View* (a BBC viewers' feedback programme), which failed to make an impact as not a single letter was either published or broadcast. One group of fans even campaigned for funds to mount a legal challenge against the BBC's decision to drop the series, but (as detailed in Chapter 7) this was ultimately abandoned.

Off-air audio recordings of sixties *Doctor Who* episodes, including all those subsequently wiped by the BBC, had long been in circulation among the series' fans. In the nineties, however, much clearer copies became available, mostly from the respective collections of Graham Strong, David Holman and David Butler. These have since been used by a number of fans to create video 'reconstructions' of the missing episodes (the picture usually consisting of a mixture of still photographs and video images, sometimes accompanied by captions describing the action and dialogue) and also in a few instances by the BBC to replace poor-quality soundtracks on episodes held in their archives.

The period beginning in 1987 and continuing into the 1990s was, overall, something of a golden age for fandom. Rather than withering away after the demise of *Doctor Who* as an ongoing series, it arguably became stronger and more focused than ever before.

Viewer Reaction

by Ian Wheeler

Press coverage of McCoy's first season may have been far from enthusiastic, but it would be wrong to say that reaction to the arrival of the new Doctor was entirely negative. The response from the general viewing public – arguably those whose views mattered the most – was often very different. *Radio Times* ran a number of letters of comment from readers who had seen the new Doctor's debut adventure and enjoyed it. S. Lancaster from Stoke-on-Trent wrote: 'The real Doctor is back . . . For the first time in six-and-a-half years I can't wait to see the next episode . . .' Michael Proctor from Hertfordshire was equally impressed, referring to McCoy as 'an inspired choice'. In Scotland, the *Sunday Post* had some equally positive feedback. 'Sylvester didn't do much for me in the first episode,' wrote Miss

J. Napier of Glasgow, 'but now I have to admit he's got me hooked.' J. Robertson of Aberdeen appeared to agree: 'Sylvester is a good new Doctor and the story is fine. The series has definitely improved from last year.'

It wasn't all plain sailing for the series, however, and Margaret Francis of Bristol expressed some strongly negative opinions in the pages of the *Eagle*, the long-running British adventure comic, in January 1989: 'Sylvester McCoy must be the most wimpish Doctor Who ever, as he looks more like something out of a *Carry On* film than what is supposed to be science fiction. *Doctor Who* used to be a super series, but now it's like watching a pantomime, which is a shame.' The comic's fictional editor, a cheerful computer by the name of Max, responded: 'A jokey science fiction series is okay by me. Personally, I preferred *Red Dwarf*, but anyone who takes *Doctor Who* seriously should see a Dalek Doctor!'

Viewers' letters were not the only indication that the BBC had of viewer reaction to *Doctor Who*. They also had hard statistics in the form of an Appreciation Index, or AI, for each individual episode. In much the same way as ratings are compiled by studying the viewing habits of certain households, AIs are an attempt to gauge audience enjoyment in the form of a simple percentage. The higher the percentage a programme gains, the better it was received by those who watched it. The average AI for the twenty-fourth season was 60, with a high of 64 and a low of 57. These figures would generally be considered disappointing, but fortunately things improved over the next two years: Seasons 25 and 26 both gained an average AI of 68. This was still some way below the typical figure for BBC drama – which during the period of Season 26's transmission was 76 – but it should be remembered that *Doctor Who* had always appealed to a somewhat specialist audience and its AI figures were arguably 'diluted' by the reactions of casual viewers with little interest in the series. The AIs for the McCoy stories were, in fact, generally higher than those for the earlier Doctors' eras, although, as methods of collecting the data had changed over the years, such direct comparisons can be misleading.

Other forms of statistics were collected by the BBC for Television Audience Reaction Reports. These included 'personal ratings' for the stars of programmes, based on surveys completed by a viewing panel. McCoy's rating was low to begin with but rose after the twenty-sixth season, when 78 per cent of those questioned found him 'likeable'. One viewer remarked that McCoy was '. . . naturally charming, not a mannered Doctor'. There were also three 'audience profiles' compiled during the seventh Doctor's era, giving a general picture of viewers' age, sex and social status. These were for *Time and the Rani*, *Remembrance of the Daleks* and the twenty-sixth season as a whole. From these it would appear that an even greater percentage of *Doctor Who*'s viewers than in the past were adult – 74 per cent for *Time and the Rani* and 78 per cent for both the Dalek story and the twenty-sixth season. There also existed a very even balance between male and female (an exact 50/50 split for the twenty-sixth season). If any conclusion can be drawn from this information, it would arguably be that few programmes have brought together people of different ages, sexes and backgrounds in quite the way that *Doctor Who* managed in the late eighties.

In 1989, when rumours started to spread that *Doctor Who* was coming to an end, the public were as determined as ever to have their say. The *Radio Times* letters page was once again a forum for debate. 'I hope that Jonathan Powell gets the sack as soon as possible as Controller, BBC1,' wrote Alan Dobbie from London. 'His decision to axe *Doctor Who* at the end of its present series shows that he doesn't understand what people really want. We want *Doctor Who* to continue.' Similar concerns were expressed by a contributor to the BBC's *Points of View*, who was told that there were in fact no plans to cancel the series.

It would be a long time before a new *Doctor Who* project would come to fruition, and viewer reaction to the 1996 Paul McGann television movie is covered elsewhere in this book. Later the same year, however, *Doctor Who*'s many followers finally had a real opportunity to show their appreciation. As part of the celebrations to mark the BBC's sixtieth year of television broadcasting, a telephone poll was held to determine the nation's

'Favourite Popular Drama'. There were twelve nominees to choose from, including such popular successes as *Bergerac*, *Casualty* and *EastEnders*. To the apparent surprise of many, *Doctor Who* won, and McCoy and Peter Davison collected the award as part of the televised *Auntie's All-Time Greats* birthday party. This spectacular victory subsequently attracted some sniping in the press, particularly from disgruntled *EastEnders* cast members, and suggestions were even made that well-organised *Doctor Who* fan clubs had rung in *en masse* to influence the outcome. In fact, there had been no such organised fan campaign to try to influence the vote. In the hearts of many, and by a simple majority vote, the award had gone to the series that most deserved it.

Ratings

by Ian Wheeler

When considering the viewing figures for McCoy's time as the Doctor, it is important to place the raw numerical data in context. From 1987 to 1989, *Doctor Who* was scheduled against the toughest possible opposition in the form of Granada's *Coronation Street*, the UK's oldest and mightiest soap opera. The ratings were thus bound to be lower on average than for earlier eras of the series' history. It should also be borne in mind that many families are likely to have watched *Coronation Street* and recorded *Doctor Who* on video, a factor not allowed for at this time as only those viewers who had seen a programme on transmission were counted for ratings purposes.

The ratings for Season 24 were modest but consistent. All the episodes fell within a relatively small range, with a minimum of 4.2 and a maximum of 5.5 million viewers. A notable fall occurred between the first and second episodes of the opening story, but this was nothing new: it had happened on many previous occasions in the series' history as numerous casual viewers tuned in out of curiosity to see how the season began and then lost interest. The average figure for the season was a somewhat disappointing 5.0 million viewers (although this was still higher than that for the previous run – consisting of the single fourteen-part story *The Trial of a Time Lord* – which had had the advantage of a traditional Saturday evening timeslot). There are five factors that would seem to account for this rather low figure. First, and most importantly, the scheduling of the series opposite *Coronation Street.* Secondly, the actual transmission time of 7.35 p.m., which was rather late for some children and also gave *Doctor Who*'s opponents on other channels a five-minute advantage (shows tending to start on the hour or half-hour). Thirdly, McCoy had a relatively low public profile (certainly in comparison with, say, Peter Davison, who had already acquired a major following on *All Creatures Great and Small* before coming to *Doctor Who*). Fourthly, after the hiatus of 1985 (when the series had been taken off the air for eighteen months by BBC1 Controller Michael Grade), people had got out of the habit of watching *Doctor Who* and in many cases simply did not bother to tune in when it returned. And finally, the season itself was arguably of a relatively poor quality, with high levels of humour resulting in negative press reviews. Poor publicity has been cited by some commentators as an additional factor, but this is not entirely valid as *Radio Times* coverage of the series was good and numerous on-screen trailers were shown.

The ratings for Season 25 were far more respectable, averaging 5.4 million viewers and peaking at 6.6 million. McCoy had by now established himself in the role of the Doctor and the season had the added advantage of beginning transmission in October rather than September, which was when many new shows made their debut and competition for viewers was more fierce, and running on into January, when ratings are traditionally higher. The combination of an important anniversary and the return of the Daleks and the Cybermen created a considerable 'nostalgia factor' and the season itself was of a high quality, receiving supportive reviews in the press. Interestingly, the second episode of the opening story, *Remembrance of the Daleks*, gained a higher rating than the first, suggesting that there may have been good 'word of mouth' about the quality of the latter and its exciting 'hovering Dalek' cliffhanger.

Season 26 did less well, and in fact received the worst viewing figures of the McCoy era. *Battlefield* Part One was seen by only 3.1 million viewers, *Doctor Who*'s all-time lowest rating. The figures for *Ghost Light* and *The Curse of Fenric* hovered around the four million mark, but only *Survival* gained what could be described as a healthy rating, with five million viewers for Parts One and Three. This time there can be little doubt that a major factor accounting for the season's relative failure was a lack of publicity. There was virtually no effort made to promote the series in the *Radio Times*; and, although there had been some press coverage of the stories at the time of their production, a press call (with John Nathan-Turner, Sophie Aldred and Jean Marsh) on 16 August 1989 to publicise their imminent transmission failed to generate any significant interest and a second one (with Nicholas Parsons) did not take place until 19 October, by which point only *The Curse of Fenric* and *Survival* remained to be transmitted. Given that the viewing figures had been steadily rising during the course of the season, it is tempting to wonder how much more successful it would have become had it continued for a few more episodes. Looking at these figures alone, however, it is perhaps not entirely surprising that *Doctor Who* was taken off the air at this point.

The series bounced back in 1993 when the Children in Need special *Dimensions in Time* achieved an average viewing figure of 13.7 million. This, however, was somewhat misleading as the annual charity telethon is always popular and the ratings quoted were only for the quarter-hour segments in which the *Doctor Who* skit happened to be transmitted. Rather more impressive was the 9.08 million figure won by the 1996 *Doctor Who* television movie. This placed it ninth in the top one hundred most watched programmes that week, the second highest position attained by a drama show. This was, by any standard, a remarkably good figure and showed that many of the viewers who had deserted *Doctor Who* in the late eighties had returned, along with a whole new audience of youngsters.

Sylvester McCoy/Paul McGann Stories in Order of Average Viewing Figures

(Figures in millions of viewers)

Doctor Who	9.08
Silver Nemesis	5.50
The Greatest Show in the Galaxy	5.43
Remembrance of the Daleks	5.35
Delta and the Bannermen	5.27
Dragonfire	5.07
The Happiness Patrol	5.07
Survival	4.93
Paradise Towers	4.93
Time and the Rani	4.63
The Curse of Fenric	4.13
Ghost Light	4.07
Battlefield	3.65

Production Credits

	TITLE	AUTHOR	DIRECTOR	COSTUME	MAKE-UP	VISUAL EFFECTS	MUSIC	DESIGNER
	SEASON TWENTY-FOUR **Producer *John Nathan-Turner*. Script Editor *Andrew Cartmel***							
7D	Time and the Rani	Pip and Jane Baker	Andrew Morgan	Ken Trew	Lesley Rawstorne	Colin Mapson	Keff McCulloch	Geoff Powell
7E	Paradise Towers	Stephen Wyatt	Nicholas Mallett	Janet Tharby	Shaunna Harrison	Simon Tayler	Keff McCulloch	Martin Collins
7F	Delta and the Bannermen	Malcolm Kohll	Chris Clough	Richard Croft	Gillian Thomas	Andy McVean	Keff McCulloch	John Asbridge
7G	Dragonfire	Ian Briggs	Chris Clough	Richard Croft	Gillian Thomas	Andy McVean	Dominic Glynn	John Asbridge
	SEASON TWENTY-FIVE							
7H	Remembrance of the Daleks	Ben Aaronovitch	Andrew Morgan	Ken Trew	Christine Greenwood	Stuart Brisdon	Keff McCulloch	Martin Collins
7L	The Happiness Patrol	Graeme Curry	Chris Clough	Richard Croft	Dorka Nieradzik	Perry Brahan	Dominic Glynn	John Asbridge
7K	Silver Nemesis	Kevin Clarke	Chris Clough	Richard Croft	Dorka Nieradzik	Perry Brahan	Keff McCulloch	John Asbridge
7J	The Greatest Show in the Galaxy	Stephen Wyatt	Alan Wareing	Rosalind Ebbutt	Denise Baron	Steve Bowman	Mark Ayres	David Laskey
	SEASON TWENTY-SIX							
7N	Battlefield	Ben Aaronovitch	Michael Kerrigan	Anushia Nieradzik	Juliette Mayer	Dave Bezkorowajny	Keff McCulloch	Martin Collins
7Q	Ghost Light	Marc Platt	Alan Wareing	Ken Trew	Joan Stribling	Malcolm James	Mark Ayres	Nick Somerville
7M	The Curse of Fenric	Ian Briggs	Nicholas Mallett	Ken Trew	Denise Baron	Graham Brown	Mark Ayres	David Laskey
7P	Survival	Rona Munro	Alan Wareing	Ken Trew	Joan Stribling	Malcolm James	Dominic Glynn	Nick Somerville

Afterword

With this volume we reach the end of a seven-book series charting the ups and downs of one of the most enduring, innovative and enjoyable television series ever made. From humble beginnings, *Doctor Who* reached heights of popularity that the producers of other shows could only dream of, and in the process became an integral part of the formative years of three generations.

Since its debut in 1963, the show has been praised – and sometimes pilloried – by fans, critics and the general public alike. In 1996 it won a vote as the most popular BBC drama series of the last sixty years, and it has inspired and informed the vast majority of science fiction on television today. It has spawned impressive and enduring ranges of merchandise – including original novels and videos based on some of the characters and situations – and even introduced new words into the English language. No other television show can claim to have been so enduring or influential.

But what comes next?

Since 1989 the BBC has steadfastly refused to make any meaningful comment on or commitment to the future production of the series. All the indicators are that this public corporation is embarrassed by one of its most popular creations, and that it would like it to sink quietly into history and be forgotten. It will not produce further episodes itself, and it refuses to let others do so either. It no longer even runs repeats of the past stories residing in its archives, preferring to leave this to the satellite channel UK Gold.

Even the 1996 television movie, made as a co-production with Universal in America, was transmitted just once by the BBC, despite the fact that on that occasion it drew over nine million viewers and was among the week's top five rated dramas, and number nine in the overall chart. Apparently the BBC regarded this as a failure.

However, this 'failure' resulted in BBC Worldwide, the commercial arm of the BBC, deciding to claw back the licence to publish original *Doctor Who* novels from Virgin Publishing, the latest in a succession of publishers dating back to 1973 to bring out books associated with the series. BBC Worldwide decided that this 'failure' should spawn not only a series of original novels featuring the eighth Doctor, but also a parallel series featuring earlier Doctors, not to mention short-story collections and factual books based on the series. BBC Worldwide also continue to release videos of the earlier stories, and have even dabbled in audio releases where these no longer exist in a visual form.

All this stemming from a show that the BBC claimed did not reach the audience for which it was intended.

It is easy to criticise, however, when one is not privy to all the behind-the-scenes discussions and negotations. Even the series' fans are not entirely in agreement about what they would like to see happen in the future. Some have suggested that the BBC should commission a new *Doctor Who* movie every year and release it direct to video. Others feel that nothing less than a new series will do. Some would like to see an animated series produced, while others are quite happy with the new books and the old videos. As this book goes to press, there are rumours that Philip David Segal, the man behind the 1996 movie, is again in negotiation with the BBC over a possible new *Doctor Who* project. Whatever happens, *Doctor Who* has a 35-year history to sustain it, and its legions of fans and admirers will never let it be forgotten.

Errata

Despite our best efforts to ensure that everything contained within the Handbooks has been accurate, occasionally errors have slipped through.

This section details those that we have spotted ourselves, or that have been pointed out to us over the years. Our thanks to everyone who has pointed out these glitches and, if anyone finds any others, please let us know care of the publishers so that they may be noted in any future editions of this volume. We have decided, for reasons of space, to include only corrections here and not to try to include a great deal of additional information, although some has been included as we felt it was of interest.

Story Titles

Over the course of the publication of the series of Handbooks, further information has come to light regarding story titles. The following are those subject to most change and are those titles currently believed to be correct at time of first transmission: Serial A: *100,000 BC* (aka *An Unearthly Child, The Tribe of Gum*); Serial B: *The Mutants* (aka *The Daleks*); Serial C: *Inside the Spaceship* (aka *The Edge of Destruction, Beyond the Sun*); Serial T/A (or DC): *Mission to the Unknown* (aka *Dalek Cutaway*).

First Doctor Handbook

Page 69

The final two studio dates for *The Keys of Marinus* should be 17.04.64 and 24.04.64.

Page 75
The Sensorites was novelised in 1987.

Page 92
The Web Planet was novelised in 1965.

Page 99
The transmission date for *The Chase: The Planet of Decision* should be 26.06.65.

Page 103
The durations for the repeat of *The Time Meddler* should be 24'18", 25'18", 24'01" and 23'47".

Page 108
In the list of actors playing Varga plants, 'Tony Starn' should be 'Tony Starr'.

Page 134
The transmission dates for *The Smugglers* should be 10.09.66, 17.09.66, 24.09.66 and 01.10.66.

Page 135
The author of the novelisation of *The Smugglers* was Terrance Dicks.

Page 230–231
The BBC's Assistant Head of Design, I Beynon-Lewis, is misspelt 'Beynon Lewis'.

Page 340
Doctor Who screening began in New Zealand on 18 September 1964 in Christchurch on the regional channel CHTV-3 (not in Auckland on AKTV-2). Auckland was the second channel to begin screening the series, six weeks later. *Marco Polo*, from 27 October to 8 December 1968, was the only story that screened on AKTV-2 before the other regions.

Although the dates given for the run of *The Reign of Terror* to *The Romans* are correct for the Auckland region, this was the last of the four channels to screen these stories. These stories first aired in New Zealand on CHTV-3 from 26 January to 3 May 1968.

The fourth and final run first screened on CHTV-3 from 27 October 1968 to 24 October 1969. The date given of 3 November 1968 was the day that the last first Doctor episode aired on AKTV-2.

Page 342
CBC did air *The Mutants: The Dead Planet*, and the run finished on 2 July not 7 July.

Transmissions debuted with *100,000 BC: An Unearthly Child* on 23 January 1965 in a 5 p.m. timeslot. There was a two week break between *100,000 BC: The Cave of Skulls* and *100,000 BC: The Forest of Fear* so the story finished on 20 February.

After *The Mutants: The Rescue* on 10 April the timeslot was changed to Wednesdays at 5 p.m. starting with *Inside the Spaceship: The Edge of Destruction* on 21 April and running until *The Keys of Marinus: The Sea of Death* on 23 June.

The final five episodes of *The Keys of Marinus* were shown in a daily 5 p.m. slot from 28 June to 2 July. After this, CBC never aired *Doctor Who* again.

Page 347
In the listing of stories, the entry for *Mission to the Unknown* (aka *Dalek Cutaway*) is missing. This had a viewing figure of 8.3, which places it alongside *The Celestial Toymaker*.

Page 348
In the entry for *The Dalek Invasion of Earth*, Tony Pearce, listed under Make-Up, should really be listed under Costume.

Page 349
In the entry for *The Daleks' Master Plan*, some of the entries have become transposed between columns. Dennis Spooner was *writer* of episodes 6, 8–12, not *co-director*.

Second Doctor Handbook

Page 84

There are several apparent errors in the table of differences to the opening and closing incidental music for the Troughton stories. It has come to light that many of the fan-recorded audios that exist have had their opening and closing music tampered with and so therefore it is not possible to tell with certainty which episodes originally had which versions of the music.

By way of a compromise on what has turned out to be a very difficult and complex area, the following, revised, table lists only those stories and episodes that are known to exist in an original format in the BBC's archives.

STORY	OPENING TITLES	CLOSING TITLES
Details for 'standard' existing Troughton episodes:	New Music	Old music, starting from 15 seconds into the piece
The Faceless Ones 1, 3	Old music for first episode, new music for third episode	Old music, starting from 15 seconds into the piece
The Tomb of the Cybermen	New music	New music, starting at the beginning of the piece
The Abominable Snowmen 2	New music	New music, starting at the beginning of the piece
The Web of Fear 1	New music	Old music, starting at the beginning of the piece
The War Games	New music	Music from commercial record release on episodes 7–9 only. Remainder: Old music, starting from 15 seconds into the piece

Page 178

Terence Bayler is mis-spelt 'Terence Baylor'.

Page 150

Emrys Jones is mis-spelt 'Emrys James'.

Page 289
In the paragraph on the discovery of the sequences cut by the Australian censors, it should be recorded that, as well as Dallas Jones and Damian Shanahan, other Australian fans were also involved in the hunt for such material, notably Rod Scott, and all this activity resulted in the final confirmation of their existence by Shanahan and their eventual return to the BBC.

Page 292
The last paragraph of the section on New Zealand transmissions suggests that some of the film prints were obtained through Australia. While this appears to be true of some stories screened in the eighties, no evidence has been found to suggest that the Troughton stories came to New Zealand through Australia.

Page 307
The visual effects for *The Mind Robber* were handled by Jack Kine and Bernard Wilkie.

Third Doctor Handbook

Page 9
Jon Pertwee was born on 7 July 1919.

Pages 69–70
The spelling of Philips is incorrect throughout the synopsis for *Terror of the Autons*.

Page 73
Shakira Baksh is mis-spelt 'Shakira Batsh'.

Page 265
The title of the first *Doctor Who* cinema film is *Dr Who and the Daleks*.

Page 273
The Green Death did not feature edits made by the ABC. The one edit (in Episode Three) was apparently made by TVNZ.

Additional Overseas Information on Pertwee transmissions by TVOntario, North America.
TV Ontario started airing specially selected *Doctor Who* episodes in 1976. They aired two 'seasons' worth of Pertwee serials. Each story was introduced by commentator Dr Jim Dator who discussed various philosophical and scientific elements of the show as well as continuity with previously aired stories. TVO also published an educational viewers' guide to *Doctor Who* in 1976.

Their first 'season' was broadcast from 18 September 1976 to 12 March 1977 and consisted of *The Three Doctors, Day of the Daleks*, *The Curse of Peladon*, *The Claws of Axos*, *The Mutants* and *The Time Warrior*. All of which bar *The Claws of Axos* and *The Time Warrior* were repeated in 1979.

Their second 'season' was broadcast from 16 September 1977 to 25 March 1978 and contained *The Time Monster*, *The Green Death*, *Death to the Daleks*, *The Monster of Peladon* and *Planet of the Spiders. The Time Monster*, *The Green Death* and *The Monster of Peladon* were repeated in 1980.

Fourth Doctor Handbook

Page 78
The production details for *Masque of Mandragora* are incorrect:
Location Filming: 03.05.76–06.05.76
Studio Recording: 24.05.76–25.05.76, 06.06.76–08.06.76 in TC3.

Page 79
The transmission date for *The Hand of Fear* Part Two is incorrect. It should be 09.10.76.

Page 96
Maximillian Stael is spelt incorrectly.

Page 108
Emilia Rumford is spelt incorrectly.

Pages 167, 169 and 170
Graeme McDonald is mis-spelt 'Graeme MacDonald'.

Page 170
Graham Williams talks about the '*Crackerjack* clock' union disputes. Although this was what these seem to have been generally known as, the dispute was actually over the clock from the pre-school programme *Play School* and not *Crackerjack*, which did not feature a clock.

Page 218
The location filming in Portmerion was for the story *The Masque of Mandragora* (the text does not identify the story title).

Page 224
The Maltings in Suffolk is mis-spelt 'The Moultings'.

Page 227 & 229
The story title *Nightmare of Eden* has been mis-spelt [*The*] *Nightmare on Eden.*

Page 241
'When Baker came along, the show was aired almost all year round, giving New Zealanders repeat after repeat of the Doctor's exploits.' This statement is incorrect as Tom Baker's stories did not screen almost all year round – at least not for the first year – and his stories have been repeated only once. His first three stories were aired from 4 February to 8 April 1978, followed by a four-month gap. The show resumed with *Revenge of the Cybermen*, *Terror of the Zygons*, *Pyramids of Mars* and *Planet of Evil* from 12 August to 25 November 1978. *The Android Invasion* was screened from 29 December 1978 to 19 January 1979, and only then a solid run of Tom Baker stories commenced from 12 May 1979 with *The Brain of Morbius* and continued to screen weekly (with a one-month break in March 1981) finally ending with *The Keeper of Traken* on 1 September 1981. *Logopolis* was finally screened from 20 September to 18 October 1982. The entire Tom Baker era – including four stories that had been omitted the first time around: *Genesis of the Daleks*, *Horror of Fang Rock*, *The Sun Makers* and *The Invasion of Time* – were

screened without a break from 30 December 1986 to 19 August 1988. This is the only repeat run to date of the fourth Doctor's stories.

Fifth Doctor Handbook

Page 69
The Fairlight is a dedicated sampler and not a computer synthesiser.

Page 133
The duration of the repeat of *The Awakening* should be 47'50".

Page 263
Dick Mills joined the Radiophonic Workshop in 1958.

Page 265
The sequence in which Peter Davison's jacket was offered for auction following transmission of *The Five Doctors* is also known to have been shown in the BBC Wales and North West regions.

Pages 293 and 294
The two listing pages have been transposed. Page 294 should come before page 293.

Page 293
Jill Hagger is mis-spelt 'Jill Hagar' in the entry for *The Five Doctors.*

Page 294
The visual effects designer for *Castrovalva* was Simon McDonald.

Sixth Doctor Handbook

Page 12
Sarah Greene is mis-spelt 'Sarah Green'.

Page 13
Patrick Ryecart is mis-spelt 'Patrick Rycart'.

Page 90
Marc Brunel is mis-spelt 'Mark Brunell'.

Page 95
Frazer Hines should be credited as playing Jamie in the synopsis for *The Two Doctors*.

Page 110
The first OB date for *The Trial of a Time Lord* should be 08.04.86.

In compiling this list we are grateful to the following people who helped with corrections: David Brunt, Michael J. Doran, Chris Fieldhouse, Rosemary Howe, Dan Kukwa, Steve Manfred, John Molyneux, Paul Scoones and Martin Wiggins.

Index

1st, 2nd, etc denotes to which Handbook the page number(s) following refer.

Story titles appear in italics. '*' after a story title denotes a working title; '+' denotes an unmade story.